Student Companion

Boston, Massachusetts • Chandler, Arizona • Glenview, Illinois • Upper Saddle River, New Jersey

Acknowledgements Illustration: Stephen Durke: 29, 124; Jeff Grunwald represented by Wilkinson Studios, Inc.: 156, 164, 189, 192, 200; Phil Guzy: 229, 276; XNR Productions: 232 **Photo:** All photographs not listed are the property of Pearson Education; **Back Cover,** © Bon Appetit/Almay; **Page 16,** Pete Saloutos/zefa/Corbis; **108,** John Wells/Photo Researchers, Inc.; **151,** Eric Hood/iStockphoto; **236,** Ron Kimball/kimballstock; **240,** iStockphoto; Andy Crawford/Dorling Kindersley; **251,** M.C. Escher's "Symmetry E56" © 2009 The M.C. Escher Company-Holland. All rights reserved. www.mcescher.com; **279,** Matthias Tunger/Photonica/Getty Images; **285,** amana images inc./Alamy.

ISBN-13: 978-0-13-318594-2
ISBN-10: 0-13-318594-X
5 6 7 8 9 10   V016   15 14 13

Contents

Chapter 1   **Tools of Geometry** 2
1-1 Nets and Drawings for Visualizing Geometry 2
1-2 Points, Lines, and Planes 6
1-3 Measuring Segments 10
1-4 Measuring Angles 14
1-5 Exploring Angle Pairs 18
1-6 Basic Constructions 22
1-7 Midpoint and Distance in the Coordinate Plane 26
1-8 Perimeter, Circumference, and Area 30

Chapter 2   **Reasoning and Proof** 34
2-1 Patterns and Inductive Reasoning 34
2-2 Conditional Statements 38
2-3 Biconditionals and Definitions 42
2-4 Deductive Reasoning 46
2-5 Reasoning in Algebra and Geometry 50
2-6 Proving Angles Congruent 54

Chapter 3   **Parallel and Perpendicular Lines** 58
3-1 Lines and Angles 58
3-2 Properties of Parallel Lines 62
3-3 Proving Lines Parallel 66
3-4 Parallel and Perpendicular Lines 70
3-5 Parallel Lines and Triangles 74
3-6 Constructing Parallel and Perpendicular Lines 78
3-7 Equations of Lines in the Coordinate Plane 82
3-8 Slopes of Parallel and Perpendicular Lines 86

Chapter 4   **Congruent Triangles** 90
4-1 Congruent Figures 90
4-2 Triangle Congruence by SSS and SAS 94
4-3 Triangle Congruence by ASA and AAS 98
4-4 Using Corresponding Parts of Congruent Triangles 102
4-5 Isosceles and Equilateral Triangles 106
4-6 Congruence in Right Triangles 110
4-7 Congruence in Overlapping Triangles 114

Chapter 5 **Relationships Within Triangles** 118
    5-1 Midsegments of Triangles 118
    5-2 Perpendicular and Angle Bisectors 122
    5-3 Bisectors in Triangles 126
    5-4 Medians and Altitudes 130
    5-5 Indirect Proof 134
    5-6 Inequalities in One Triangle 138
    5-7 Inequalities in Two Triangles 142

Chapter 6 **Polygons and Quadrilaterals** 146
    6-1 The Polygon-Angle Sum Theorems 146
    6-2 Properties of Parallelograms 150
    6-3 Proving That a Quadrilateral Is a Parallelogram 154
    6-4 Properties of Rhombuses, Rectangles, and Squares 158
    6-5 Conditions for Rhombuses, Rectangles, and Squares 162
    6-6 Trapezoids and Kites 166
    6-7 Polygons in the Coordinate Plane 170
    6-8 Applying Coordinate Geometry 174
    6-9 Proofs Using Coordinate Geometry 178

Chapter 7 **Similarity** 182
    7-1 Ratios and Proportions 182
    7-2 Similar Polygons 186
    7-3 Proving Triangles Similar 190
    7-4 Similarity in Right Triangles 194
    7-5 Proportions in Triangles 198

Chapter 8 **Right Triangles and Trigonometry** 202
    8-1 The Pythagorean Theorem and Its Converse 202
    8-2 Special Right Triangles 206
    8-3 Trigonometry 210
    8-4 Angles of Elevation and Depression 214
    8-5 Law of Sines 218
    8-6 Law of Cosines 222

Chapter 9 **Transformations** 226
    9-1 Translations 226
    9-2 Reflections 230
    9-3 Rotations 234
    9-4 Compositions of Isometries 238
    9-5 Triangle Congruence 242
    9-6 Dilations 246
    9-7 Similarity Transformations 250

Chapter 10   **Area**. 254
             10-1 Areas of Parallelograms and Triangles 254
             10-2 Areas of Trapezoids, Rhombuses, and Kites 258
             10-3 Areas of Regular Polygons 262
             10-4 Perimeters and Areas of Similar Figures 266
             10-5 Trigonometry and Area 270
             10-6 Circles and Arcs. 274
             10-7 Areas of Circles and Sectors 278
             10-8 Geometric Probability. 282

Chapter 11   **Surface Area and Volume** 286
             11-1 Space Figures and Cross Sections. 286
             11-2 Surface Areas of Prisms and Cylinders 290
             11-3 Surface Areas of Pyramids and Cones 294
             11-4 Volumes of Prisms and Cylinders 298
             11-5 Volumes of Pyramids and Cones 302
             11-6 Surface Areas and Volumes of Spheres 306
             11-7 Areas and Volumes of Similar Solids. 310

Chapter 12   **Circles**. 314
             12-1 Tangent Lines 314
             12-2 Chords and Arcs. 318
             12-3 Inscribed Angles. 322
             12-4 Angle Measures and Segment Lengths 326
             12-5 Circles in the Coordinate Plane 330
             12-6 Locus: A Set of Points 334

Chapter 13   **Probability** 338
             13-1 Experimental and Theoretical Probability 338
             13-2 Probability Distributions and Frequency Tables 342
             13-3 Permutations and Combinations. 346
             13-4 Compound Probability 350
             13-5 Probability Models 354
             13-6 Conditional Probability Formulas 358
             13-7 Modeling Randomness 362

Welcome to **Geometry!**

Your Prentice Hall Geometry program is designed to help you achieve mastery of Geometry topics. Your *Prentice Hall Geometry Student Companion* is written to support you as you study. Your Student Companion is designed to work with your Student Edition textbook and PowerGeometry.com by providing a place to practice the concepts, skills, and vocabulary you'll learn in each lesson.

Using the Geometry Student Companion

Your Student Companion provides daily support for each lesson by targeting the following areas:

- **Vocabulary** Building your math vocabulary is an important part of success this year. You'll use your Student Companion to learn and understand the vocabulary words you need for Geometry.

- **Got It?** You'll use your Student Companion to check your understanding of example problems from your Student Edition.

- **Lesson Check** You'll use your Student Companion to make sure you're ready to tackle your homework.

Together, these sections will help you prepare to master the topics covered in your Student Edition — and lead to a successful year in Geometry.

Using PowerGeometry.com

All your Student Companion pages are available for downloading and printing from PowerGeometry.com.

1-1 Nets and Drawings for Visualizing Geometry

Vocabulary

● **Review**

Identify each figure as *two-dimensional* or *three-dimensional*.

1.

_____

2.

_____

3.

_____

● **Vocabulary Builder**

polygon

polygon (noun) PAHL ih gahn

Definition A **polygon** is a two-dimensional figure with three or more sides, where each side meets exactly two other sides at their endpoints.

Main Idea: A **polygon** is a closed figure, so all sides meet. No sides cross each other.

Examples: Triangles, rectangles, pentagons, hexagons, and octagons are **polygons**.

● **Use Your Vocabulary**

Underline the correct word(s) to complete each sentence.

4. A *polygon* is formed by two / three or more straight sides.

5. A circle is / is not a *polygon*.

6. A triangle / rectangle is a *polygon* with three sides.

7. The sides of a *polygon* are curved / straight .

8. Two / Three sides of *polygon* meet at the same point.

Cross out the figure(s) that are NOT *polygons*.

9.

10.

11.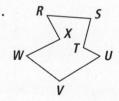

Underline the correct word(s) to complete the sentence.

12. A *net* is a <mark>two-dimensional / three-dimensional</mark> diagram that you can fold to form

a <mark>two-dimensional / three-dimensional</mark> figure.

13. Circle the *net* that you can NOT fold into a cube.

Use the net of a cube at the right for Exercises 14 and 15.

14. Suppose you fold the net into a cube. What number will be opposite each face?

1	3	4
_____	_____	_____

15. Suppose you fold the net into a cube. What number is missing from each view?

_____	_____	_____

✓ **Problem 1** **Identifying a Solid From a Net**

Got It? The net at the right folds into the cube shown.
Which letters will be on the top and right side of the cube?

16. Four of the five other letters will touch some side of Face B when
the net is folded into a cube. Cross out the letter of the side that
will NOT touch some side of Face B.

A	C	D	E	F

17. Which side of the cube will that letter be on? Circle your answer.

Top	Bottom	Right	Left	Back

18. Use the net. Which face is to the right of Face B? How do you know?

_____

_____

19. Use the net. Which face is on the top of the cube? How do you know?

_____

_____

Lesson 1-1

Problem 2 Drawing a Net From a Solid

Got It? What is a net for the figure at the right? Label the net with its dimensions.

Write T for _true_ or F for _false_.

_____ **20.** Three of the faces are rectangles.

_____ **21.** Four of the faces are triangles.

_____ **22.** The figure has five faces in all.

23. Now write a description of the net.

_____

_____

24. Circle the net that represents the figure above.

Problem 3 Isometric Drawing

Got It? What is an isometric drawing of this cube structure?

25. The cube structure has

_____ edges that you can see and

_____ vertices that you can see.

26. The isometric dot paper shows 2 vertices and 1 edge of the cube structure. Complete the isometric drawing.

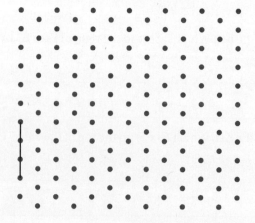

Problem 4   Orthographic Drawing

Got It? What is the orthographic drawing for this isometric drawing?

Front   Right

27. Underline the correct word to complete the sentence.

     If you built the figure out of cubes, you would use seven / eight cubes

28. Cross out the drawing below that is NOT part of the orthographic drawing.
Then label each remaining drawing. Write *Front, Right,* or *Top*.

Lesson Check • Do you UNDERSTAND?

Vocabulary Tell whether each drawing is *isometric, orthographic,* a *net,* or *none.*

29. Write *dot paper, one view, three views* or *none.* Then label each figure.

Top

Front   Right

Front   Right

Math Success

Check off the vocabulary words that you understand.

☐ net   ☐ isometric drawing   ☐ orthographic drawing

Rate how well you can *use nets, isometric drawings, and orthographic drawings.*

Need to review   0   2   4   6   8   10   Now I get it!

Lesson 1-1

Vocabulary

● Review

Draw a line from each *net* in Column A to the three-dimensional figure it represents in Column B.

Column A   Column B

1.

2.

3.

● Vocabulary Builder

conjecture (noun, verb) **kun** JEK **chur**	

Main Idea: A **conjecture** is a guess or a prediction.

Definition: A **conjecture** is a conclusion reached by using inductive reasoning.

● Use Your Vocabulary

Write *noun* or *verb* to identify how the word *conjecture* is used in each sentence.

4. You make a *conjecture* that your volleyball team will win.

5. Assuming that your sister ate the last cookie is a *conjecture*.

6. You *conjecture* that your town will build a swimming pool.

Key Concept   Undefined and Defined Terms

Write the correct word from the list on the right. Use each word only once.

	Undefined or Defined Term	Diagram	Name
7.	_____	•A	A
8.	_____	(line ℓ through B and A)	$\overleftrightarrow{AB}$
9.	_____	(plane P containing A, B, C)	P
10.	_____	A•———•B	$\overline{AB}$
11.	_____	A•———→ B	$\overrightarrow{AB}$
12.	_____	←•———•———•→ A C B	$\overrightarrow{CA}$, $\overrightarrow{CB}$

line
opposite rays
plane
point
ray
segment

Draw a line from each item in Column A to its description in Column B.

Column A	Column B
13. plane *HGE*	intersection of $\overline{AB}$ and line *z*
14. $\overline{BF}$	plane *AEH*
15. plane *DAE*	line through points *F* and *E*
16. line *y*	intersection of planes *ABF* and *CGF*
17. point *A*	plane containing points *E*, *F*, and *G*

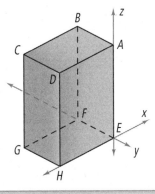

Postulates 1-1, 1-2, 1-3, and 1-4

18. Complete each postulate with *line*, *plane*, or *point*.

Postulate 1-1 Through any two points there is exactly one _?_.

Postulate 1-2 If two distinct lines intersect, then they intersect in exactly one _?_.

Postulate 1-3 If two distinct planes intersect, then they intersect in exactly one _?_.

Postulate 1-4 Through any three noncollinear points there is exactly one _?_.

Lesson 1-2

Write P if the statement describes a *postulate* or U if it describes an *undefined term*.

_____ **19.** A point indicates a location and has no size.

_____ **20.** Through any two points there is exactly one line.

_____ **21.** A line is represented by a straight path that has no thickness and extends in two opposite directions without end.

_____ **22.** If two distinct planes intersect, then they intersect in exactly one line.

_____ **23.** If two distinct lines intersect, then they intersect in exactly one point.

_____ **24.** Through any three nontcollinear points there is exactly one plane.

Problem 2 Naming Segments and Rays

Got It? Reasoning $\overrightarrow{EF}$ and $\overrightarrow{FE}$ form a line. Are they opposite rays? Explain.

For Exercises 25–29, use the line below.

←———————————————————————→

25. Draw and label points E and F. Then draw $\overrightarrow{EF}$ in one color and $\overrightarrow{FE}$ in another color.

26. Do $\overrightarrow{EF}$ and $\overrightarrow{FE}$ share an endpoint?   Yes / No

27. Do $\overrightarrow{EF}$ and $\overrightarrow{FE}$ form a line?   Yes / No

28. Are $\overrightarrow{EF}$ and $\overrightarrow{FE}$ opposite rays?   Yes / No

29. Explain your answer to Exercise 28.

_____

_____

Problem 3 Finding the Intersection of Two Planes

Got It? Each surface of the box at the right represents part of a plane. What are the names of two planes that intersect in $\overleftrightarrow{BF}$?

30. Circle the points that are on $\overleftrightarrow{BF}$ or in one of the two planes.

A	B	C	D	E	F	G	H

31. Circle another name for plane *BFG*. Underline another name for plane *BFE*.

ABF	BCD	BCG	CDH	FGH

32. Now name two planes that intersect in $\overleftrightarrow{BF}$.

_____   _____

Problem 4 Using Postulate 1-4

Got It? What plane contains points *L*, *M*, and *N*? Shade the plane.

33. Use the figure below. Draw $\overline{LM}$, $\overline{LN}$, and $\overline{MN}$ as dashed segments. Then shade plane *LMN*.

Underline the correct word to complete the sentence.

34. $\overline{LM}$, $\overline{LN}$, and $\overline{MN}$ form a triangle / rectangle .

35. Name the plane.

_____

Lesson Check • Do you UNDERSTAND?

Are $\overrightarrow{AB}$ and $\overrightarrow{BA}$ the same ray? Explain.

Underline the correct symbol to complete each sentence.

36. The endpoint of $\overrightarrow{AB}$ is *A* / *B* .

37. The endpoint of $\overrightarrow{BA}$ is *A* / *B* .

38. Use the line. Draw and label points *A* and *B*. Then draw $\overrightarrow{AB}$ and $\overrightarrow{BA}$.

39. Are $\overrightarrow{AB}$ and $\overrightarrow{BA}$ the same ray? Explain.

_____

Math Success

Check off the vocabulary words that you understand.

☐ point ☐ line ☐ plane ☐ segment ☐ ray ☐ postulate ☐ axiom

Rate how well you *understand points, lines, and planes.*

Lesson 1-2

1-3 Measuring Segments

Vocabulary

● Review

Draw an example of each.

1. *point*

2. $\overleftrightarrow{AB}$

3. $\overrightarrow{DF}$

● Vocabulary Builder

segment HJ

H ● ——— ● J

segment (noun) SEG **munt**

Definition: A **segment** is part of a line that consists of two endpoints and all points between them.

Main Idea: You name a **segment** by its endpoints.

● Use Your Vocabulary

Complete each sentence with *endpoint, endpoints, line,* or *points.*

4. A *ray* has one __?__.

5. A *line* contains infinitely many __?__.

6. A *segment* has two __?__.

7. A *segment* is part of a __?__.

Place a check ✓ if the phrase describes a *segment.* Place an ✗ if it does not.

_____ **8.** Earth's equator   _____ **9.** the right edge of a book's cover   _____ **10.** one side of a triangle

take note

Postulate 1–5   Ruler Postulate

Every point on a line can be paired with a real number, called the *coordinate* of the point.

Problem 1 **Measuring Segment Lengths**

Got It? What are *UV* and *SV* on the number line?

11. Label each point on the number line with its coordinate.

```
        S                           U       V
  ←──┼──●──┼──┼──┼──┼──┼──┼──●──┼──●──┼──→
    -6  ▢  -2  0  2  4  6  8  ▢  12  ▢  16
```

12. Find *UV* and *SV*. Write a justification for each statement.

$UV = \left| \boxed{} - \boxed{} \right|$ _____ $SV = \left| \boxed{} - \boxed{} \right|$

$UV = \left| \boxed{} \right|$ _____ $SV = \left| \boxed{} \right|$

$UV = \boxed{}$ _____ $SV = \boxed{}$

Postulate 1-6 **Segment Addition Postulate**

If three points *A*, *B*, and *C* are collinear and *B* is between *A* and *C*, then $AB + BC = AC$.

Given points *A*, *B*, and *C* are collinear and *B* is between *A* and *C*, complete each equation.

13. $AB = 5$ and $BC = 4$, so $AB + BC = \boxed{} + \boxed{}$ and $AC = \boxed{}$.

14. $AC = 12$ and $BC = 7$, so $AC - BC = \boxed{} - \boxed{}$ and $AB = \boxed{}$.

Problem 2 **Using the Segment Addition Postulate**

Got It? In the diagram, $JL = 120$. What are *JK* and *KL*?

```
        4x + 6        7x + 15
      ●─────────●──────────────●
      J         K              L
```

15. Write a justification for each statement.

$JK + KL = JL$ _____

$(4x + 6) + (7x + 15) = 120$ _____

$11x + 21 = 120$ _____

$11x = 99$ _____

$x = 9$ _____

16. You know that $JK = 4x + 6$ and $KL = 7x + 15$. Use the value of *x* from Exercise 15 to to find *JK* and *KL*. Find *JK* and *KL*.

17. $JK = \boxed{}$ and $KL = \boxed{}$.

11

Lesson 1-3

Got It? Use the diagram below. Is $\overline{AB}$ congruent to $\overline{DE}$?

In Exercises 18 and 19, circle the expression that completes the equation.

18. $AB = \blacksquare$

| $-2 - 2$ | $\lvert -2 - 2 \rvert$ | $\lvert -2 - 3 \rvert$ | $\lvert -2 - 4 \rvert$ |

19. $DE = \blacksquare$

| $3 - 14$ | $10 + 14$ | $\lvert 5 - 14 \rvert$ | $\lvert 10 - 14 \rvert$ |

20. After simplifying, $AB = $ ▭ and $DE = $ ▭ .

21. Is $\overline{AB}$ congruent to $\overline{DE}$? Explain.

_____

The *midpoint* of a segment is the point that divides the segment into two congruent segments.

Use the number line below for Exercises 22–25.

22. Point ▭ is halfway between points B and J.   **23.** The midpoint of $\overline{AE}$ is point ▭ .

24. Point ▭ divides $\overline{EK}$ into two congruent segments.

25. Find the midpoint of each segment. Then write the coordinate of the midpoint.

	$\overline{AG}$	$\overline{DH}$	$\overline{AK}$
Midpoint	▭	▭	▭
Coordinate	▭	▭	▭

26. Find the coordinate of the midpoint of each segment.

	segment with endpoints at -4 and 2	segment with endpoints at -2 and 4
Coordinate of midpoint	▭	▭

27. Circle the expression that relates the coordinate of the midpoint to the coordinates of the endpoints.

| $x_1 + x_2$ | $\dfrac{(x_1 + x_2)}{2}$ | $\dfrac{(x_1 - x_2)}{2}$ |

Problem 4 Using the Midpoint

Got It? *U* is the midpoint of $\overline{TV}$. What are *TU*, *UV*, and *TV*?

$$\overset{8x + 11 \qquad 12x - 1}{\underset{T \qquad\qquad U \qquad\qquad V}{\rule{5cm}{0.4pt}}}$$

28. Use the justifications at the right to complete the steps below.

Step 1 Find *x*.

$TU = UV$	Definition of midpoint
$8x + 11 = \boxed{}$	Substitute.
$8x + 11 + \boxed{} = \boxed{} + \boxed{}$	Add 1 to each side.
$\boxed{} = \boxed{}$	Subtract 8*x* from each side.
$\boxed{} = x$	Divide each side by 4.

Step 2 Find *TU* and *UV*.

$TU = 8 \cdot \boxed{} + 11 = \boxed{}$ Substitute $\boxed{}$ for *x*.

$UV = 12 \cdot \boxed{} - 1 = \boxed{}$ Substitute.

Step 3 Find *TV*.

$TV = TU + UV$	Definition of midpoint
$= \boxed{} + \boxed{}$	Substitute.
$= \boxed{}$	Simplify.

Lesson Check • Do you UNDERSTAND?

Vocabulary Name two segment bisectors of $\overline{PR}$.

Underline the correct word or symbol to complete each sentence.

29. A bisector / midpoint may be a point, line, ray, or segment.

30. The midpoint of $\overline{PR}$ is point *P / Q / R* .

31. Line ℓ passes through point *P / Q / R* .

32. Two bisectors of $\overline{PR}$ are $\boxed{}$ and $\boxed{}$.

Math Success

Check off the vocabulary words that you understand.

☐ congruent segments   ☐ coordinate   ☐ midpoint   ☐ segment bisector

Rate how well you can *find lengths of segments.*

Lesson 1-3

Vocabulary

● **Review**

Write T for *true* or F for *false*.

_____ **1.** $\overrightarrow{AB}$ names a *ray* with endpoints *A* and *B*.

_____ **2.** You name a *ray* by its endpoint and another point on the *ray*.

● **Vocabulary Builder**

> **angle** (noun, verb) ANG **gul**
>
> **Other Word Forms:** angular (adjective), angle (verb), angled (adjective)
>
> **Definition:** An **angle** is formed by two rays with the same endpoint.

● **Use Your Vocabulary**

Name the rays that form each *angle*.

3. and

4. and

---

take note

Key Concept   Angle

Definition	How to Name It	Diagram
An **angle** is formed by two rays with the same endpoint. The rays are the **sides** of the angle. The endpoint is the **vertex** of the angle.	You can name an angle by • its vertex • a point on each ray and the vertex • a number	

For Exercises 5–8, use the diagram in the Take Note on page 14. Name each part of the angle.

5. the *vertex*

6. two points that are NOT the vertex

and

7. the *sides*

→ and →

8. Name the angle three ways.

by its *vertex*

by a point on each side and the vertex

by a number

 Problem 1 **Naming Angles**

Got It? What are two other names for ∠*KML*?

9. Cross out the ray that is NOT a ray of ∠*KML*.

$\overrightarrow{MK}$ $\overrightarrow{MJ}$ $\overrightarrow{ML}$

10. Circle all the possible names of ∠*KML*.

∠1   ∠2   ∠*JKL*   ∠*JMK*   ∠*JML*   ∠*KMJ*   ∠*LMK*

 Key Concept **Types of Angles**

11. Draw your own example of each type of angle.

acute

$0 < x <$ ▢

right

$x =$ ▢

obtuse

▢ $< x <$ ▢

straight

$x =$ ▢

In the diagram, $m\angle ABC = 70$ and $m\angle BFE = 90$. Describe each angle as *acute*, *right*, *obtuse* or *straight*. Give an angle measure to support your description.

12. ∠*ABC*

13. ∠*CBD*

14. ∠*CFG*

15. ∠*CFH*

Lesson 1-4

Measuring and Classifying Angles

Got It? What are the measures of ∠LKH, ∠HKN, and ∠MKH in the art below?
Classify each angle as *acute, right, obtuse,* or *straight.*

16. Write the measure of each angle. Then classify each angle.

∠LKH   ∠HKN   ∠MKH

°   °   °

_____   _____   _____

 Problem 3 **Using Congruent Angles**

Got It? Use the photo at the right. If m∠ABC = 49,
what is m∠DEF?

17. ∠ABC has [ ] angle mark(s).

18. The other angle with the same number of

marks is ∠ [ ].

19. Underline the correct word to complete the sentence.

The measure of ∠ABC and the measure of the angle

in Exercise 18 are equal / unequal .

20. m∠DEF = [ ]

 Postulate 1–8 **Angle Addition Postulate**

If point *B* is in the interior of ∠AOC, then m∠AOB + m∠BOC = m∠AOC.

21. Draw ∠ABT with point *L* in the interior and ∠ABL and ∠LBT.

22. Complete: m∠ABL + m∠ [ ] = m∠ [ ]

Problem 4 **Using the Angle Addition Postulate**

Got It? ∠*DEF* is a straight angle. What are *m*∠*DEC* and *m*∠*CEF*?

23. Write a justification for each statement.

$m\angle DEF = 180$ _____

$m\angle DEC + m\angle CEF = 180$ _____

$(11x - 12) + (2x + 10) = 180$ _____

$13x - 2 = 180$ _____

$13x = 182$ _____

$x = 14$ _____

24. Use the value of *x* to find *m*∠*DEC* and *m*∠*CEF*.

$m\angle DEC = 11x - 12 = 11(\boxed{}) - 12 = \boxed{}$

$m\angle CEF = $

 Lesson Check • **Do you know How?**

Algebra If *m*∠*ABD* = 85, what is an expression to represent *m*∠*ABC*?

25. Use the justifications at the right to complete the statements below.

$m\angle ABC + m\angle CBD = m\angle ABD$ Angle Addition Postulate

$m\angle ABC + \boxed{} = \boxed{}$ Substitute.

$m\angle ABC + \boxed{} - \boxed{} = \boxed{} - \boxed{}$ Subtract $\boxed{}$ from each side.

$m\angle ABC = \boxed{}$ Simplify.

Math Success

Check off the vocabulary words that you understand.

☐ acute angle ☐ obtuse angle ☐ right angle ☐ straight angle

Rate how well you can *classify angles.*

Need to review 0 2 4 6 8 10 Now I get it!

Vocabulary

● **Review**

Use a word from the list below to complete each sentence. Use each word just once.

> interior   rays   vertex

1. The __?__ of an *angle* is the region containing all of the points
between the two sides of the angle.

2. When you use three points to name an *angle*, the __?__ must go in the middle.

3. The sides of ∠*QRS* are __?__ *RS* and *RQ*.

Use the figure below for Exercises 4–7. Identify each
angle as *acute, right, obtuse,* or *straight.*

4. ∠*SRV*

5. ∠*TRS*

6. ∠*TRQ*

7. ∠*VRQ*

● **Vocabulary Builder**

> **conclusion** (noun) **kun KLOO zhun**
>
> **Other Word Forms:** conclude (verb)
>
> **Definition:** A **conclusion** is the end of an event or the last step in a
> reasoning process.

● **Use Your Vocabulary**

Complete each sentence with *conclude* or *conclusion.*

8. If it rains, you can __?__ that soccer practice will be canceled.

9. The last step of the proof is the __?__.

Key Concept   Types of Angle Pairs

Angle Pair	Definition
Adjacent angles	Two coplanar angles with a common side, a common vertex, and no common interior points
Vertical angles	Two angles whose sides are opposite rays
Complementary angles	Two angles whose measures have a sum of 90
Supplementary angles	Two angles whose measures have a sum of 180

Draw a line from each word in Column A to the angles it describes in Column B.

Column A

10. supplementary

11. adjacent

12. vertical

13. complementary

Column B

∠1 and ∠2

∠2 and ∠3

∠2 and ∠5

∠3 and ∠6

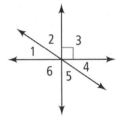

Problem 1 Identifying Angle Pairs

Got It? Use the diagram at the right. Are ∠AFE and ∠CFD vertical angles? Explain.

14. The rays of ∠AFE are $\overrightarrow{FE}$ and $\overrightarrow{FC}$ / $\overrightarrow{FA}$.

15. The rays of ∠CFD are $\overrightarrow{FC}$ and $\overrightarrow{FD}$ / $\overrightarrow{FA}$.

Complete each statement.

16. $\overrightarrow{FE}$ and ▢ are opposite rays.

17. $\overrightarrow{FA}$ and ▢ are opposite rays.

18. Are ∠AFE and ∠CFD vertical angles?   Yes / No

Problem 2 Making Conclusions From a Diagram

Got It? Can you conclude that $\overline{TW} \cong \overline{WV}$ from the diagram? Explain.

19. Circle the items marked as congruent in the diagram.

$\overline{PW}$ and $\overline{WQ}$ $\overline{TW}$ and $\overline{WV}$

∠TWQ and ∠PWT   ∠TWQ and ∠VWQ

20. Can you conclude that $\overline{TW} \cong \overline{WV}$? Why or why not?

_____

_____

Postulate 1-9 Linear Pair Postulate

If two angles form a linear pair, then they are supplementary.

21. If $\angle A$ and $\angle B$ form a linear pair, then $m\angle A + m\angle B = $ ☐ .

Problem 3 Finding Missing Angle Measures

Got It? Reasoning $\angle KPL$ and $\angle JPL$ are a linear pair, $m\angle KPL = 2x + 24$, and $m\angle JPL = 4x + 36$. How can you check that $m\angle KPL = 64$ and $m\angle JPL = 116$?

22. What is one way to check solutions? Place a ✓ in the box if the response is correct. Place an ✗ in the box if it is incorrect.

☐   Draw a diagram. If it looks good, the solutions are correct.

☐   Substitute the solutions in the original problem statement.

23. Use your answer(s) to Exercise 22 to check the solutions.

24. How does your check show that you found the correct angle measurements?

_____

_____

Problem 4 Using an Angle Bisector to Find Angle Measures

Got It? $\overrightarrow{KM}$ bisects $\angle JKL$. If $m\angle JKL = 72$, what is $m\angle JKM$?

25. Write a justification for each step.

$m\angle JKM = m\angle MKL$

$m\angle JKM + m\angle MKL = m\angle JKL$

$2m\angle JKM = m\angle JKL$

$m\angle JKM = \frac{1}{2}m\angle JKL$

26. Complete.

$m\angle JKL =$ ⬜ , so $m\angle JKM =$ ⬜ .

27. Now complete the diagram below.

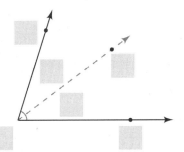

Lesson Check • Do you UNDERSTAND?

Error Analysis Your friend calculated the value of x below. What is her error?

$$4x + 2x = 180$$
$$6x = 180$$
$$x = 30$$

28. Circle the best description of the largest angle in the figure.

acute	obtuse	right	straight

29. Complete: $4x + 2x =$ ⬜

30. What is your friend's error? Explain.

_____

_____

_____

Math Success

Check off the vocabulary words that you understand.

☐ angle   ☐ complementary   ☐ supplementary   ☐ angle bisector   ☐ vertical

Rate how well you can *find missing angle measures*.

Need to review   0   2   4   6   8   10   Now I get it!

1-6 Basic Constructions

Vocabulary

● Review

Draw a line from each word in Column A to its symbol or picture in Column B.

Column A   Column B

1. congruent

2. point

• W

3. ray

4. vertex

5. intersection of segments   ≅

● Vocabulary Builder

> **perpendicular** (adjective) **pur pun** DIK **yoo lur**
>
> **Definition:** **Perpendicular** means at right angles to a given line or plane.
>
> **Example:** Each corner of this paper is formed by **perpendicular** edges of the page.
>
> **Non-Examples:** Acute, obtuse, and straight angles do not have **perpendicular** rays.

● Use Your Vocabulary

6. Circle the figure that shows *perpendicular* segments.

Problem 1 Constructing Congruent Segments

Got It? Use a straightedge to draw $\overline{XY}$. Then construct $\overline{RS}$ so that $RS = 2XY$.

7. A student did the construction at the right. Describe each step of the construction.

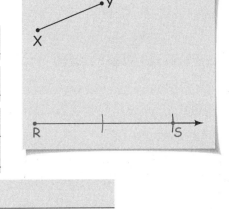

Step 1 _____

Step 2 _____

Step 3 _____
_____

Step 4 _____

Step 5 _____

Problem 2 Constructing Congruent Angles

Got It? Construct $\angle F$ so that $m\angle F = 2m\angle B$ at the right.

8. Use *arc* or *compass* to complete the sentence(s) in each step. In the large box, construct $\angle F$.

Step 1 Use a straightedge to construct a ray with endpoint *F*.

Step 2 With your __?__ point on vertex *B*, draw a(n) __?__ that intersects both sides of $\angle B$. Label the points of intersection *A* and *C*.
_____

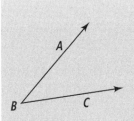

Step 3 Use the same compass setting. Put the __?__ point on point *F*. Draw a long __?__ and label its intersection with the ray as *S*.
_____

Step 6 Draw $\overrightarrow{FR}$.

Step 5 Use the same compass setting. Put the __?__ point on point *T*. Draw an __?__ and label its intersection with the first __?__ as point *R*.
_____

Step 4 Open the __?__ to the length of $\overline{AC}$. With the compass point on point *S*, draw an __?__. Label where this arc intersects the other arc as point *T*.
_____

Lesson 1-6

A *perpendicular bisector* of a segment is a line, segment, or ray that is perpendicular to the segment at its midpoint.

9. Circle the drawing that shows the perpendicular bisector of a segment.

Problem 3 **Constructing the Perpendicular Bisector**

Got It? Draw $\overline{ST}$. Construct its perpendicular bisector.

10. Error Analysis A student's construction of the perpendicular bisector of $\overline{ST}$ is shown below. Describe the student's error.

11. Do the construction correctly in the box below.

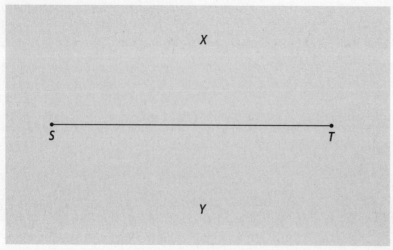

Problem 4 Constructing the Angle Bisector

Got It? Draw obtuse ∠*XYZ*. Then construct its bisector $\overrightarrow{YP}$.

12. Obtuse ∠*XYZ* is drawn in the box at the right. Complete the flowchart and do each step of the construction.

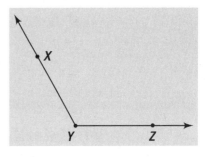

Step 1 Put the compass point on vertex ☐ . Draw an arc that intersects the sides of ☐ . Label the points of intersection *A* and *B*.

↓

Step 2 Put the compass point on point *A* and draw an arc. With the same / a different compass setting, draw an arc using point *B*. Be sure the arcs intersect. Label the point where the two arcs intersect *P*.

↓

Step 3 Draw ☐ .

Lesson Check • Do you UNDERSTAND?

Vocabulary What two tools do you use to make constructions?

Draw a line from each task in Column A to the tool used in Column B.

Column A	Column B
13. measure lines	compass
14. measure angles	protractor
15. construct arcs	ruler
16. construct lines	straightedge

Math Success

Check off the vocabulary words that you understand.

☐ straightedge   ☐ compass   ☐ construction   ☐ perpendicular bisector

Rate how well you can *construct angles and bisectors*.

Need to review   0   2   4   6   8   10   Now I get it!

Lesson 1-6

1-7 Midpoint and Distance in the Coordinate Plane

Vocabulary

● Review

Use the figure at the right for Exercises 1–6. Write T for *true* or F for *false*.

_____ **1.** Points *A* and *B* are both at the *origin*.

_____ **2.** If $AB = BC$, then *B* is the midpoint of $\overline{AC}$.

_____ **3.** The *midpoint* of $\overline{AE}$ is *F*.

_____ **4.** The *Pythagorean Theorem* can be used for any triangle.

_____ **5.** Point *C* is at (6, 0).

_____ **6.** Point *E* has a *y-coordinate* of −8.

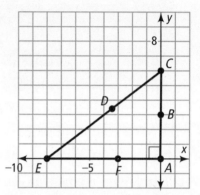

● Vocabulary Builder

> **midpoint** (noun) MID **poynt**
>
> **Definition:** A *midpoint* of a segment is a point that divides the segment into two congruent segments.

● Use Your Vocabulary

Use the figure at the right for Exercises 7–9.

7. The *midpoint* of $\overline{EF}$ is $G(\quad, \quad)$.

8. The *midpoint* of $\overline{AB}$ is $(\quad, \quad)$, or the origin.

9. The *midpoint* of $\overline{CD}$ is $(\quad, \quad)$.

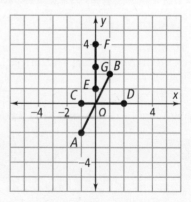

Key Concept Midpoint Formulas

On a Number Line	In the Coordinate Plane
The coordinate of the midpoint M of $\overline{AB}$ with endpoints at a and b is $\dfrac{a+b}{2}$.	Given $A(x_1, y_1)$ and $B(x_2, y_2)$, the coordinates of the midpoint of $\overline{AB}$ are $M\left(\dfrac{x_1 + x_2}{2}, \dfrac{y_1 + y_2}{2}\right)$

Find the coordinate of the midpoint M of each segment with the given endpoints on a number line.

10. endpoints 5 and 9

11. endpoints −3 and 5

12. endpoints −10 and −3

13. endpoints −8 and −1

14. Complete the diagram below.

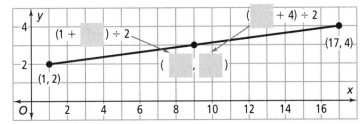

Problem 2 Finding an Endpoint

Got It? The midpoint of $\overline{AB}$ has coordinates $(4, -9)$. Endpoint A has coordinates $(-3, -5)$. What are the coordinates of B?

15. Complete the equations below.

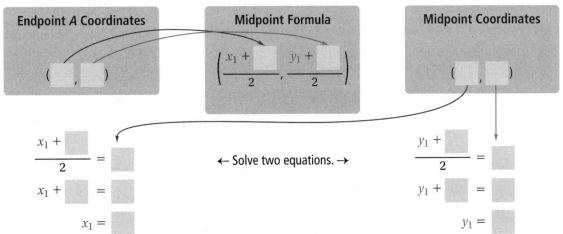

16. The coordinates of endpoint B are (___).

Lesson 1-7

take note

Formula The Distance Formula

The distance between two points $A(x_1, y_1)$ and $B(x_2, y_2)$ is $d = \sqrt{(x_2 - x_1)^2 + (y_2 - y_1)^2}$.

The Distance Formula is based on the Pythagorean Theorem.

$$a^2 + b^2 = c^2$$

Use the diagrams above. Draw a line from each triangle side in Column A to the corresponding triangle side in Column B.

Column A	Column B
17. $y_2 - y_1$	a
18. $x_2 - x_1$	b
19. distance, d	c

Problem 3 **Finding Distance**

Got It? $\overline{SR}$ has endpoints $S(-2, 14)$ and $R(3, -1)$. What is SR to the nearest tenth?

20. Complete the diagram at the right.

21. Let $S(-2, 14)$ be (x_1, y_1) and let $R(3, -1)$ be (x_2, y_2). Use the justifications and complete the steps below to find SR.

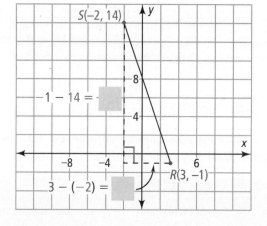

$d = \sqrt{\left(\boxed{} - x_1\right)^2 + \left(\boxed{} - y_1\right)^2}$ Use the Distance Formula.

$SR = \sqrt{\left(\boxed{} - (-2)\right)^2 + \left(\boxed{} - 14\right)^2}$ Substitute.

$= \sqrt{\left(\boxed{}\right)^2 + \left(\boxed{}\right)^2}$ Subtract.

$= \sqrt{\boxed{} + \boxed{}}$ Simplify powers.

$= \sqrt{\boxed{}}$ Add.

$\approx \boxed{}$ Use a calculator.

Problem 4 Finding Distance

Got It? On a zip-line course, you are harnessed to a cable that travels through the treetops. You start at Platform *A* and zip to each of the other platforms. How far do you travel from Platform *D* to Platform *E*? Each grid unit represents 5 m.

22. The equation is solved below. Write a justification for each step.

$$d = \sqrt{(x_2 - x_1)^2 + (y_2 - y_1)^2}$$

_____

$$DE = \sqrt{(30 - 20)^2 + (-15 - 20)^2}$$

_____

$$= \sqrt{10^2 + (-35)^2} = \sqrt{100 + 1225} = \sqrt{1325}$$

_____

23. To the nearest tenth, you travel about _____ m.

Lesson Check • Do you UNDERSTAND?

Reasoning How does the Distance Formula ensure that the distance between two different points is positive?

24. A radical symbol with no sign in front of it indicates a positive / negative square root.

25. Now answer the question.

_____

_____

Math Success

Check off the vocabulary words that you understand.

☐ midpoint   ☐ distance   ☐ coordinate plane

Rate how well you can *use the Midpoint and Distance Formulas*.

Need to review   0   2   4   6   8   10   Now I get it!

1-8 Perimeter, Circumference, and Area

Vocabulary

● Review

1. Cross out the shapes that are NOT *polygons*.

2. Write the name of each figure. Use each word once.

triangle   square   rectangle   circle

_____   _____   _____   _____

● Vocabulary Builder

consecutive (adjective) **kun SEK yoo tiv**

Definition: **Consecutive** means following in order without interruption.

Related Word: sequence

Example: The numbers 2, 4, 6, 8, . . . are **consecutive** even numbers.

Non-Example: The numbers 1, 3, 2, 5, 4, . . . are NOT **consecutive** numbers.

● Use Your Vocabulary

Draw a line from each sequence of letters in Column A to the next *consecutive* letter in Column B.

Column A	Column B
3. L, M, N, O, . . .	R
4. V, U, T, S, . . .	I
5. A, C, E, G. . . .	P

Key Concept Perimeter, Circumference, and Area

6. Label the parts of each of the figures below.

Square

Triangle

Rectangle

Circle

$P = 4s$ $P = a + b + c$ $P = 2b + 2h$ $C = \pi d$ or $C = 2\pi r$

$A = s^2$ $A = \frac{1}{2}bh$ $A = bh$ $A = \pi r^2$

 Problem 1 **Finding the Perimeter of a Rectangle**

Got It? You want to frame a picture that is 5 in. by 7 in. with a 1-in.-wide frame. What is the perimeter of the picture?

7. The picture is ▢ in. by ▢ in.

8. Circle the formula that gives the perimeter of the picture.

$P = 4s$ $P = 2b + 2h$ $P = a + b + c$ $C = \pi d$

9. Solve using substitution.

10. The perimeter of the picture is ▢ in.

 Problem 2 **Finding Circumference**

Got It? What is the circumference of a circle with radius 24 m in terms of π?

11. Error Analysis At the right is one student's solution. What error did the student make?

$c = \pi d$
$c = \pi(24)$
$c = 24\pi$

24 m

12. Find the correct circumference.

✓ **Problem 3** **Finding Perimeter in the Coordinate Plane**

Got It? Graph quadrilateral *JKLM* with vertices $J(-3, -3)$, $K(1, -3)$, $L(1, 4)$, and $M(-3, 1)$. What is the perimeter of *JLKM*?

13. Graph the quadrilateral on the coordinate plane at the right.

14. Use the justifications at the right to find the length of each side.

$JK = \left| -3 - 1 \right|$ Use the Ruler Postulate.

$= \boxed{}$ Simplify.

$KL = \left| 4 - \boxed{} \right|$ Use the Ruler Postulate.

$= \boxed{}$ Simplify.

$JM = \left| -3 - \boxed{} \right|$ Use the Ruler Postulate.

$= \boxed{}$ Simplify.

$ML = \sqrt{(1 - (-3))^2 + (4 - \boxed{})^2}$ Use the Distance Formula.

$= \sqrt{(\boxed{})^2 + 3^2}$ Simplify within parentheses.

$= \sqrt{(\boxed{}) + (\boxed{})}$ Simplify powers.

$= \sqrt{(\boxed{})}$ Add.

$= \boxed{}$ Take the square root.

15. Add the side lengths to find the perimeter.

$JK + KL + JM + ML = \boxed{} + \boxed{} + \boxed{} + \boxed{} = \boxed{}$

16. The perimeter of *JKLM* is $\boxed{}$ units.

✓ **Problem 5** **Finding Area of a Circle**

Got It? The diameter of a circle is 14 ft. What is its area in terms of π?

17. Label the diameter and radius of the circle at the right.

18. Use the formula $A = \pi r^2$ to find the area of the circle in terms of π.

19. The area of the circle is $\boxed{} \pi$ ft^2.

 take note

Key Concept Postulate 1-10 Area Addition Postulate

20. The area of a region is the sum / difference of the areas of its nonoverlapping parts.

Problem 6   Finding Area of an Irregular Shape

Got It? **Reasoning** The figure below shows one way to separate the figure at the left. What is another way to separate the figure?

21. Draw segments to show two different ways to separate the figure. Separate the left-hand figure into three squares.

Lesson Check • Do you UNDERSTAND?

Compare and Contrast Your friend can't remember whether $2\pi r$ computes the circumference or the area of a circle. How would you help your friend? Explain.

22. Underline the correct word(s) to complete each sentence.

Area involves   units / square units .

Circumference involves   units / square units .

The formula $2\pi r$ relates to   area / circumference   because it involves   units / square units .

Math Success

Check off the vocabulary words that you understand.

☐ perimeter   ☐ area

Rate how well you can *find the area of irregular shapes*.

Lesson 1-8

Vocabulary

● **Review**

Tell whether the statement is a *conjecture*. Explain your reasoning.

1. All apples are sweet.

2. The sun sets in the west.

● **Vocabulary Builder**

reason (noun, verb) REE zun

Related Words: reasonable (adjective), reasonably (adverb)

Definition: A **reason** is an explanation.

Main Idea: A logical argument uses **reasons** to arrive at a conclusion.

● **Use Your Vocabulary**

3. Complete each statement with the appropriate form of the word *reason*.

NOUN	In a logical argument, you state each _?_ .	
ADJECTIVE	The student did a _?_ job on the last math test.	
ADVERB	The workers cleaned up _?_ well after the party.	
VERB	To make a good decision, we _?_ together.	

Write R if the estimate is *reasonable* or U if it is *unreasonable*.

4. $32 + 11 + 6 \approx 60$

5. A 15% tip on $36 is $6.

Problem 1 Finding and Using a Pattern

Got It? What are the next two terms in the sequence?

45, 40, 35, 30, . . .

For Exercises 6–9, circle the correct answer.

6. Do the numbers increase or decrease?

    Increase / Decrease

7. Does the amount of change *vary* or remain *constant*?

    Vary / Constant

8. Which operation helps you form the next term?

    Addition / Subtraction

9. Which number helps you form the next term?

    5 / 15

10. Now find the next two terms in the sequence.

 Problem 2 Using Inductive Reasoning

Got It? What conjecture can you make about the twenty-first term in
R, W, B, R, W, B, ...?

11. Complete the table.

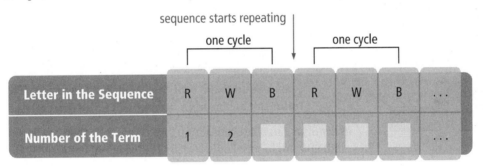

sequence starts repeating

one cycle   one cycle

Letter in the Sequence	R	W	B	R	W	B	. . .
Number of the Term	1	2					. . .

12. There are ▯ letters in the pattern before it starts repeating.

13. R is the 1st term, 4th term, ▯ term, ...

    W is the 2nd term, ▯ term, ▯ term, ...

    B is the 3rd term, ▯ term, ▯ term, ...

Underline the correct words to complete the sentence.

14. The twenty-first term is

    one more than a multiple of 3 / two more than a multiple of 3 / a multiple of 3 .

15. Now make a conjecture.

    The twenty-first term of the sequence is ▯ .

Lesson 2-1

Got It? What conjecture can you make about the sum of the first 30 odd numbers?

16. Complete the table.

Number of Terms	Sum		
1	1	= 1	= 1 • 1
2	1 + 3	= 4	= 2 • ☐
3	1 + ☐ + ☐	= 9	= ☐ • ☐
4	☐ + ☐ + ☐ + ☐	= ☐	= ☐ • ☐
5	☐ + ☐ + ☐ + ☐ + ☐	= ☐	= ☐ • ☐
⋮	⋮		

17. Now make a conjecture.

The sum of the first 30 odd numbers is • ☐ , or ☐ .

 ✓ **Problem 4** Making a Prediction

Got It? What conjecture can you make about backpack sales in June?

For Exercises 18–22, write T for *true* or F for *false*.

Backpacks Sold

____ **18.** The graph shows a pattern of points.

____ **19.** Each month, the number of backpacks sold increases.

____ **20.** The change in sales varies from month to month, so you need to estimate this change.

____ **21.** If sales change by about 500 each month, you can subtract 500 from April's sales to estimate May's sales.

____ **22.** If sales change by about 500 each month, you can add 500 to May's sales to estimate June's sales.

23. Now make a conjecture about backpack sales in June.

About ☐ backpacks will be sold in June.

Problem 5 **Finding a Counterexample**

Got It? What is a counterexample for the conjecture?

If a flower is red, it is a rose.

24. Circle the flowers below that are or can be red.

| rose | bluebell | carnation | geranium | tulip |

25. Is every flower you named a rose?   Yes / No

26. Write a word to complete the counterexample.

A __?__ is a red flower but it is not a rose.

_____
_____

 Lesson Check • **Do you UNDERSTAND?**

Compare and Contrast Clay thinks the next term in the sequence 2, 4, . . . is 6. Given the same pattern, Ott thinks the next term is 8, and Stacie thinks the next term is 7. What conjecture is each person making? Is there enough information to decide who is correct?

Choose the letter that describes the rule for each sequence.

A Multiply by 2   **B** Add 2, add 3, add 4, . . .   **C** Add 2

____ 27. 2, 4, 6, 8, . . .   ____ 28. 2, 4, 8, 16, . . .   ____ 29. 2, 4, 7, 1, . . .

____ 30. Clay's conjecture   ____ 31. Ott's conjecture   ____ 32. Stacie's conjecture

33. Circle the correct answer.

Are two numbers enough to show a pattern?   Yes / No

Math Success

Check off the vocabulary words that you understand.

☐ inductive reasoning   ☐ conjecture   ☐ counterexample

Rate how well you can *use inductive reasoning*.

| Need to review | 0 | 2 | 4 | 6 | 8 | 10 | Now I get it! |

2-2 Conditional Statements

Vocabulary

● **Review**

Underline the *conclusion* of each statement.

1. If the weather is nice, we will go swimming.

2. If I ride my bike to softball practice, then I will get there on time.

● **Vocabulary Builder**

---

converse (noun) KAHN **vurs**

Related Words: convert, conversion

Definition: The **converse** of something is its opposite.

Word Source: The prefix *con-*, which means "together," and *vertere*, which means "to turn," come from Latin. So, a **converse** involves changing the order of more than one thing.

● **Use Your Vocabulary**

Finish writing the *converse* of each statement.

3. **Statement:** If I study, then I pass the Geometry test.

   Converse: If __?__ , then I study.

   _____

4. **Statement:** If I am happy, then I laugh.

   Converse: If __?__ , then __?__ .

   _____   _____

5. **Statement:** If I have a summer job, then I can buy a new bicycle.

   Converse: __?__ .

   _____

Key Concept · Conditional Statements

Definition	Symbols	Diagram
A **conditional** is an if-then statement. The **hypothesis** is the part p following *if*. The **conclusion** is the part q following *then*.	$p \rightarrow q$ Read as "If p then q" or "p implies q."	

6. If $p = $ tears and $q = $ sadness, what are two ways to read $p \rightarrow q$?

_____   _____

Problem 1 Identifying the Hypothesis and the Conclusion

Got It? What are the hypothesis and the conclusion of the conditional?

If an angle measures 130, then the angle is obtuse.

Complete each sentence with *if* or *then*.

7. The hypothesis is the part following __?__.

_____

8. The conclusion is the part following __?__.

_____

9. Circle the hypothesis. Underline the conclusion.

If an angle measures 130, then the angle is obtuse.

Problem 2 Writing a Conditional

Got It? How can you write "Dolphins are mammals" as a conditional?

10. Circle the correct statement.

All dolphins are mammals.   All mammals are dolphins.

Underline the correct words to complete each statement.

11. The set of dolphins / mammals is inside the set of dolphins / mammals .

12. The smaller/larger set is the hypothesis and the smaller / larger set is the conclusion.

13. Use your answers to Exercises 11 and 12 to write the conditional.

If __?__ , then __?__ .

If an animal is _____ ,

then it is _____ .

Lesson 2-2

Finding the Truth Value of a Conditional

Got It? Is the conditional *true* or *false*? If it is false, find a counterexample.

If a month has 28 days, then it is February.

14. Cross out the month(s) that have at least 28 days.

January	February	March	April	May	June
July	August	September	October	November	December

15. Is the conditional *true* or *false*? Explain.

_____

_____

take note

Key Concept **Related Conditional Statements**

Statement	How to Write It	Symbols	How to Read It
Conditional	Use the given hypothesis and conclusion.	$p \rightarrow q$	If p, then q.
Converse	Exchange the hypothesis and the conclusion.	$q \rightarrow p$	If q, then p.
Inverse	Negate both the hypothesis and the conclusion of the conditional.	$\sim p \rightarrow \sim q$	If not p, then not q.
Contrapositive	Negate both the hypothesis and the conclusion of the converse.	$\sim q \rightarrow \sim p$	If not q, then not p.

Use the statement below to write each conditional.

$\angle A$ measures 98, so $\angle A$ is obtuse.

16. Conditional If _?_, then _?_.

If $\angle A$ measures 98, then _____.

17. Converse If _?_, then _?_.

If _____, then _____.

18. Inverse If *not* _?_, then *not* _?_.

If _____,

then _____.

19. Contrapositive If *not* _?_, then *not* _?_.

If _____,

then _____.

Problem 4 Writing and Finding Truth Values of Statements

Got It? What are the converse, inverse, and contrapositive of the conditional statement below? What are the truth values of each? If a statement is false, give a counterexample.

> If a vegetable is a carrot, then it contains beta carotene.

20. **Converse:** If a vegetable contains beta carotene, then __?__ .

21. **Inverse:** If a vegetable is not a carrot, then __?__ .

22. **Contrapositive:** If a vegetable does not contain beta carotene, then __?__ .

23. The converse is true / false . The inverse is true / false . The contrapositive is true / false .

24. Give counterexamples for the statements that are false.

 Lesson Check • **Do you UNDERSTAND?**

Error Analysis Your classmate rewrote the statement "You jog every Sunday" as "If you jog, then it is Sunday." What is your classmate's error? Correct it.

25. Circle the hypothesis and underline the conclusion of your classmate's conditional.

> If you jog, then it is Sunday.

26. Circle the counterexample for your classmate's conditional.

> You don't jog, and it is not Sunday.   You also jog on Saturday.

27. Write the conditional that best represents "You jog every Sunday."

 Math Success

Check off the vocabulary words that you understand.

☐ conditional   ☐ hypothesis   ☐ conclusion

Rate how well you can *write conditional statements.*

Need to review 0 2 4 6 8 10 Now I get it!

Lesson 2-2

2-3 Biconditionals and Definitions

Vocabulary

Review

Underline the *hypothesis* in each statement.

1. If it rains on Friday, I won't have to cut the grass on Saturday.

2. If I go to sleep early tonight, then I won't be late for school tomorrow.

3. A triangle is equilateral if it has three congruent sides.

4. I'll know how to write biconditionals if I can identify a hypothesis and a conclusion.

Vocabulary Builder

bi- (prefix) **by**

Definition: *bi-* is a prefix that means having two.

Examples: A *bicycle* has two wheels. Someone who is *bilingual* speaks two languages fluently.

Use Your Vocabulary

Draw a line from each word in Column A to its meaning in Column B.

Column A	Column B
5. biannually (adverb)	occurring every two hundred years
6. biathlon (noun)	a two-footed animal
7. bicentennial (adjective)	having two coasts
8. bicoastal (adjective)	supported by two parties
9. biped (noun)	occurring every two weeks
10. bipartisan (adjective)	occurring every two years
11. biplane (noun)	a plane with two sets of wings
12. biweekly (adjective)	a two-event athletic contest

Key Concept   Biconditional Statements

A *biconditional* combines $p \to q$ and $q \to p$ as $p \leftrightarrow q$.

You read $p \leftrightarrow q$ as "p if and only if q."

13. Complete the biconditional.

A ray is an angle bisector __?__ it divides an angle into two congruent angles.

_____

Problem 1   Writing a Biconditional

Got It? What is the converse of the following true conditional? If the converse is also true, rewrite the statements as a biconditional.

If two angles have equal measure, then the angles are congruent.

14. Identify the hypothesis (p) and the conclusion (q).

p: _____ q: _____

15. Circle the converse ($q \to p$) of the conditional.

| If two angles do *not* have equal measure, then the angles are *not* congruent. | If two angles are congruent, then the angles have equal measure. | If two angles are *not* congruent, then the angles do *not* have equal measure. |

16. Now write the statements as a biconditional ($p \leftrightarrow q$).

_____   if and only if   _____.

Problem 2   Identifying the Conditionals in a Biconditional

Got It? What are the two conditionals that form this biconditional?

Two numbers are reciprocals if and only if their product is 1.

17. Identify p and q.

p: _____ q: _____

18. Write the conditional $p \to q$.

If _____,

then _____.

19. Write the conditional $q \to p$.

If _____,

then _____.

Lesson 2-3

Problem 3 Writing a Definition as a Biconditional

Got It? Is this definition of *straight angle* reversible? If yes, write it as a true biconditional.

A straight angle is an angle that measures 180.

20. *Reversible* means you can reverse p and [ ] in the conditional.

21. Write the conditional.

If _____,

then _____.

22. Write the converse.

If _____,

then _____.

23. Write the biconditional.

_____,

if and only if _____.

 Problem 4 Identifying Good Definitions

Got It? Is the following statement a good definition? Explain.

A square is a figure with four right angles.

24. Write the *conditional*.

_____

_____

25. Write the *converse*.

_____

_____

26. Which statement is true, the *conditional*, the *converse*, or *both*?

_____

27. Is the definition of a square a good definition? Explain.

_____

_____

Chapter 2

44

Lesson Check • Do you UNDERSTAND?

Compare and Contrast Which of the following statements is a better definition of a linear pair?

A linear pair is a pair of supplementary angles.

A linear pair is a pair of adjacent angles with noncommon sides that are opposite rays.

Use the figures below for Exercises 28–31.

Figure 1   Figure 2   Figure 3   Figure 4

Underline the correct number or numbers to complete each sentence.

28. Figure(s) 1 / 2 / 3 / 4 show(s) linear pairs.

29. Figure(s) 1 / 2 / 3 / 4 show(s) supplementary angles.

30. Figure(s) 1 / 2 / 3 / 4 show(s) adjacent angles.

31. Figure(s) 1 / 2 / 3 / 4 show(s) adjacent angles whose noncommon sides are opposite rays.

32. Underline the correct word to complete the sentence.

Supplementary angles are always / sometimes / never linear pairs.

33. Write the better definition of a linear pair.

_____

_____

_____

Math Success

Check off the vocabulary words that you understand.

☐ biconditional   ☐ conditional   ☐ hypothesis   ☐ conclusion

Rate how well you can *use biconditionals*.

Lesson 2-3

Vocabulary

● Review

Write the *converse* of each conditional.

1. If I am thirsty, then I drink water.

_____

2. If the car outside is wet, then it rained.

_____

● Vocabulary Builder

deduce (verb) **dee DOOS**

Related Words: deductive (adjective), deduction (noun)

Definition: To **deduce** is to use known facts to reach a conclusion.

Main Idea: When you use general principles and facts to come to a conclusion, you **deduce** the conclusion.

Example: Your friend is wearing red today. He wears red only when there is a home game. You use these facts to **deduce** that there is a home game today.

● Use Your Vocabulary

Complete each statement with a word from the list. Use each word only once.

deduce   deduction   deductive

3. You use __?__ reasoning to draw a conclusion based on facts.

4. The conclusion of your reasoning is a __?__ .

5. The teacher will not __?__ that a dog ate your homework.

Property Law of Detachment

Law

If the hypothesis of a true conditional is true, then the conclusion is true.

Symbols

If $p \rightarrow q$ is true and p is true, then q is true.

Problem 1 Using the Law of Detachment

Got It? What can you conclude from the given information?

If there is lightning, then it is not safe to be out in the open.
Marla sees lightning from the soccer field.

6. Underline the hypothesis of the conditional. Circle the conclusion.

If there is lightning, then it is not safe to be out in the open.

Underline the correct word or phrase to complete each sentence.

7. "Marla sees lightning from the soccer field" fits / does not fit the hypothesis of the conditional.

8. It is safe / not safe to be on the soccer field.

Property Law of Syllogism

You can state a conclusion from two true conditional statements when the conclusion of one statement is the hypothesis of the other statement.

If $p \rightarrow q$ is true and $q \rightarrow r$ is true, then $p \rightarrow r$ is true.

Complete each conclusion.

9. If it is July, then you are on summer vacation.

If you are on summer vacation, then you work in a smoothie shop.

Conclusion: If it is July, then _____.

10. If a figure is a rhombus, then it has four sides.

If a figure has four sides, then it is a quadrilateral.

Conclusion: If a figure is a rhombus, then _____.

Problem 2 Using the Law of Syllogism

Got It? What can you conclude from the given information? What is your reasoning?

If a number ends in 0, then it is divisible by 10.
If a number is divisible by 10, then it is divisible by 5.

11. Identify p, q, and r.

p: a number ends in ☐ q: a number is divisible by ☐ r: a number is divisible by ☐

Lesson 2-4

12. Decide whether each part of the given information is *true* or *false*. Write T for *true* or F for *false*.

_____ $p \rightarrow q$ _____ $q \rightarrow r$ _____ $p \rightarrow r$

13. Circle the part of the Law of Syllogism that you will write.

| $p \rightarrow q$ | $q \rightarrow r$ | $p \rightarrow r$ |

14. Now write your conclusion.

If _____ , then _____ .

Problem 3   Using the Laws of Syllogism and Detachment

Got It? What can you conclude from the given information? What is your reasoning?

If a river is more than 4000 mi long, then it is longer than the Amazon.
If a river is longer than the Amazon, then it is the longest river in the world.
The Nile is 4132 mi long.

15. Identify p, q, and r in the given information.

p: _____

q: _____

r: _____

16. Use the Law of Syllogism to complete the conditional.

If a river is more than _____ .

then it _____ .

17. Use the Law of Detachment and the conditional in Exercise 16 to write a conclusion.

The Nile is _____ .

Lesson Check • Do you know HOW?

If possible, make a conclusion from the given true statements. What reasoning did you use?

If a figure is a three-sided polygon, then it is a triangle.
Figure *ABC* is a three-sided polygon.

18. Identify p and q in the first statement.

p: _____

q: _____

19. Underline the correct words to complete each sentence.

The second statement matches the hypothesis / conclusion of the first statement.

I can use the Law of Detachment / Syllogism to state a conclusion.

20. Write your conclusion.

_____

Lesson Check • Do you UNDERSTAND?

Error Analysis What is the error in the reasoning below?

~~Birds that weigh more than 50 pounds cannot fly. A kiwi cannot fly. So, a kiwi weighs more than 50 pounds.~~

21. Write "Birds that weigh more than 50 pounds cannot fly" as a conditional.

_____

_____

22. Write the hypothesis of the conditional in Exercise 21.

_____

_____

Underline the correct word to complete each sentence.

23. "A kiwi cannot fly" matches the hypothesis / conclusion of the conditional.

24. The student incorrectly applied the Law of Detachment / Syllogism .

Math Success

Check off the vocabulary words that you understand.

☐ Law of Detachment ☐ Law of Syllogism ☐ deductive reasoning ☐ conditional

Rate how well you can use *deductive reasoning*.

Need to review 0 2 4 6 8 10 Now I get it!

Lesson 2-4

Reasoning in Algebra and Geometry

Vocabulary

● Review

1. Circle each *equation*.

$2(a - 5)^2$ $\qquad$ $3x + 2 = 4$ $\qquad$ $5 + 3^4$ $\qquad$ $9 < x - 2$

Write an *equation* to represent each problem.

2. Sara has five more than twice the number of apples that Gregg has. If Sara has 21 apples, how many apples does Gregg have?

3. Your brother does one less than twice the number of chores that you do. If he does seven chores, how many chores do you do?

● Vocabulary Builder

justify (verb) ᴊᴜs **tuh fy**

Related Words: justice (noun), justification (noun), justifiable (adjective), justly (adverb)

Definition: To **justify** a step in a solution means to provide a mathematical reason why the step is correct.

Main Idea: When you **justify** an action, you explain why it is reasonable.

● Use Your Vocabulary

4. Draw a line from each equation in Column A to the property you would use to *justify* it in Column B.

Column A	Column B
$3 + 7 = 7 + 3$	Associative Property of Addition
$12(4) = 4(12)$	Associative Property of Multiplication
$2 \cdot (5 \cdot x) = (2 \cdot 5) \cdot x$	Commutative Property of Addition
$1 + (9 + 53) = (1 + 9) + 53$	Commutative Property of Multiplication

Key Concept   Properties of Equality

5. Complete the graphic organizer.

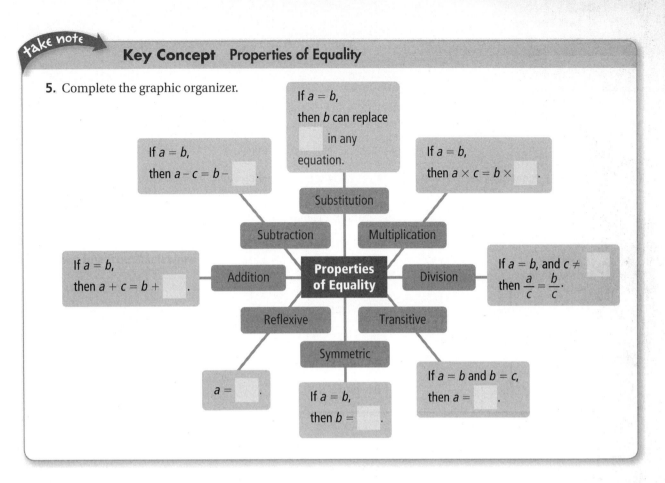

If $a = b$,
then b can replace ☐ in any equation.

Substitution

If $a = b$,
then $a - c = b -$ ☐.

Subtraction

If $a = b$,
then $a \times c = b \times$ ☐.

Multiplication

If $a = b$,
then $a + c = b +$ ☐.

Addition

Properties of Equality

Division

If $a = b$, and $c \neq$ ☐,
then $\dfrac{a}{c} = \dfrac{b}{c}$.

Reflexive

Transitive

Symmetric

$a =$ ☐.

If $a = b$,
then $b =$ ☐.

If $a = b$ and $b = c$,
then $a =$ ☐.

Key Concept   The Distributive Property

Use multiplication to distribute a to each term of the sum or difference within the parentheses.

Sum
$a(b + c) = ab + ac$

Difference
$a(b - c) = ab - ac$

Use the Distributive Property to simplify each expression.

6. $5(24) = 5(20 + $ ☐ $)$
$= 5($ ☐ $) + 5($ ☐ $)$
$= $ ☐ $ + $ ☐
$= $ ☐

7. $17(3) = (20 - 3)($ ☐ $)$
$= 20($ ☐ $) - 3($ ☐ $)$
$= $ ☐ $ - $ ☐
$= $ ☐

Problem 1   Justifying Steps When Solving an Equation

Got It? What is the value of x? Justify each step.

Given: $\overrightarrow{AB}$ bisects $\angle RAN$.

8. Circle the statement you can write from the given information.

$\angle RAB$ is obtuse. $\angle RAB \cong \angle NAB$ $\angle NAB \cong \angle RAN$

9. Use the justifications below to find the value of x.

$\overrightarrow{AB}$ bisects $\angle RAN$.   Given

$\angle RAB \cong \angle$ [ ]   Definition of angle bisector

$m\angle RAB = m\angle$ [ ]   Congruent angles have equal measures.

$x =$ [ ]   Substitute.

$0 =$ [ ]   Subtraction Property of Equality

$75 =$ [ ]   Addition Property of Equality

take note

Key Concept   Properties of Congruence

Reflexive   **Symmetric**   **Transitive**

$\overline{AB} \cong \overline{AB}$ If $\overline{AB} \cong \overline{CD}$, then $\overline{CD} \cong \overline{AB}$.   If $\overline{AB} \cong \overline{CD}$ and $\overline{CD} \cong \overline{EF}$, then $\overline{AB} \cong \overline{EF}$.

$\angle A \cong \angle A$ If $\angle A \cong \angle B$, then $\angle B \cong \angle A$.   If $\angle A \cong \angle B$ and $\angle B \cong \angle C$, then $\angle A \cong \angle C$.

Complete each statement.

10. If $\angle P \cong \angle R$ and $\angle R \cong \angle A$, then $\angle P \cong \angle$ [ ] .

11. If $\angle X \cong \angle N$ and $\angle$ [ ] $\cong \angle Y$, then $\angle X \cong \angle Y$.

12. If $\angle L \cong \angle T$ and $\angle T \cong \angle$ [ ] , then $\angle L \cong \angle Q$.

Problem 3   Writing a Two-Column Proof

Got It? Write a two-column proof.

Given: $\overline{AB} \cong \overline{CD}$ **Prove:** $\overline{AC} \cong \overline{BD}$

13. The statements are given below. Write a reason for each statement.

Statements	Reasons
1) $\overline{AB} \cong \overline{CD}$	1) _____
2) $AB = CD$	2) _____
3) $BC = BC$	3) _____
4) $AB + BC = BC + CD$	4) _____
5) $AC = BD$	5) _____
6) $\overline{AC} \cong \overline{BD}$	6) _____

Lesson Check • Do you UNDERSTAND?

Developing Proof Fill in the reasons for this algebraic proof.

Given: $5x + 1 = 21$

Prove: $x = 4$

Statements	Reasons
1) $5x + 1 = 21$	1) __?__
2) $5x = 20$	2) __?__
3) $x = 4$	3) __?__

14. The first step in a proof is what you are given / to prove .

Underline the correct word(s) to complete each sentence. Then circle the property of equality that justifies the step.

15. First, the number 1 was added to / subtracted from each side of the equation.

Addition Property of Equality   Subtraction Property of Equality   Reflexive Property

16. Then, each side of the equation was multiplied / divided by 5.

Division Property of Equality   Multiplication Property of Equality   Transitive Property

17. Now write a reason for each step.

1) _____

2) _____

3) _____

Math Success

Check off the vocabulary words that you understand.

☐ Reflexive Property   ☐ Symmetric Property   ☐ Transitive Property

☐ proof   ☐ two-column proof

Rate how well you can *use properties of equality and congruence in proofs.*

Need to review   0   2   4   6   8   10   Now I get it!

2-6 Proving Angles Congruent

Vocabulary

● Review

Complete each sentence with *proof* or *prove*.

1. Galileo wanted to __?__ that the planets revolve around the sun.

2. His observations and discoveries supported his theory but were not a __?__ of it.

● Vocabulary Builder

theorem (noun) THEE **uh rum**

Definition: A **theorem** is a conjecture or statement that you prove true.

Main Idea: You use definitions, postulates, properties, and previously proven theorems to prove **theorems.**

● Use Your Vocabulary

Write T for *true* or F for *false*.

_____ 3. A postulate is a *theorem*.

_____ 4. A *theorem* may contain definitions.

_____ 5. An axiom is a *theorem*.

Complete each statement with *lines*, *planes*, or *points*.

6. **Postulate 1-1** Through any two __?__ there is exactly one line.

7. **Postulate 1-2** If two distinct __?__ intersect, then they intersect in exactly one point.

8. **Postulate 1-3** If two distinct __?__ intersect, then they intersect in exactly one line.

9. **Postulate 1-4** Through any three noncollinear __?__ there is exactly one plane.

Chapter 2 54

Theorem 2-1   Vertical Angles Theorem

Vertical angles are congruent.

10. If $\angle A$ and $\angle B$ are vertical angles and $m\angle A = 15$, then $m\angle B =$ _____ .

Problem 1   **Using the Vertical Angles Theorem**

Got It? What is the value of x?

11. Circle the word that best describes the labeled angle pair in the diagram.

| corresponding | perpendicular | vertical |

12. Circle the word that best describes the relationship between the labeled angles in the diagram.

| congruent | perpendicular | supplementary |

13. Use the labels in the diagram to write an equation.

$3x =$ _____

14. Now solve the equation.

15. The value of x is _____ .

Problem 2   **Proof Using the Vertical Angles Theorem**

Got It? Use the Vertical Angles Theorem to prove the following.

Given: $\angle 1 \cong \angle 2$

Prove: $\angle 1 \cong \angle 2 \cong \angle 3 \cong \angle 4$

16. Write a reason for each statement below.

Statements	Reasons
1) $\angle 1 \cong \angle 2$	1) _____
2) $\angle 1 \cong \angle 3$	2) _____
3) $\angle 2 \cong \angle 4$	3) _____
4) $\angle 1 \cong \angle 2 \cong \angle 3 \cong \angle 4$	4) _____

Lesson 2-6

Theorem 2-2 Congruent Supplements Theorem

If two angles are supplements of the same angle (or of congruent angles), then the two angles are congruent.

If ∠1 and ∠3 are supplements and ∠2 and ∠3 are supplements, then ∠1 ≅ ∠2.

17. Complete the diagram below to illustrate Theorem 2-2.

18. If $m\angle D = 135$ and $m\angle G = 45$ and ∠F and ∠G are supplements, then $m\angle F =$ ☐ .

If ∠A and ∠B are supplements and $m\angle C = 85$ and $m\angle B = 95$, then $m\angle A =$ ☐ .

Problem 3 Writing a Paragraph Proof

Got It? Write a paragraph proof for the Vertical Angles Theorem.

    Given: ∠1 and ∠3 are vertical angles.

    Prove: ∠1 ≅ ∠3

Circle the correct word to complete each sentence.

19. ∠1 and ∠3 are __?__ angles because it is given.   supplementary / vertical

20. ∠1 and ∠2 are __?__ angles because they form a linear pair.   supplementary / vertical

21. ∠2 and ∠3 are __?__ angles because they form a linear pair.   supplementary / vertical

22. $m\angle 1 + m\angle 2 = 180$ because the sum of the measures of __?__ angles is 180.   complementary / supplementary

23. $m\angle 2 + m\angle 3 = 180$ because the sum of the measures of __?__ angles is 180.   complementary / supplementary

24. By the __?__ Property of Equality, $m\angle 1 + m\angle 2 = m\angle 2 + m\angle 3$.   Reflexive / Transitive

25. By the __?__ Property of Equality, $m\angle 1 = m\angle 3$.   Subtraction / Symmetric

26. Angles with the same __?__ are congruent, so ∠1 ≅ ∠3.   properties / measure

Theorem 2-3 Congruent Complements Theorem

If two angles are complements of the same angle (or of congruent angles), then the two angles are congruent.

27. ∠A is a supplement of a 165° angle. ∠B is a complement of a 75° angle. Circle the relationship between ∠A and ∠B.

    complementary   congruent   supplementary

Theorems 2-4 and 2-5

Theorem 2-4 All right angles are congruent.

Theorem 2-5 If two angles are congruent and supplementary, then each is a right angle.

28. If ∠R and ∠S are right angles, then ☐ ≅ ☐ .

29. If ∠H ≅ ∠J and ∠H and ∠J are supplements, then m∠H = m ☐ = ☐ .

Lesson Check • Do you know HOW?

What are the measures of ∠1, ∠2, and ∠3?

30. Cross out the theorem you CANNOT use to find an angle measure.

| Congruent Complements Theorem | Congruent Supplements Theorem | Vertical Angles Theorem |

31. m∠1 = ☐   **32.** m∠2 = ☐   **33.** m∠3 = ☐

Lesson Check • Do you UNDERSTAND?

Reasoning If ∠A and ∠B are supplements, and ∠A and ∠C are supplements, what can you conclude about ∠B and ∠C? Explain.

34. Since ∠A and ∠B are supplements, m∠A + m∠B = ☐ .

35. Since ∠A and ∠C are supplements, m∠A + m∠C = ☐ .

36. By the Transitive Property of Equality, ☐ + m∠B = ☐ + m∠C.

37. By the Subtraction Property of Equality, m∠B = ☐ , so ∠B ≅ ☐ .

Math Success

Check off the vocabulary words that you understand.

☐ theorem   ☐ paragraph proof   ☐ complementary   ☐ supplementary   ☐ right angle

Rate how well you can *write proofs*.

Need to review   0   2   4   6   8   10   Now I get it!

Lesson 2-6

3-1 Lines and Angles

Vocabulary

● Review

Write T for *true* or F for *false*.

_____ **1.** You can name a *plane* by a capital letter, such as *A*.

_____ **2.** A *plane* contains a finite number of lines.

_____ **3.** Two points lying on the same *plane* are coplanar.

_____ **4.** If two distinct *planes* intersect, then they intersect in exactly one line.

● Vocabulary Builder

parallel (noun) PA ruh lel

The symbol for **parallel** is ∥.

Definition: *Parallel* lines lie in the same plane but never intersect, no matter how far they extend.

● Use Your Vocabulary

5. Circle the segment(s) that are *parallel* to the *x*-axis.

$\overline{AB}$ $\overline{BC}$ $\overline{CD}$ $\overline{AD}$

6. Circle the segment(s) that are *parallel* to the *y*-axis.

$\overline{AB}$ $\overline{BC}$ $\overline{CD}$ $\overline{AD}$

7. Circle the polygon(s) that have two pairs of *parallel* sides.

rectangle   parallelogram   square   trapezoid

Complete each statement below with *line* or *segment*.

8. A __?__ consist of two endpoints and all the points between them.

9. A __?__ is made up of an infinite number of points.

Parallel lines are coplanar lines that do not intersect.

Skew lines are noncoplanar; they are not parallel and do not intersect.

Parallel planes are planes that do not intersect.

10. Write each word, phrase, or symbol in the correct oval.

noncoplanar   coplanar   do not intersect

intersect $\overleftrightarrow{AE}$ and $\overleftrightarrow{CG}$ $\overleftrightarrow{CB}$ and $\overleftrightarrow{AE}$

Parallel   **Skew**

Use arrows to show
$\overleftrightarrow{AE} \parallel \overleftrightarrow{BF}$ and $\overleftrightarrow{AD} \parallel \overleftrightarrow{BC}$.

Problem 1   **Identifying Nonintersecting Lines and Planes**

Got It? Use the figure at the right. Which segments are parallel to $\overline{AD}$?

11. In plane *ADHE*, [   ] is parallel to $\overline{AD}$.

12. In plane *ADBC*, [   ] is parallel to $\overline{AD}$.

13. In plane *ADGF*, [   ] is parallel to $\overline{AD}$.

Got It? **Reasoning** Explain why $\overline{FE}$ and $\overline{CD}$ are *not* skew.

14. Cross out the words or phrases below that do NOT describe skew lines.

coplanar	do not intersect	intersect
parallel	noncoplanar	not parallel

15. Circle the correct statement below.

Segments and rays can be skew if they lie in skew lines.

Segments and rays are never skew.

16. Underline the correct words to complete the sentence.

$\overline{FE}$ and $\overline{CD}$ are in a plane that slopes from the bottom / top left edge to the

bottom / top right edge of the figure.

17. Why are $\overline{FE}$ and $\overline{CD}$ NOT skew?

Lesson 3-1

Key Concept   Angle Pairs Formed by Transversals

Alternate interior angles are nonadjacent interior angles that lie on opposite sides of the transversal.

Same-side interior angles are interior angles that lie on the same side of the transversal.

Corresponding angles lie on the same side of a transversal *t* and in corresponding positions.

Alternate exterior angles are nonadjacent exterior angles that lie on opposite sides of the transversal.

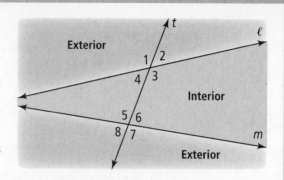

Use the diagram above. Draw a line from each angle pair in Column A to its description in Column B.

Column A	Column B
18. ∠4 and ∠6	alternate exterior angles
19. ∠3 and ∠6	same-side interior angles
20. ∠2 and ∠6	alternate interior angles
21. ∠2 and ∠8	corresponding angles

Problem 2 **Identifying an Angle Pair**

Got It? What are three pairs of corresponding angles in the diagram at the right?

Underline the correct word(s) or letter(s) to complete each sentence.

22. The transversal is line *m* / *n* / *r* .

23. Corresponding angles are on the same side / different sides of the transversal.

24. Name three pairs of corresponding angles.

∠ ☐ and ∠ ☐   ∠ ☐ and ∠ ☐   ∠ ☐ and ∠ ☐   ∠ ☐ and ∠ ☐

Problem 3 **Classifying an Angle Pair**

Got It? Are angles 1 and 3 *alternate interior angles, same-side interior angles, corresponding angles,* or *alternate exterior angles*?

25. Are ∠1 and ∠3 on the same side of the transversal?   Yes / No

26. Cross out the angle types that do NOT describe ∠1 and ∠3.

alternate exterior   alternate interior   corresponding   same-side interior

27. ∠1 and ∠3 are _?_ angles.

Lesson Check • Do you know HOW?

Name one pair each of the segments or planes.

28. parallel segments

$\overline{AB} \parallel$ _____

29. skew segments

$\overline{HD}$ and _____

30. parallel planes

$ABCD \parallel$ _____

Name one pair each of the angles.

31. alternate interior

∠8 and ∠ _____

32. same-side interior

∠8 and ∠ _____

33. corresponding

∠1 and ∠ _____

34. alternate exterior

∠7 and ∠ _____

Lesson Check • Do you UNDERSTAND?

Error Analysis Carly and Juan examine the figure at the right. Carly says $\overline{AB} \parallel \overline{HG}$. Juan says $\overline{AB}$ and $\overline{HG}$ are skew. Who is correct? Explain.

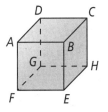

Write T for *true* or F for *false*.

_____ **35.** Parallel segments are coplanar.

_____ **36.** There are only six planes in a cube.

_____ **37.** No plane contains $\overline{AB}$ and $\overline{HG}$.

38. Who is correct? Explain.

_____

_____

Math Success

Check off the vocabulary words that you understand.

☐ angle   ☐ parallel   ☐ skew   ☐ transversal

Rate how well you can *classify angle pairs*.

| Need to review | 0 | 2 | 4 | 6 | 8 | 10 | Now I get it! |

Lesson 3-1

Properties of Parallel Lines

Vocabulary

● Review

1. Circle the symbol for *congruent*.

≅   =   ‖

Identify each angle below as *acute*, *obtuse*, or *right*.

2.
125°

_____

3.

_____

4.
72°

_____

● Vocabulary Builder

interior (noun) in TEER ee ur

m   interior   ℓ

Main Idea: The **interior** is the inside of a figure.

Related Words: inside (noun), exterior (noun, antonym)

Definition: The **interior** of a pair of lines is the region between the two lines.

Example: A painter uses **interior** paint for the inside of a house.

● Use Your Vocabulary

Use the diagram at the right for Exercises 5 and 6. Underline the correct point to complete each sentence.

5. The *interior* of the circle contains point A / B / C .

6. The *interior* of the angle contains point A / B / C .

7. Underline the correct word to complete the sentence.

The endpoint of an *angle* is called its ray / vertex .

8. Write two other names for ∠ABC in the diagram at the right.

_____   _____

take note

Postulate 3-1, Theorems 3-1, 3-2, 3-3

Then...

If...

a transversal intersects two parallel lines,

corresponding angles are congruent.
Theorem 3-2 Corresponding Angles Theorem

alternate interior angles are congruent.
Theorem 3-1 Alternate Interior Angles Theorem

same-side interior angles are supplementary.
Postulate 3-1 Same-Side Interior Angles Postulate

alternate exterior angles are congruent.
Theorem 3-3 Alternate Exterior Angles Theorem

Use the graphic organizer and the diagram to find each congruent angle.

9. Theorem 3-2
$\angle 3 \cong$ ☐

10. Theorem 3-1
$\angle 3 \cong$ ☐

11. Theorem 3-3
$\angle 1 \cong$ ☐

 Problem 1 Identifying Congruent Angles

Got It? Reasoning Can you always find the measure of all 8 angles when two parallel lines are cut by a transversal? Explain.

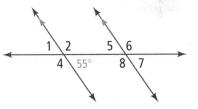

Yes, because $m\angle 1 = 55$ by the Vertical Angles Theorem.

$m\angle 5 = 55$ by the Corresponding Angles Postulate because $\angle 1$ and $\angle 5$ are corresponding angles.

12. Write a reason for each statement.

$m\angle 7 = 55$

$m\angle 5 = m\angle 7$

$m\angle 5 = 55$

$m\angle 2 = 125$

$m\angle 4 = 125$

$m\angle 6$ and $m\angle 8 = 125$

Lesson 3-2

Problem 2 Proving an Angle Relationship

Got It? Given: $a \parallel b$

Prove: $\angle 1 \cong \angle 7$

13. Use the reasons at the right to write each step of the proof.

Statements	Reasons
1)	1) Given
2)	2) If lines are $\parallel$, then corresp. angles are $\cong$.
3)	3) Congruent angles have equal measure.
4)	4) Vertical angles are congruent.
5)	5) Congruent angles have equal measure.
6)	6) Transitive Property of $\cong$
7)	7) Angles with equal measure are $\cong$.

Problem 3 Finding Measures of Angles

Got It? Find the measure of $\angle 1$. Justify your answer.

14. There are two sets of parallel lines. Each parallel line also acts as a __?__ .

15. The steps to find $m\angle 1$ are given below. Justify each step.

Statements	Reasons
1) $\angle 1 \cong \angle 4$	1)
2) $m\angle 1 = m\angle 4$	2)
3) $\angle 4$ and $\angle 6$ are supplementary.	3)
4) $m\angle 4 + m\angle 6 = 180$	4)
5) $m\angle 1 + m\angle 6 = 180$	5)
6) $m\angle 5 = 105$	6)
7) $m\angle 6 = 105$	7)
8) $m\angle 1 + 105 = 180$	8)
9) $m\angle 1 = 75$	9)

Problem 4 Using Algebra to Find an Angle Measure

Got It? In the figure at the right, what are the values of x and y?

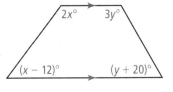

16. The bases of a trapezoid are parallel / perpendicular .

17. Use the Same-Side Interior Angles Postulate to complete each statement.

$2x + \boxed{} = 180$ $3y + \boxed{} = 180$

18. Solve each equation.

 Lesson Check • **Do you UNDERSTAND?**

In the diagram at the right, $\angle 1$ and $\angle 8$ are supplementary. What is a good name for this pair of angles? Explain.

19. Circle the best name for lines a and b.

| parallel | perpendicular | skew | transversals |

20. Circle the best name from the list below for $\angle 1$ and $\angle 8$.

| alternate | congruent | corresponding | same-side |

21. Circle the best name from the list below for $\angle 1$ and $\angle 8$.

| exterior | interior |

22. Use your answers to Exercises 20 and 21 to write a name for $\angle 1$ and $\angle 8$.

_____

Math Success

Check off the vocabulary words that you understand.

☐ alternate interior angles   ☐ alternate exterior angles

Rate how well you can *prove angle relationships*.

Need to review   0   2   4   6   8   10   Now I get it!

Vocabulary

● Review

Write the *converse* of each statement.

1. Statement: If you are cold, then you wear a sweater.

Converse: If __?__ , then __?__ .

If _____ , then _____ .

2. Statement: If an angle is a right angle, then it measures 90°.

Converse: _____

3. The *converse* of a true statement is always / sometimes / never true .

● Vocabulary Builder

exterior (adjective) **ek STEER ee ur**

Related Words: **exterior** (noun), external, interior (antonym)

Definition: **Exterior** means on the outside or in an outer region.

Example: Two lines crossed by a transversal form four **exterior** angles.

● Use Your Vocabulary

Underline the correct word to complete each sentence.

4. To paint the outside of your house, buy interior / exterior paint.

5. The protective cover prevents the interior / exterior of the book from being damaged.

6. In the diagram at the right, angles 1 and 7 are alternate interior / exterior angles.

7. In the diagram at the right, angles 4 and 5 are same-side interior / exterior angles.

Underline the *hypothesis* and circle the *conclusion* in the following statements.

8. If the lines do not intersect, then they are parallel lines.

9. If the angle measures 180°, then it is a straight angle.

Theorems 3-2 and 3-4   Corresponding Angles Theorem and Its Converse

Theorem 3-2 Corresponding Angles Theorem

If a transversal intersects two parallel lines, then corresponding angles are congruent.

10. Complete the statement of Theorem 3-2.

Theorem 3-4 Converse of the Corresponding Angles Theorem

If two lines on a transversal form corresponding angles that are congruent, then the lines are __?__ .

11. Use the diagram below. Place appropriate marking(s) to show that ∠1 and ∠2 are congruent.

12. Circle the diagram that models Theorem 3-4.

Theorems 3-5, 3-6, and 3-7

Theorem 3-5 Converse of the Alternate Interior Angles Theorem

If two lines and a transversal form alternate interior angles that are congruent, then the two lines are parallel.

Theorem 3-6 Converse of the Same-Side Interior Angles Theorem

If two lines and a transversal form same-side interior angles that are supplementary, then the two lines are parallel.

Theorem 3-7 Converse of the Alternate Exterior Angles Theorem

If two lines and a transversal form alternate exterior angles that are congruent, then the two lines are parallel.

13. Use the diagram at the right to complete each example.

Theorem 3-5	**Theorem 3-6**	**Theorem 3-7**
If ∠4 ≅ ▢, then $b\|c$.	If ∠3 and ▢ are supplementary, then $b\|c$.	If ∠1 ≅ ▢, then $b\|c$.

Lesson 3-3

Problem 1 Identifying Parallel Lines

Got It? Which lines are parallel if ∠6 ≅ ∠7? Justify your answer.

14. Underline the correct word(s) to complete each sentence.

∠6 ≅ ∠7 is given / to prove .

∠6 and ∠7 are alternate / same-side angles.

∠6 and ∠7 are corresponding / exterior / interior angles.

I can use Theorem 3-2 / Theorem 3-4 to prove the lines parallel.

Using ∠6 ≅ ∠7, lines a and b / ℓ and m are parallel and the transversal is a/ b / ℓ/ m .

Problem 2 Writing a Flow Proof of Theorem 3-6

Got It? Given that ∠1 ≅ ∠7. Prove that ∠3 ≅ ∠5 using a flow proof.

15. Use the diagram at the right to complete the flow proof below.

```
[_____]
  Given  ──────────┐
                    ↓
              ┌──────────┐     ┌──────────┐     ┌──────────┐
              │ ∠3 ≅ ∠7  │ ──▶ │ ∠7 ≅ [ ] │ ──▶ │ ∠3 ≅ ∠5  │
              └──────────┘     └──────────┘     └──────────┘
┌──────────┐       │                │                │
│ ∠1 ≅ ∠3  │ ──────┘          Vertical angles
└──────────┘                    are ≅.
┌──────────┐
│          │
│          │
└──────────┘
```

Problem 3 Determining Whether Lines Are Parallel

Got It? Given that ∠1 ≅ ∠2, you can use the Converse of the Alternate Exterior Angles Theorem to prove that lines *r* and *s* are parallel. What is another way to explain why *r* ‖ *s*? Justify your answer.

16. Justify each step.

∠1 ≅ ∠2 _____

∠2 ≅ ∠3 _____

∠1 ≅ ∠3 _____

17. Angles 1 and 3 are alternate / corresponding .

18. What postulate or theorem can you now use to explain why *r* ‖ *s*?

_____

Got It? What is the value of *w* for which *c* ∥ *d*?

Underline the correct word to complete each sentence.

19. The marked angles are on opposite sides / the same side of the transversal.

20. By the Corresponding Angles Theorem, if *c* ∥ *d* then corresponding angles are complementary / congruent / supplementary .

21. Use the theorem to solve for *w*.

Lesson Check • Do you UNDERSTAND?

Error Analysis A classmate says that $\overleftrightarrow{AB} \parallel \overleftrightarrow{DC}$ based on the diagram at right. Explain your classmate's error.

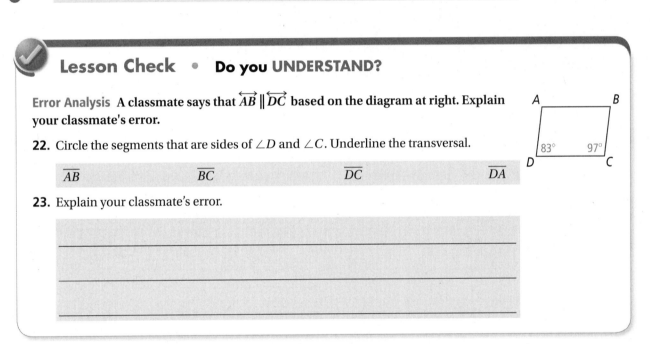

22. Circle the segments that are sides of ∠D and ∠C. Underline the transversal.

| $\overline{AB}$ | $\overline{BC}$ | $\overline{DC}$ | $\overline{DA}$ |

23. Explain your classmate's error.

_____

_____

_____

Math Success

Check off the vocabulary words that you understand.

☐ flow proof   ☐ two-step proof   ☐ parallel lines

Rate how well you can *prove that lines are parallel.*

Vocabulary

Review

Complete each statement with *always, sometimes* or *never*.

1. A *transversal* __?__ intersects at least two lines.

2. A *transversal* __?__ intersects two lines at more than two points.

3. A *transversal* __?__ intersects two parallel lines.

4. A *transversal* __?__ forms angles with two other lines.

Vocabulary Builder

transitive (adjective) TRAN **si tiv**

Related Words: transition, transit, transitivity

Main Idea: You use the **Transitive** Property in proofs when what you know implies a statement that, in turn, implies what you want to prove.

Definition: **Transitive** describes the property where one element in relation to a second element and the second in relation to the third implies the first element is in relation to the third element.

> **Transitive**
>
> If $A \to B$
> and $B \to C$
> then $A \to C$.

Use Your Vocabulary

Complete each example of the *Transitive* Property.

5. If $a > b$
and $b > c$,
then _____.

6. If Joe is younger than Ann
and Ann is younger than
Sam, then
_____
_____.

7. If you travel from
Station 2 to Station 3
and you travel from
_____
_____,
then you travel from
Station 2 to Station 4.

8. Complete the table below.

	Theorem 3-8 Transitive Property of Parallel Lines	Theorem 3-9
	If two lines are parallel to the same line, then they are parallel to each other.	In a plane, if two line are perpendicular to the same line, then they are parallel to each other.
If	$a \parallel b$	$m \perp t$
and	☐ $\parallel$ ☐	$n \perp t$
then	$a \parallel c$	m ☐ n

Problem 1 Solving a Problem With Parallel Lines

Got It? Can you assemble the pieces at the right to form a picture frame with opposite sides parallel? Explain.

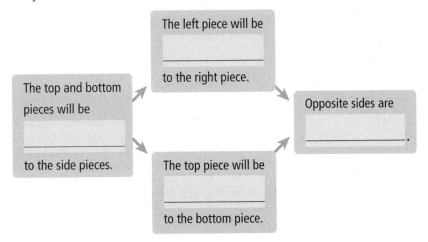

9. Circle the correct phrase to complete the sentence.

To make the picture frame, you will glue __?__.

the same angle to the same angle   two different angles together

10. The angles at each connecting end measure ☐° and ☐°.

11. When the pieces are glued together, each angle of the frame will measure ☐°.

12. Complete the flow chart below with *parallel* or *perpendicular*.

The left piece will be _____ to the right piece.

The top and bottom pieces will be _____ to the side pieces.

The top piece will be _____ to the bottom piece.

Opposite sides are _____.

13. Underline the correct words to complete the sentence.

Yes / No , I can / cannot assemble the pieces to form a picture frame with opposite sides parallel.

Lesson 3-4

Theorem 3-10 Perpendicular Transversal Theorem

In a plane, if a line is perpendicular to one of two parallel lines, then it is also perpendicular to the other.

14. Place a right angle symbol in the diagram at the right to illustrate Theorem 3-10.

Use the information in each diagram to complete each statement.

15.

16.

$a \parallel$ [ ] and $a \perp$ [ ], so [ ] $\perp$ [ ].

$c \perp$ [ ] and $n \parallel$ [ ], so [ ] $\perp$ [ ].

Problem 2 Proving a Relationship Between Two lines

Got It? Use the diagram at the right. In a plane, $c \perp b$, $b \perp d$, and $d \perp a$. Can you conclude that $a \parallel b$? Explain.

17. Circle the line(s) perpendicular to a. Underline the line(s) perpendicular to b.

| a | b | c | d |

18. Lines that are perpendicular to the same line are parallel / perpendicular .

19. Can you conclude that $a \parallel b$? Explain.

_____

_____

Lesson Check • Do you know HOW?

In one town, Avenue A is parallel to Avenue B. Avenue A is also perpendicular to Main Street. How are Avenue B and Main Street related? Explain.

20. Label the streets in the diagram A for *Avenue A*, B for *Avenue B*, and M for *Main Street.*

21. Underline the correct word(s) to complete each sentence.

The Perpendicular Transversal Theorem states that, in a plane, if a line is

 parallel / perpendicular to one of two parallel / perpendicular lines, then it is

also parallel / perpendicular to the other.

Avenue B and Main Street are parallel / perpendicular streets.

Lesson Check • Do you UNDERSTAND?

Which theorem or postulate from earlier in the chapter supports the conclusion in Theorem 3-9? In the Perpendicular Transversal Theorem? Explain.

Use the diagram at the right for Exercises 22 and 23.

22. Complete the conclusion to Theorem 3-9.

    In a plane, if two lines are perpendicular to the same line, then __?__ .

    _____

23. Complete the statement of Theorem 3-4.

    If two lines and a transversal form __?__ angles that are congruent, then the lines are parallel.

Use the diagram at the right for Exercises 24 and 25.

24. Complete the conclusion to the Perpendicular Transversal Theorem.

    In a plane, if a line is perpendicular to one of two parallel lines, then it is also __?__ .

    _____

25. Explain how any congruent angle pairs formed by parallel lines support the conclusion to the Perpendicular Transversal Theorem.

    _____

    _____

    _____

    _____

Math Success

Check off the vocabulary words that you understand.

☐ parallel   ☐ perpendicular

Rate how well you can *understand parallel and perpendicular lines.*

Need to review   0   2   4   6   8   10   Now I get it!

Vocabulary

● Review

Identify the part of speech for the word *alternate* in each sentence below.

1. You vote for one winner and one *alternate*.

2. Your two friends *alternate* serves during tennis.

3. You and your sister babysit on *alternate* nights.

4. Write the *converse* of the statement.

Statement: If it is raining, then I need an umbrella.

Converse:

● Vocabulary Builder

tri- (prefix) **try**

Related Word: triple

Main Idea: **Tri-** is a prefix meaning three that is used to form compound words.

Examples: triangle, tricycle, tripod

● Use Your Vocabulary

Write T for *true* or F for *false*.

5. A *tri*pod is a stand that has three legs.

6. A *tri*angle is a polygon with three or more sides.

7. A *tri*atholon is a race with two events — swimming and bicycling.

8. In order to *tri*ple an amount, multiply it by three.

Postulate 3-2 Parallel Postulate

Through a point not on a line, there is one and only one line parallel to the given line.

9. You can draw ___ line(s) through P parallel to line ℓ.

Theorem 3-11 Triangle Angle-Sum Theorem

The sum of the measures of the angles of a triangle is 180.

Find each angle measure.

10.

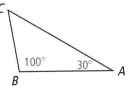

$m\angle C =$ ___

11.

$m\angle L =$ ___

Problem 1 Using the Triangle Angle-Sum Theorem

Got It? Use the diagram at the right. What is the value of z?

Complete each statement.

12. $m\angle A =$ ___

13. $m\angle ABC =$ ___ $+$ ___ $=$ ___

14. $m\angle A + m\angle ABC + m\angle C =$ ___

___ $+$ ___ $+ z =$ ___

$z =$ ___ $-$ ___ $-$ ___ $=$ ___

Check your result by solving for z another way.

15. Find $m\angle BDA$.

16. Then find $m\angle BDC$.

17. Use your answers to Exercises 15 and 16 to find the value of z.

Lesson 3-5

Theorem 3-12 Triangle Exterior Angle Theorem

take note

An **exterior angle of a polygon** is an angle formed by a side and an extension of an adjacent side. For each exterior angle of a triangle, the two nonadjacent interior angles are its **remote interior angles.**

The measure of each exterior angle of a triangle equals the sum of the measures of its two remote interior angles.

18. [   ] $= m\angle 2 + m\angle 3$

Circle the number of each exterior angle and draw a box around the number of each remote interior angle.

19.

20.

Problem 2 Using the Triangle Exterior Angle Theorem

Got It? Two angles of a triangle measure 53. What is the measure of an exterior angle at each vertex of the triangle?

21. Use the diagram at the right.

Label the interior angles 53°, 53°, and a.

Label the exterior angles adjacent to the 53° angles as x and y. Label the third exterior angle z.

22. Complete the flow chart.

Triangle Angle-Sum

$53 + 53 + a =$ [   ]

$a =$ [   ] $-$ [   ]

$=$ [   ]

Exterior Angle

$x = a +$ [   ]

$=$ [   ] $+$ [   ]

$=$ [   ]

Exterior Angle

$y = a +$ [   ]

$=$ [   ] $+$ [   ]

$=$ [   ]

Exterior Angle

$z =$ [   ] $+$ [   ]

$=$ [   ]

Chapter 3

76

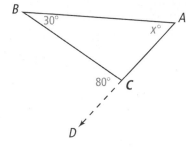

Problem 3 Applying the Triangle Theorems

Got It? **Reasoning** Can you find $m\angle A$ without using the
Triangle Exterior Angle Theorem? Explain.

23. $\angle ACB$ and $\angle DCB$ are complementary / supplementary angles.

24. Find $m\angle ACB$.

25. Can you find $m\angle A$ if you know two of the angle measures? Explain.

_____

Lesson Check • Do you UNDERSTAND?

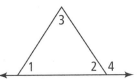

Explain how the Triangle Exterior Angle Theorem makes sense based on the
Triangle Angle-Sum Theorem.

26. Use the triangle at the right to complete the diagram below.

| Triangle Angle-Sum Theorem | ➡ | [ ] $+ m\angle 2 = 180$ |

$m\angle 1 + m\angle 3 = m\angle 4$

| Linear Pair Postulate | ➡ | [ ] $+ m\angle 2 = 180$ |

27. Explain how the Triangle Exterior Angle Theorem makes sense based on the
Triangle Angle-Sum Theorem.

_____

_____

Math Success

Check off the vocabulary words that you understand.

☐ exterior angle ☐ remote interior angles

Rate how well you can *use the triangle theorems.*

Lesson 3-5

3-6 Constructing Parallel and Perpendicular Lines

Vocabulary

● **Review**

Write T for *true* or F for *false*.

_____ **1.** A rectangle has two pairs of *parallel* segments.

_____ **2.** A rectangle has two pairs of *perpendicular* segments.

Write *alternate exterior, alternate interior,* or *corresponding* to describe each angle pair.

3.

4.

5.

_____   _____   _____

● **Vocabulary Builder**

construction (noun) **kun STRUCK shun**

Other Word Forms: construct (verb), constructive (adjective)

Main Idea: Construction means how something is built or *constructed*.

Math Usage: A **construction** is a geometric figure drawn using a straightedge and a compass.

● **Use Your Vocabulary**

6. Complete each statement with the correct form of the word *construction*.

VERB   You __?__ sand castles at the beach.

NOUN   The __?__ on the highway caused quite a traffic jam.

ADJECTIVE   The time you spent working on your homework was __?__.

Problem 1 Constructing Parallel Lines

Got It? Reasoning The diagram at the right shows the construction of line *m* through point *N* with line *m* parallel to line ℓ. Why must lines ℓ and *m* be parallel?

7. The diagram shows the construction of congruent

   angles [   ] and [   ].

8. Circle the description(s) of the angle pairs that were constructed.

   alternate interior   congruent   corresponding   same-side interior

9. Now explain why lines ℓ and *m* must be parallel.

   _____

   _____

   _____

Problem 2 Constructing a Special Quadrilateral

Got It? Draw a segment. Label its length *m*. Construct quadrilateral *ABCD* with $\overleftrightarrow{AB} \parallel \overleftrightarrow{CD}$, so that $AB = m$ and $CD = 2m$.

Underline the correct word or symbol to complete each sentence.

10. Construct parallel / perpendicular lines.

11. Draw $\overleftrightarrow{AB}$. Draw point *D* not on $\overleftrightarrow{AB}$. Draw $\overleftrightarrow{AD}$. The length of
    $\overline{AB} / \overline{AD}$ is *m*.

12. At *D*, construct $\angle TDZ$ perpendicular / congruent to $\angle DAB$ so that $\angle TDZ$ and
    $\angle DAB$ are corresponding angles. Then $\overleftrightarrow{DZ} \parallel \overleftrightarrow{AB}$.

13. Now, you need a side of length 2*m*. Construct *C* on $\overleftrightarrow{DZ}$ so that $DC = 2m$.
    Draw $\overline{BC} / \overline{BA}$.

14. Do the construction below.

Lesson 3-6

Problem 3 Perpendicular at a Point on a Line

Got It? Use a straightedge to draw $\overleftrightarrow{EF}$. Construct $\overleftrightarrow{FG}$ so that $\overleftrightarrow{FG} \perp \overleftrightarrow{EF}$ at point F.

15. Use the diagram at the right. Write each construction step.

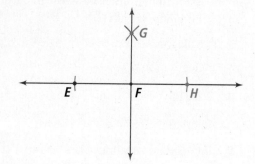

Step 1 _____

_____

Step 2 _____

_____

_____

Step 3 _____

_____

_____

Step 4 _____

_____

_____

_____

Step 5 _____

---

take note

Postulate 3-3   Perpendicular Postulate

Complete the statement of Postulate 3-3 below.

16. Through a point not on a line, there is one and only one line parallel / perpendicular
to the given line.

17. Circle the diagram that models Postulate 3-3.

Problem 4 Perpendicular From a Point to a Line

Got It? Draw a line $\overleftrightarrow{CX}$ and a point Z not on $\overleftrightarrow{CX}$. Construct $\overleftrightarrow{ZB}$ so that $\overleftrightarrow{ZB} \perp \overleftrightarrow{CX}$.

Underline the correct word(s) to complete each sentence.

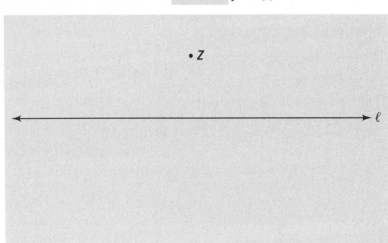

18. Open your compass to a size equal to / greater than the distance from Z to line ℓ.

19. With the compass tip on point Z, draw an arc that intersects line ℓ at one / two point(s).

20. Label the point(s) C and X / Z.

21. Place the compass point on C / Z and make an arc below line ℓ.

22. With the same opening and the compass tip on C / X, draw an arc that intersects the arc you made in Exercise 21. Label the point of intersection B.

23. Draw $\overleftrightarrow{ZB} / \overleftrightarrow{CX}$.

24. Use line ℓ and point Z at the right. Construct a line through point Z perpendicular to line ℓ.

Lesson Check • Do you UNDERSTAND?

Suppose you use a wider compass setting in Exercise 18. Will you construct a different perpendicular line? Explain.

25. Explain why you will NOT construct a different perpendicular line.

_____

_____

Math Success

Check off the vocabulary words that you understand.

☐ construction   ☐ parallel   ☐ perpendicular

Rate how well you can *construct parallel and perpendicular lines.*

| Need to review | 0 | 2 | 4 | 6 | 8 | 10 | Now I get it! |

Lesson 3-6

3-7

Equations of Lines in the Coordinate Plane

Vocabulary

● Review

Write T for *true* or F for *false*.

_____ **1.** An *ordered pair* describes the location of a point in a coordinate grid.

_____ **2.** An *ordered pair* can be written as (*x*-coordinate, *y*-coordinate) or (*y*-coordinate, *x*-coordinate).

_____ **3.** The *ordered pair* for the origin is (0, 0).

● Vocabulary Builder

| **slope** (noun, verb) **slohp** | $\text{Slope} = \dfrac{\text{rise}}{\text{run}}$ |

Definition: The **slope** of a line m between two points (x_1, y_1) and (x_2, y_2) on a coordinate plane is the ratio of the vertical change (rise) to the horizontal change (run). $\quad m = \dfrac{\text{rise}}{\text{run}} = \dfrac{y_2 - y_1}{x_2 - x_1}$

● Use Your Vocabulary

Complete each statement with the appropriate word from the list. Use each word only once.

slope   sloping   sloped

4. The __?__ of the hill made it difficult for bike riding.

5. The driveway __?__ down to the garage.

6. The __?__ lawn led to the river.

Draw a line from each word in Column A to its corresponding part of speech in Column B.

Column A   Column B

7. linear   ADJECTIVE

8. line   NOUN

Problem 1 Finding Slopes of Lines

Got It? Use the graph at the right. What is the slope of line *a*?

9. Complete the table below to find the slope of line *a*.

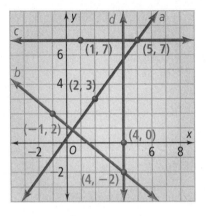

Think	Write
I know the slope is the ratio $\dfrac{\text{change in } y\text{-coordinates}}{\text{change in } x\text{-coordinates}}$.	$m = \dfrac{y_2 - y_1}{x_2 - x_1}$
Two points on line *a* are (2, 3) and (5, 7).	$= \dfrac{\boxed{} - \boxed{}}{\boxed{} - \boxed{}}$
Now I can simplify.	$= \boxed{}$

Key Concept Forms of Linear Equations

Definition

The **slope-intercept form** of an equation of a nonvertical line is $y = mx + b$, where *m* is the slope and *b* is the *y*-intercept.

The **point-slope form** of an equation of a nonvertical line is $y - y_1 = m(x - x_1)$, where *m* is the slope and (x_1, y_1) is a point on the line.

Symbols

$$y = mx + b$$

slope   *y*-intercept

$$y - y_1 = m(x - x_1)$$

y-coordinate   slope   *x*-coordinate

Problem 2 Graphing Lines

Got It? Graph $y = 3x - 4$.

10. In what form is the given equation written?

_____

11. Written as a fraction, the slope is $\boxed{}$.

12. One point on the graph is ($\boxed{}$, −4).

13. From that point, move $\boxed{}$ unit(s) *up* and $\boxed{}$ unit (s) *to the right*.

14. Graph $y = 3x - 4$ on the coordinate plane.

Lesson 3-7

Problem 3 Writing Equations of Lines

Got It? What is an equation of the line with slope $-\frac{1}{2}$ and y-intercept 2?

15. Complete the problem-solving model below.

Know

slope $m = \boxed{}$

y-intercept $= \boxed{}$

Need

Write an equation of a line.

Plan

Use $\boxed{}$, the slope-intercept form of a linear equation.

16. Now write the equation.

 Problem 4 Using Two Points to Write an Equation

Got It? You can use the two points given on the line at the right to show that the slope of the line is $\frac{6}{5}$. So one equation of the line is $y - 5 = \frac{6}{5}(x - 3)$. What is an equation of the line if you use $(-2, -1)$ instead of $(3, 5)$ in the point-slope form of the equation?

17. The equation is found below. Write a justification for each step.

$y - y_1 = m(x - x_1)$ Write in _____

$y - (-1) = \frac{6}{5}(x - (-2))$

$y + 1 = \frac{6}{5}(x + 2)$

Got It? Use the two equations for the line shown above. Rewrite the equations in slope-intercept form and compare them. What can you conclude?

18. Write each equation in slope-intercept form.

$y - 5 = \frac{6}{5}(x - 3)$ $y + 1 = \frac{6}{5}(x + 2)$

19. Underline the correct word(s) to complete each sentence.

The equations are different / the same .

Choosing $(-2, -1)$ gives a different / the same equation as choosing $(3, 5)$.

The equations $y - 5 = \frac{6}{5}(x - 3)$ and $y + 1 = \frac{6}{5}(x + 2)$ are / are not equivalent.

Problem 5 Writing Equations of Horizontal and Vertical Lines

Got It? What are the equations for the horizontal and vertical lines through $(4, -3)$?

Write T for *true* or F for *false*.

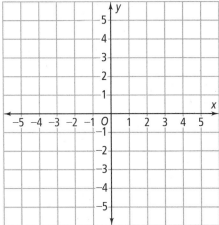

_____ **20.** Every point on a horizontal line through $(4, -3)$ has y-coordinate of -3.

_____ **21.** The equation of a vertical line through $(4, -3)$ is $y = -3$.

_____ **22.** The equation of a vertical line through $(4, -3)$ is $x = 4$.

23. Graph the horizontal and vertical lines through $(4, -3)$ on the coordinate plane at the right.

Lesson Check • Do you UNDERSTAND?

Error Analysis A classmate found the slope of the line passing through $(8, -2)$ and $(8, 10)$ as shown at the right. Describe your classmate's error. Then find the correct slope of the line passing through the given points.

$$m = \frac{8 - 8}{10 - (-2)}$$
$$m = \frac{0}{12}$$
$$m = 0$$

24. What is your classmate's error?

_____

25. Find the slope, m.

_____

26. The run is $8 - 8 =$ [ ] , so the slope is _____ .

Math Success

Check off the vocabulary words that you understand.

☐ slope   ☐ slope-intercept form   ☐ point-slope form

Rate how well you can write and graph *linear equations*.

Need to review 0 2 4 6 8 10 Now I get it!

Lesson 3-7

3-8 Slopes of Parallel and Perpendicular Lines

Vocabulary

● Review

Use the graph at the right for Exercises 1–4. Write *parallel* or *perpendicular* to complete each sentence.

1. Line *b* is ___?___ to line *a*.

2. Line *b* is ___?___ to the *x*-axis.

3. Line *a* is ___?___ to the *y*-axis.

4. The *x*-axis is ___?___ to the *y*-axis.

Write the *converse, inverse,* and *contrapositive* of the statement below.

If a polygon is a triangle, then the sum of the measures of its angles is 180.

5. **CONVERSE** If the sum of the measures of the angles of a polygon is 180, then ___?___.

6. **INVERSE** If a polygon is *not* a triangle, then ___?___.

7. **CONTRAPOSITIVE** If the sum of the measures of the angles of a polygon is *not* 180, then ___?___.

● Vocabulary Builder

The **reciprocal** of x is $\frac{1}{x}$.

reciprocal (noun) **rih SIP ruh kul**

Other Word Forms: reciprocate (verb)

Definition: The **reciprocal** of a number is a number such that the product of the two numbers is 1. The **reciprocal** of $\frac{\text{numerator}}{\text{denominator}}$ is $\frac{\text{denominator}}{\text{numerator}}$.

● Use Your Vocabulary

Complete each statement with *reciprocal* or *reciprocate*. Use each word only once.

8. VERB After your friend helps you with your homework, you _?_ by helping your friend with his chores.

9. NOUN The _?_ of $\frac{2}{3}$ is $\frac{3}{2}$.

---

 take note

Key Concept   Slopes of Parallel Lines

- If two nonvertical lines are parallel, then their slopes are equal.
- If the slopes of two distinct nonvertical lines are equal, then the lines are parallel.
- Any two vertical lines or horizontal lines are parallel.

Circle the correct statement in each exercise.

10.   A vertical line is parallel to any other vertical line.

A vertical line is parallel to any horizontal line.

11.   Any two nonvertical lines have the same slope.

Any two nonvertical lines that are parallel have the same slope.

✓ Problem 1 Checking for Parallel Lines

Got It? Line ℓ_3 contains $A(-13, 6)$ and $B(-1, 2)$. Line ℓ_4 contains $C(3, 6)$ and $D(6, 7)$. Are ℓ_3 and ℓ_4 parallel? Explain.

12. To determine whether lines ℓ_3 and ℓ_4 are are parallel check whether the lines have the same _?_ .

13. Find the slope of each line.

slope of ℓ_3

$$\frac{2 - 6}{-1 - (-13)} = \frac{\quad}{\quad} = \boxed{}$$

slope of ℓ_4

14. Are the slopes equal?   Yes / No

15. Are lines ℓ_3 and ℓ_4 parallel? Explain.

Lesson 3-8

Problem 2 Writing Equations of Parallel Lines

Got It? What is an equation of the line parallel to $y = -x - 7$ that contains $(-5, 3)$?

16. The slope of the line $y = -x - 7$ is ☐ .

17. The equation of the line parallel to $y = -x - 7$ will have slope $m = $ ☐ .

18. Find the equation of the line using point-slope form. Complete the steps below.

$y - y_1 =$	☐	Write in point-slope form.
$y - 3 =$	☐	Substitute point and slope into equation.
$y - 3 =$	☐	Simplify.
$y =$	☐	Add 3 to both sides.

take note

Key Concept Slopes of Perpendicular Lines

- If two nonvertical lines are perpendicular, then the product of their slopes is -1.
- If the slopes of two lines have a product of -1, then the lines are perpendicular.
- Any horizontal line and vertical line are perpendicular.

Write T for *true* or F for *false*.

___ **19.** The second bullet in the Take Note is the contrapositive of the first bullet.

___ **20.** The product of the slopes of any horizontal line and any vertical line is -1.

Problem 3 Checking for Perpendicular Lines

Got It? Line ℓ_3 contains $A(2, 7)$ and $B(3, -1)$. Line ℓ_4 contains $C(-2, 6)$ and $D(8, 7)$. Are ℓ_3 and ℓ_4 perpendicular? Explain.

21. Find the slopes and multiply them.

$m_3 = $ ☐ $m_4 = $ ☐

$m_3 \times m_4 = $ ☐

22. Underline the correct words to complete the sentence.

Lines ℓ_3 and ℓ_4 are / are not perpendicular because the product of their slopes

does / does not equal -1.

Problem 4 **Writing Equations of Perpendicular Lines**

Got It? What is an equation of the line perpendicular to $y = -3x - 5$ that contains $(-3, 7)$?

23. Complete the reasoning model below.

Think	Write
I can identify the slope, m_1, of the given line.	$y = -3x - 5$ is in point-slope form, so $m_1 = $ ☐ .
I know that the slope, m_2, of the perpendicular line is the negative reciprocal of m_1.	m_2 is $\dfrac{\ \ }{\ \ }$ because ☐ $\times \dfrac{\ \ }{\ \ } = -1$.
I can use m_2 and $(-3, 7)$ to write the equation of the perpendicular line in point-slope form.	$y - y_1 = m(x - x_1)$

 Lesson Check • **Do you UNDERSTAND?**

Error Analysis Your classmate tries to find an equation for a line parallel to $y = 3x - 5$ that contains $(-4, 2)$. What is your classmate's error?

24. Parallel lines have the same / different slopes.

25. Show a correct solution in the box below.

slope of given line = 3
slope of parallel line = $\frac{1}{3}$
$y - y_1 = m(x - x_1)$
$y - 2 = \frac{1}{3}(x + 4)$

 Math Success

Check off the vocabulary words that you understand.

☐ slope   ☐ reciprocal   ☐ parallel   ☐ perpendicular

Rate how well you *understand perpendicular lines.*

Lesson 3-8

4-1 Congruent Figures

Vocabulary

● **Review**

1. Underline the correct word to complete the sentence.

   A *polygon* is a two-dimensional figure with two / three or more segments that meet exactly at their endpoints.

2. Cross out the figure(s) that are NOT *polygons*.

● **Vocabulary Builder**

congruent (adjective) **kahng GROO unt**

Main Idea: **Congruent** figures have the same size and shape.

Related Word: congruence (noun)

● **Use Your Vocabulary**

3. Circle the triangles that appear to be *congruent*.

Write T for *true* or F for *false*.

_____ 4. *Congruent* angles have different measures.

_____ 5. A prism and its net are *congruent* figures.

_____ 6. The corresponding sides of *congruent* figures have the same measure.

Key Concept   Congruent Figures

Congruent polygons have congruent corresponding parts—their matching sides and angles. When you name congruent polygons, you must list corresponding vertices in the same order.

$ABCD \cong EFGH$

7. Use the figures at the right to complete each congruence statement.

$\overline{AB} \cong$ ☐ $\overline{BC} \cong$ ☐ $\overline{CD} \cong$ ☐ $\overline{DA} \cong$ ☐

$\angle A \cong$ ☐ $\angle B \cong$ ☐ $\angle C \cong$ ☐ $\angle D \cong$ ☐

Problem 1   Using Congruent Parts

Got It? If $\triangle WYS \cong \triangle MKV$, what are the congruent corresponding parts?

8. Use the diagram at the right.
Draw an arrow from each vertex of the first triangle to the corresponding vertex of the second triangle.

$$\triangle W\ Y\ S \cong \triangle M\ K\ V$$

9. Use the diagram from Exercise 8 to complete each congruence statement.

Sides $\overline{WY} \cong$ ☐ $\overline{YS} \cong$ ☐ $\overline{WS} \cong$ ☐

Angles $\angle W \cong$ ☐ $\angle Y \cong$ ☐ $\angle S \cong$ ☐

Problem 2   Finding Congruent Parts

Got It? Suppose that $\triangle WYS \cong \triangle MKV$. If $m\angle W = 62$ and $m\angle Y = 35$, what is $m\angle V$? Explain.

Use the congruent triangles at the right.

10. Use the given information to label the triangles. Remember to write corresponding vertices in order.

11. Complete each congruence statement.

$\angle W \cong$ ☐

$\angle Y \cong$ ☐

$\angle S \cong$ ☐

12. Use the Triangle Angle-Sum theorem.

$m\angle S + m$ ☐ $+ m$ ☐ $= 180$, so $m\angle S = 180 - ($ ☐ $+$ ☐ $)$, or ☐ .

13. Complete.

Since $\angle S \cong$ ☐ and $m\angle S =$ ☐ , $m\angle V =$ ☐ .

Lesson 4-1

Problem 3 Finding Congruent Triangles

Got It? Is △ABD ≅ △CBD? Justify your answer.

14. Underline the correct word to complete the sentence.

   To prove two triangles congruent, show that all adjacent / corresponding
   parts are congruent.

15. Circle the name(s) for △ACD.

acute	isosceles	right	scalene

16. Cross out the congruence statements that are NOT supported by the information in
   the figure.

$\overline{AD} \cong \overline{CD}$	$\overline{BD} \cong \overline{BD}$	$\overline{AB} \cong \overline{CB}$
$\angle A \cong \angle C$	$\angle ABD \cong \angle CBD$	$\angle ADB \cong \angle CDB$

17. You need [ ] congruence statements to prove two triangles congruent, so you

   can / cannot prove that △ABD ≅ △CBD.

---

take note

Theorem 4-1 Third Angles Theorem

Theorem	If . . .	Then . . .
If two angles of one triangle are congruent to two angles of another triangle, then the third angles are congruent.	$\angle A \cong \angle D$ and $\angle B \cong \angle E$	$\angle C \cong \angle F$

Use △ABC and △DEF above.

18. If $m\angle A = 74$, then $m\angle D = $ [ ].

19. If $m\angle B = 44$, then $m\angle E = $ [ ].

20. If $m\angle C = 62$, then $m\angle F = $ [ ].

Problem 4 Proving Triangles Congruent

Got It? Given: $\angle A \cong \angle D$, $\overline{AE} \cong \overline{DC}$,
   $\overline{EB} \cong \overline{CB}$, $\overline{BA} \cong \overline{BD}$

   Prove: △AEB ≅ △DCB

21. You are given four pairs of congruent parts. Circle the additional information you
   need to prove the triangles congruent.

A third pair of congruent sides	A second pair of congruent angles	A third pair of congruent angles

22. Complete the steps of the proof.

1) $\overline{AE} \cong$ ☐ , $\overline{EB} \cong$ ☐ , $\overline{BA} \cong$ ☐   1) Given

2) $\angle A \cong$ ☐   2) Given

3) $\angle ABE \cong$ ☐   3) Vertical angles are congruent.

4) $\angle E \cong$ ☐   4) Third Angles Theorem

5) $\triangle AEB \cong$ ☐   5) Definition of $\cong$ triangles

Lesson Check • Do you UNDERSTAND?

If each angle in one triangle is congruent to its corresponding angle in another triangle, are the two triangles congruent? Explain.

23. Underline the correct word to complete the sentence.

To disprove a conjecture, you need one / two / many counterexample(s).

24. An equilateral triangle has three congruent sides and three 60° angles. Circle the equilateral triangles below.

25. Use your answers to Exercise 24 to answer the question.

_____
_____
_____

Math Success

Check off the vocabulary words that you understand.

☐ congruent   ☐ polygons

Rate how well you can *identify congruent polygons*.

Need to review   0   2   4   6   8   10   Now I get it!

Lesson 4-1

Vocabulary

● **Review**

1. Use the diagram at the right. Find each.

included angle between $\overline{AB}$ and $\overline{CA}$

included side between $\angle A$ and $\angle C$

included angle between $\overline{BC}$ and $\overline{CA}$

included side between $\angle B$ and $\angle C$

included angle between $\overline{BC}$ and $\overline{AB}$

included side between $\angle B$ and $\angle A$

● **Vocabulary Builder**

postulate (noun) PAHS chuh lit

Definition: A **postulate** is a statement that is accepted as true without being proven true.

Main Idea: In geometry, you use what you know to be true to prove new things true. The statements that you accept as true without proof are called **postulates** or axioms.

● **Use Your Vocabulary**

2. Underline the correct word to complete the sentence.

You can use properties, *postulates*, and previously proven theorems as reasons / statements in a proof.

3. **Multiple Choice** What is a *postulate*?

   Ⓐ   a convincing argument using deductive reasoning

   Ⓑ   a conjecture or statement that you can prove true

   Ⓒ   a statement accepted as true without being proven true

   Ⓓ   a conclusion reached by using inductive reasoning

Postulate 4–1 Side-Side-Side (SSS) Postulate

Postulate 4-1 Side-Side-Side (SSS) Postulate

If the three sides of one triangle are congruent to the three sides of another triangle, then the two triangles are congruent.

4. Use the figures at the right to complete the sentence.

If $\overline{AB} \cong \overline{DE}$, $\overline{BC} \cong \overline{EF}$, and $\overline{AC} \cong$ ☐, then $\triangle ABC \cong \triangle$ ☐.

Problem 1 Using SSS

Got It? Given: $\overline{BC} \cong \overline{BF}$, $\overline{CD} \cong \overline{FD}$
Prove: $\triangle BCD \cong \triangle BFD$

5. You know two pairs of sides that are congruent. What else do you need to prove the triangles congruent by SSS?

_____

6. The triangles share side ☐ .

7. Complete the steps of the proof.

Statement	Reason
1) $\overline{BC} \cong$ ☐	1) Given
2) $\overline{CD} \cong$ ☐	2) Given
3) $\overline{BD} \cong$ ☐	3) Reflexive Property of $\cong$
4) $\triangle BCD \cong$ ☐	4) SSS

Postulate 4–2 Side-Angle-Side (SAS) Postulate

Postulate 4–2 Side-Angle-Side (SAS) Postulate

If two sides and the included angle of one triangle are congruent to two sides and the included angle of another triangle, then the two triangles are congruent.

Use the figures below to complete each statement.

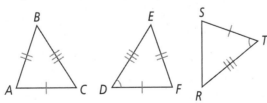

8. $\triangle DEF \cong$ ☐ by SAS.

9. $\triangle ABC \cong$ ☐ by SSS.

Lesson 4-2

Got It? What other information do you need to prove
$\triangle LEB \cong \triangle BNL$ by SAS?

10. Circle the angles that are marked congruent in the diagram.

$\angle EBL$	$\angle ELB$	$\angle NBL$	$\angle NLB$

11. Circle the sides that form the angles that are marked congruent in the diagram.

$\overline{BE}$	$\overline{BL}$	$\overline{BN}$	$\overline{LB}$	$\overline{LE}$	$\overline{LN}$

12. Complete each congruence statements.

$\overline{LB} \cong$ ☐ $\angle BLE \cong$ ☐

Underline the correct word(s) to complete each sentence.

13. Proving $\triangle LEB \cong \triangle BNL$ by SAS requires one / two pair(s) of congruent sides and
one / two pair(s) of congruent angles.

14. The diagram shows congruency of zero / one / two pair(s) of congruent sides and
zero / one / two pair(s) of congruent angles.

15. To prove the triangles congruent by SAS, you still need zero / one / two pair(s) of
congruent sides and zero / one / two pair(s) of congruent angles .

16. To prove the triangles congruent, you need to prove ☐ and ☐ congruent.

 Problem 3 Identifying Congruent Triangles

Got It? Would you use SSS or SAS to prove the triangles below congruent? Explain.

Complete each statement with *SSS* or *SAS*.

17. Use _?_ if you have three pairs of sides congruent.

18. Use _?_ if you have two pairs of sides and the included angle congruent.

Write T for *true* or F for *false*.

____ **19.** The diagram shows congruence of three sides.

____ **20.** In the triangle on the left, the marked angle is the included angle of the side
with two marks and the side with three marks.

____ **21.** In the triangle on the right, the marked angle is the included angle of the side
with two marks and the side with three marks.

22. Would you use SSS or SAS to prove the triangles congruent? Explain.

Lesson Check • Do you UNDERSTAND?

Error Analysis Your friend thinks that the triangles below are congruent by SAS. Is your friend correct? Explain.

23. Are two pairs of corresponding sides congruent?   Yes / No

24. Is there a pair of congruent angles?   Yes / No

25. Are the congruent angles the included angles between the corresponding congruent sides?   Yes / No

26. Are the triangles congruent by SAS? Explain.

Math Success

Check off the vocabulary words that you understand.

☐ congruent   ☐ corresponding

Rate how well you can *use SSS and SAS to prove triangles congruent.*

Need to review   0   2   4   6   8   10   Now I get it!

4-3 Triangle Congruence by ASA and AAS

Vocabulary

● Review

1. Cross out the figure(s) that are NOT *triangle*(s).

2. A *triangle* is a polygon with ▢ sides.

3. A *triangle* with a right angle is called a(n)
obtuse / right / scalene *triangle*.

● Vocabulary Builder

corresponding (adjective) **kawr uh SPAHN ding**

Other Word Forms: correspond (verb); correspondence (noun)

Definition: Corresponding means similar in position, purpose, or form.

Math Usage: Congruent figures have congruent **corresponding** parts.

corresponding sides

● Use Your Vocabulary

Draw a line from each part of △*ABC* in Column A to the *corresponding* part of △*XYZ* in Column B.

Column A	Column B
4. $\overline{BC}$	∠Z
5. ∠A	∠Y
6. $\overline{AB}$	$\overline{YZ}$
7. ∠C	∠X
8. $\overline{AC}$	$\overline{XY}$
9. ∠B	$\overline{XZ}$

Postulate 4-3 Angle-Side-Angle (ASA) Postulate

Postulate	If . . .	Then . . .
If two angles and the included side of one triangle are congruent to two angles and the included side of another triangle, then the two triangles are congruent.	$\angle A \cong \angle D$, $\overline{AC} \cong \overline{DF}$, $\angle C \cong \angle F$	$\triangle ABC \cong \triangle DEF$

10. Explain how the ASA Postulate is different from the SAS Postulate.

_____

_____

_____

 Problem 1 Using ASA

Got It? Which two triangles are congruent by ASA? Explain.

11. Name the triangles. List the vertices in corresponding order: list the vertex with the one arc first, the vertex with the two arcs second, and the third vertex last.

12. $\angle G \cong \angle$ ☐ $\cong \angle$ ☐

13. $\angle H \cong \angle$ ☐ $\cong \angle$ ☐

14. $\overline{HG} \cong$ ☐ $\cong$ ☐

15. The congruent sides that are included between congruent angles are ☐ and ☐ .

16. Write a congruence statement. Justify your reasoning.

$\triangle$ ☐ $\cong \triangle$ ☐

_____

_____

Problem 2 · Writing a Proof Using ASA

Got It? Given: ∠CAB ≅ ∠DAE, $\overline{BA}$ ≅ $\overline{EA}$, ∠B and ∠E are right angles
Prove: △ABC ≅ △AED

17. Complete the flow chart to prove △ABC ≅ △AED.

take note

Theorem 4-2 Angle-Angle-Side (AAS) Theorem

Theorem	If . . .	Then . . .
If two angles and a nonincluded side of one triangle are congruent to two angles and the corresponding nonincluded side of another triangle, then the two triangles are congruent.	∠A ≅ ∠D, ∠B ≅ ∠E, $\overline{AC}$ ≅ $\overline{DF}$	△ABC ≅ △DEF

18. The nonincluded congruent sides of △ABC and △DEF are ▢ and ▢.

Problem 3 · Writing a Proof Using AAS

Got It? Given: ∠S ≅ ∠Q, $\overline{RP}$ bisects ∠SRQ
Prove: △SRP ≅ △QRP

19. How do you know which angles in the diagram are corresponding angles?

20. Complete the statements to prove △SRP ≅ △QRP.

Statements	Reasons
1) ∠S ≅ ▢	1) Given
2) $\overline{RP}$ bisects ▢	2) Given
3) ∠SRP ≅ ▢	3) Definition of an angle bisector
4) $\overline{RP}$ ≅ ▢	4) Reflexive Property of Congruence
5) △SRP ≅ ▢	5) AAS

Problem 4 Determining Whether Triangles Are Congruent

Got It? Are △*PAR* and △*SIR* congruent? Explain.

21. The congruence marks show that ∠*A* ≅ [ ] and $\overline{PR}$ ≅ [ ].

22. What other corresponding congruent parts exist? Explain.

_____

_____

23. Are △*PAR* and △*SIR* congruent? If so, what theorem proves them congruent?

_____

_____

Lesson Check • Do you UNDERSTAND?

Reasoning Suppose ∠*E* ≅ ∠*I* and $\overline{FE}$ ≅ $\overline{GI}$. What else must you know in order to prove △*FDE* and △*GHI* are congruent by ASA? By AAS?

24. Label the diagram at the right.

25. To prove the triangles congruent by ASA, what do you need?

_____

_____

26. To prove the triangles congruent by AAS, what do you need?

_____

_____

_____

27. If you want to use ASA, ∠ [ ] and ∠ [ ] must also be congruent.

28. If you want to use AAS, ∠ [ ] and ∠ [ ] must also be congruent.

Math Success

Check off the vocabulary words that you understand.

☐ included   ☐ nonincluded   ☐ corresponding

Rate how well you can *use ASA and AAS*.

Need to review	0	2	4	6	8	10	Now I get it!

Vocabulary

● Review

Underline the correct word(s) to complete each sentence.

1. The *Reflexive* Property of Congruence states that any geometric figure is congruent / similar to itself.

2. The *Reflexive* Property of Equality states that any quantity is equal to / greater than / less than itself.

3. Circle the expressions that illustrate the *Reflexive* Property of Equality.

$a = a$	If $AB = 2$, then $2 = AB$.
$3(x + y) = 3x + 3y$	$5 + c = 5 + c$

4. Circle the expressions that illustrate the *Reflexive* Property of Congruence.

If $\angle A \cong \angle B$, then $\angle B \cong \angle A$.	If $\overline{CD} \cong \overline{LM}$ and $\overline{LM} \cong \overline{XY}$, then $\overline{CD} \cong \overline{XY}$.
$\angle ABC \cong \angle ABC$	$\overline{CD} \cong \overline{CD}$

● Vocabulary Builder

proof (noun) <u>proof</u>

Related Word: prove (verb)

Definition: A **proof** is convincing evidence that a statement or theory is true.

Math Usage: A **proof** is a convincing argument that uses deductive reasoning.

● Use Your Vocabulary

Complete each statement with *proof* or *prove*.

5. In geometry, a __?__ uses definitions, postulates, and theorems to prove theorems.

6. No one can __?__ how our universe started.

7. He can __?__ when he bought the computer because he has a receipt.

8. Complete the steps in the *proof.*

Given: $\overline{AB} \cong \overline{AD}$, $\overline{BC} \cong \overline{DC}$,
$\angle D \cong \angle B$, $\angle DAC \cong \angle BAC$

Prove: $\triangle ABC \cong \triangle ADC$

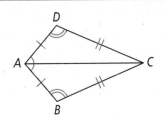

Statements	Reasons
1) $\overline{AB} \cong$ ☐ $\overline{BC} \cong$ ☐	1) Given
2) $\overline{AC} \cong$ ☐	2) Reflexive Property of $\cong$
3) $\angle D \cong$ ☐ $\angle DAC \cong$ ☐	3) Given
4) $\angle DCA \cong$ ☐	4) Third Angles Theorem
5) $\triangle ABC \cong$ ☐	5) Definition of $\cong$ triangles

Problem 1 **Proving Parts of Triangles Congruent**

Got It? **Given:** $\overline{BA} \cong \overline{DA}$, $\overline{CA} \cong \overline{EA}$

Prove: $\angle C \cong \angle E$

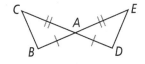

9. Name four ways you can use congruent parts of two triangles to prove that the triangles are congruent.

☐☐ ☐☐

☐☐ ☐☐

10. To prove triangles are congruent when you know two pairs of congruent corresponding sides, you can use ☐ or ☐ .

Underline the correct word to complete the sentence.

11. The *Given* states and the diagram shows that there are ⟨one / two / three⟩ pairs of congruent sides.

12. Give a reason for each statement of the proof.

Statements	Reasons
1) $\overline{BA} \cong \overline{DA}$	1)
2) $\overline{CA} \cong \overline{EA}$	2)
3) $\angle CAB \cong \angle EAD$	3)
4) $\triangle CAB \cong \triangle EAD$	4)
5) $\angle C \cong \angle E$	5)

Lesson 4-4

Got It? Given: $\overline{AB} \cong \overline{AC}$, M is the midpoint of $\overline{BC}$

Prove: $\angle AMB \cong \angle AMC$

13. Use the flow chart to complete the proof.

 ## Lesson Check • **Do you know HOW?**

Name the postulate or theorem that you can use to show the triangles are congruent. Then explain why $\overline{EA} \cong \overline{MA}$.

14. Circle the angles that are marked congruent.

$\angle E$	$\angle ETA$	$\angle M$	$\angle EAT$	$\angle MTA$

15. Circle the sides that are marked congruent.

$\overline{ET}$	$\overline{MT}$	$\overline{EA}$	$\overline{MA}$	$\overline{AT}$

16. Circle the sides that are congruent by the Reflexive Property of Congruence.

$\overline{ET}$ and $\overline{MT}$	$\overline{EA}$ and $\overline{MA}$	$\overline{AT}$ and $\overline{AT}$

17. Underline the correct postulate or theorem to complete the sentence.

$\triangle EAT \cong \triangle MAT$ by SAS / AAS / ASA / SSS .

18. Now explain why $\overline{EA} \cong \overline{MA}$.

Lesson Check • Do you UNDERSTAND?

Error Analysis Find and correct the error(s) in the proof.

Given: $\overline{KH} \cong \overline{NH}$, $\angle L \cong \angle M$ **Prove:** H is the midpoint of $\overline{LM}$.

Proof: $\overline{KH} \cong \overline{NH}$ because it is given. $\angle L \cong \angle M$ because it is given. $\angle KHL \cong \angle NHM$ because vertical angles are congruent. So, $\triangle KHL \cong \triangle MHN$ by ASA Postulate. Since corresponding parts of congruent triangles are congruent, $\overline{LH} \cong \overline{MH}$. By the definition of midpoint, H is the midpoint of $\overline{LM}$.

Place a ✓ in the box if the statement is correct. Place an ✗ if it is incorrect.

☐ **19.** $\angle KHL \cong \angle NHM$ because vertical angels are congruent.

☐ **20.** $\triangle KHL \cong \triangle MHN$ by ASA Postulate.

Underline the correct word to complete each sentence.

21. When you name congruent triangles, you must name corresponding vertices in
a different / the same order.

22. To use the ASA Postulate, you need two pairs of congruent angles and a pair of
included / nonincluded congruent sides.

23. To use the AAS Theorem, you need two pairs of congruent angles and a pair of
included / nonincluded congruent sides.

24. Identify the error(s) in the proof.

_____

_____

_____

25. Correct the error(s) in the proof.

_____

Math Success

Check off the vocabulary words that you understand.

☐ congruent   ☐ corresponding   ☐ proof

Rate how well you can *use congruent triangles*.

Need to review 0 2 4 6 8 10 Now I get it!

Vocabulary

● **Review**

Underline the correct word to complete each sentence.

1. An *equilateral* triangle has two/ three congruent sides.

2. An *equilateral* triangle has acute / obtuse angles.

3. Circle the *equilateral* triangle.

● **Vocabulary Builder**

isosceles (adjective) **eye SAHS uh leez**

Related Words: equilateral, scalene

Definition A triangle is **isosceles** if it has two congruent sides.

Main Idea: The angles and sides of **isosceles** triangles have special relationships.

isosceles

● **Use Your Vocabulary**

4. Use the triangles below. Write the letter of each triangle in the correct circle(s) at the right.

Equilateral   Isosceles   Right

Theorems 4–3, 4–4, 4–5

Theorem 4-3 Isosceles Triangle Theorem

If two sides of a triangle are congruent, then the angles opposite those sides are congruent.

Theorem 4-4 Converse of Isosceles Triangle Theorem

If two angles of a triangle are congruent, then the sides opposite those angles are congruent.

Theorem 4-5

If a line bisects the vertex angle of an isosceles triangle, then the line is also the perpendicular bisector of the base.

5. If $\overline{PQ} \cong \overline{RQ}$ in $\triangle PQR$, then $\angle$ ___ $\cong \angle$ ___ .

6. Underline the correct theorem number to complete the sentence.

   The theorem illustrated below is Theorem 4–3 / 4–4 / 4–5 .

Problem 1 Using the Isosceles Triangle Theorems

Got It? Is $\angle WVS$ congruent to $\angle S$? Is $\overline{TR}$ congruent to $\overline{TS}$? Explain.

7. The markings show that $\overline{WV} \cong$ ___ .

8. Is $\angle WVS \cong \angle S$? Explain.

9. Is $\angle R \cong \angle S$? Explain.

10. Is $\overline{TR} \cong \overline{TS}$? Explain.

Lesson 4-5

Problem 2 Using Algebra

Got It? Suppose $m\angle A = 27$. What is the value of x?

11. Since $\overline{CB} \cong$ [ ], $\triangle ABC$ is isosceles.

12. Since $\triangle ABC$ is isosceles, $m\angle A = m\angle$ [ ] = [ ].

13. Since $\overline{BD}$ bisects the vertex of an isosceles triangle, $\overline{BD} \perp$ [ ]
    and $m\angle BDC =$ [ ].

14. Use the justifications below to find the value of x.

$m\angle$ [ ] $+ m\angle BDC + x = 180$ Triangle Angle-Sum Theorem

[ ] $+$ [ ] $+ x = 180$ Substitute.

[ ] $+ x = 180$ Simplify.

$x =$ [ ]   Subtract 117 from each side.

---

take note

Corollaries to Theorems 4–3 and 4–4

Corollary to Theorem 4-3

If a triangle is equilateral, then the triangle is equiangular.

Corollary to Theorem 4-4

If a triangle is equiangular, then the triangle is equilateral.

15. Underline the correct number to complete the sentence.

The corollary illustrated below is Corollary to Theorem 4-3 / 4-4 .

If . . .   Then . . .

Problem 3 Finding Angle Measures

Got It? Suppose the triangles at the right are isosceles triangles,
where $\angle ADE$, $\angle DEC$, and $\angle ECB$ are vertex angles. If the vertex
angles each have a measure of 58, what are $m\angle A$ and $m\angle BCD$?

16. Which triangles are congruent by the Side-Angle-Side Theorem?

17. Which angles are congruent by the Isosceles Triangle Theorem?

18. By the Triangle Angle-Sum Theorem, $m\angle A + 58 + m\angle DEA = $ [   ].

19. Solve for $m\angle A$.

20. Since [   ] $\cong \angle ECD$, $m\angle ECD = $ [   ].

21. Using the Angle Addition Postulate, $m\angle BCD = 58 + m\angle ECD = $ [   ].

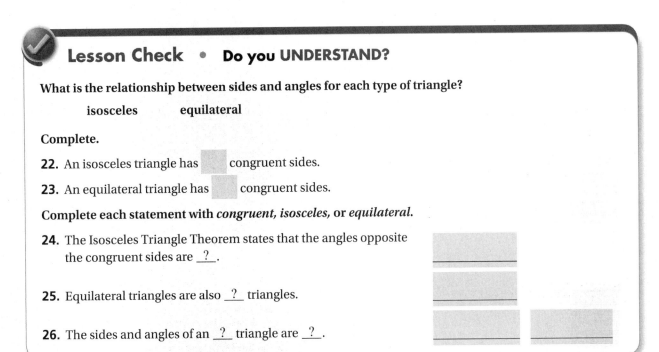

Lesson Check • Do you UNDERSTAND?

What is the relationship between sides and angles for each type of triangle?

       isosceles   equilateral

Complete.

22. An isosceles triangle has [   ] congruent sides.

23. An equilateral triangle has [   ] congruent sides.

Complete each statement with *congruent, isosceles,* or *equilateral*.

24. The Isosceles Triangle Theorem states that the angles opposite the congruent sides are ? .

25. Equilateral triangles are also ? triangles.

26. The sides and angles of an ? triangle are ? .

Math Success

Check off the vocabulary words that you understand.

☐ corollary   ☐ legs of an isosceles triangle   ☐ base of an isosceles triangle

       ☐ vertex angle of an isosceles triangle   ☐ base angles of an isosceles triangle

Rate how well you understand *isosceles and equilateral triangles*.

Lesson 4-5

4-6 Congruence in Right Triangles

Vocabulary

● **Review**

Write T for *true* or F for *false*.

_____ **1.** Segments that are *congruent* have the same length.

_____ **2.** Polygons that are *congruent* have the same shape but are not always the same size.

_____ **3.** In *congruent* figures, corresponding angles have the same measure.

● **Vocabulary Builder**

hypotenuse (noun) **hy PAH tuh noos**

Related Word: leg

Definition: The **hypotenuse** is the side opposite the right angle in a right triangle.

Main Idea: The **hypotenuse** is the longest side in a right triangle.

● **Use Your Vocabulary**

Underline the correct word(s) to complete each sentence.

4. One side of a right triangle is / is not a *hypotenuse*.

5. A right triangle has one / two / three *legs*.

6. The length of the *hypotenuse* is always equal to / greater than / less than the lengths of the *legs*.

Use the triangles at the right for Exercises 7 and 8.

7. Cross out the side that is NOT a *hypotenuse*.

| $\overline{BC}$ | $\overline{AB}$ | $\overline{GH}$ | $\overline{FD}$ |

8. Circle the *leg(s)*.

| $\overline{AC}$ | $\overline{AB}$ | $\overline{HI}$ | $\overline{ED}$ |

You can prove that two triangles are congruent without having to show that *all* corresponding parts are congruent. In this lesson, you will prove right triangles congruent by using one pair of right angles, a pair of hypotenuses, and a pair of legs.

take note

Theorem 4-6 Hypotenuse-Leg (HL) Theorem and Conditions

Theorem	**If . . .**	**Then . . .**
If the hypotenuse and a leg of one right triangle are congruent to the hypotenuse and leg of another right triangle, then the triangles are congruent.	$\triangle PQR$ and $\triangle XYZ$ are right triangles, $\overline{PR} \cong \overline{XZ}$, and $\overline{PQ} \cong \overline{XY}$	$\triangle PQR \cong \triangle XYZ$

9. To use the HL Theorem, the triangles must meet three conditions. Complete each sentence with *right* or *congruent*.

There are two ? triangles.

The triangles have ? hypotenuses.

There is one pair of ? legs.

Use the information in the Take Note for Exercises 10–12.

10. How do the triangles in the Take Note meet the first condition in Exercise 9? Explain.

11. How do the triangles in the Take Note meet the second condition in Exercise 9? Explain.

12. How do the triangles in the Take Note meet the third condition in Exercise 9? Explain.

Lesson 4-6

Problem 1 Using the HL Theorem

Got It? Given: ∠PRS and ∠RPQ are right angles, $\overline{SP} \cong \overline{QR}$

Prove: △PRS ≅ △RPQ

13. Complete each step of the proof.

Given		Given		Reflexive Prop. of ≅
∠PRS and ∠ ☐ are right angles.		$\overline{SP} \cong$ ☐		$\overline{PR} \cong$ ☐

Definition of right triangle		HL Theorem
△PRS and △ ☐ are right triangles.	→	△PRS ≅ △ ☐

Problem 2 Writing a Proof Using the HL Theorem

Got It? Given: $\overline{CD} \cong \overline{EA}$, $\overline{AD}$ is the perpendicular bisector of $\overline{CE}$

Prove: △CBD ≅ △EBA

14. Circle what you know because $\overline{AD}$ is the perpendicular bisector of $\overline{CE}$.

∠CBD and ∠EBA are right angles.	∠CBD and ∠EBA are acute angles.
B is the midpoint of $\overline{AD}$.	B is the midpoint of $\overline{CE}$.

15. Circle the congruent legs.

$\overline{AB}$	$\overline{CB}$	$\overline{DB}$	$\overline{EB}$

16. Write the hypotenuse of each triangle.

△CBD ☐   △EBA ☐

17. Complete the proof.

Statements	Reasons
1) $\overline{CD} \cong$ ☐	1) Given
2) ∠CBD and ∠ ☐ are right ∠s.	2) Definition of ⊥ bisector
3) △CBD and △ ☐ are right △s.	3) Definition of right △
4) $\overline{CB} \cong$ ☐	4) Definition of ⊥ bisector
5) △CBD ≅ ☐	5) HL Theorem

Lesson Check • Do you UNDERSTAND?

Error Analysis Your classmate says that there is not enough information to determine whether the two triangles at the right are congruent. Is your classmate correct? Explain.

Write T for *true* or F for *false*.

_____ **18.** There are three right angles.

_____ **19.** There are two right triangles.

_____ **20.** There are two congruent hypotenuses.

_____ **21.** There are no congruent legs.

_____ **22.** You need to use the Reflexive Property of Congruence.

_____ **23.** $\overline{LJ} \cong \overline{LJ}$ is given.

24. Do you always need three congruent corresponding parts to prove triangles congruent? Explain.

_____

_____

_____

25. Is your classmate correct? Explain.

_____

_____

_____

_____

Math Success

Check off the vocabulary words that you understand.

☐ hypotenuse   ☐ legs of a right triangle

Rate how well you can *use the Hypotenuse-Leg (HL) Theorem.*

Lesson 4-6

4-7 Congruence in Overlapping Triangles

Vocabulary

● Review

1. Circle the *common* side of △ABC and △ADC.

$\overline{AB}$ $\overline{AC}$ $\overline{AD}$ $\overline{BC}$

2. Circle the *common* side of △XWZ and △YWZ.

$\overline{WZ}$ $\overline{WX}$ $\overline{WY}$ $\overline{ZY}$

3. Circle the *common* side of △RST and △RPT.

$\overline{RP}$ $\overline{RS}$ $\overline{RT}$ $\overline{ST}$

● Vocabulary Builder

overlapping (adjective) **oh vur LAP ing**

Other Word Form: overlap (noun)

Definition: Overlapping events or figures have parts in common.

Math Usage: Two or more figures with common regions are **overlapping** figures.

● Use Your Vocabulary

Circle the common regions of the *overlapping*
figures in the diagram at the right.

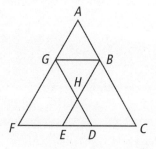

4. △FGD and △CBE

△ABG   △ACF   △EHD   △GHB

5. △BEC and △HED

△BEC   △GBH   △GDF   △HED

6. △ACF and △ABG

△ABG   △ACF   △GBH   △EHD

7. △ACF and △GBH

△ABG   △ACF   △GBH   △HED

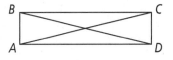

Problem 1 Identifying Common Parts

Got It? What is the common side in △*ABD* and △*DCA*?

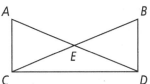

8. Separate and redraw △*ABD* and △*DCA*.

9. You drew ▢ twice, so the common side is ▢.

Problem 2 Using Common Parts

Got It? Given: △*ACD* ≅ △*BDC*

Prove: $\overline{CE} \cong \overline{DE}$

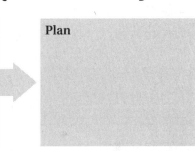

10. Use the information in the problem to complete the problem-solving model below.

Know	Need	Plan

11. Use the justifications below to complete each statement.

Statements	Reasons
1) △*ACD* ≅ ▢	1) Given
2) $\overline{AC} \cong$ ▢	2) Corresponding parts of ≅ triangles are ≅.
3) ∠*A* ≅ ▢	3) Corresponding parts of ≅ triangles are ≅.
4) ▢ ≅ ∠*BED*	4) Vertical angles are congruent.
5) ▢ ≅ △*BED*	5) Angle-Angle-Side (AAS) Theorem
6) $\overline{CE} \cong$ ▢	6) Corresponding parts of ≅ triangles are ≅.

12. How could you use the Converse of the Isosceles Triangle Theorem to prove $\overline{CE} \cong \overline{DE}$?

_____

_____

Lesson 4-7

Problem 3 Using Two Pairs of Triangles

Got It? Given: $\overline{PS} \cong \overline{RS}$, $\angle PSQ \cong \angle RSQ$

Prove: $\triangle QPT \cong \triangle QRT$

13. Give the reason for each statement in the proof.

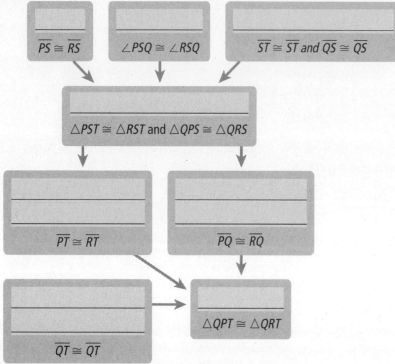

$\overline{PS} \cong \overline{RS}$

$\angle PSQ \cong \angle RSQ$

$\overline{ST} \cong \overline{ST}$ and $\overline{QS} \cong \overline{QS}$

$\triangle PST \cong \triangle RST$ and $\triangle QPS \cong \triangle QRS$

$\overline{PT} \cong \overline{RT}$

$\overline{PQ} \cong \overline{RQ}$

$\overline{QT} \cong \overline{QT}$

$\triangle QPT \cong \triangle QRT$

Problem 4 Separating Overlapping Triangles

Got It? Given: $\angle CAD \cong \angle EAD$, $\angle C \cong \angle E$

Prove: $\overline{BD} \cong \overline{FD}$

14. Circle the angles that are vertical angles.

$\angle ADB$	$\angle ADC$	$\angle ADE$	$\angle ADF$	$\angle BDC$	$\angle FDE$

15. Mark the angles that you know are congruent in each pair of separated triangles below.

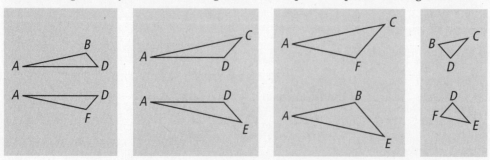

16. Which triangles are congruent by AAS? Explain.

Chapter 4

116

17. Which triangles are congruent by ASA? Explain.

_____

_____

_____

18. How can you prove $\overline{BD} \cong \overline{FD}$?

_____

_____

_____

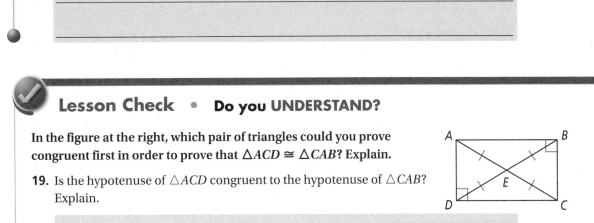

Lesson Check • Do you UNDERSTAND?

In the figure at the right, which pair of triangles could you prove congruent first in order to prove that $\triangle ACD \cong \triangle CAB$? Explain.

19. Is the hypotenuse of $\triangle ACD$ congruent to the hypotenuse of $\triangle CAB$? Explain.

_____

_____

20. What else do you need to prove right angles congruent using HL?

_____

_____

21. Which triangles can you prove congruent to find this? Explain.

_____

_____

_____

Math Success

Check off the vocabulary words that you understand.

☐ congruent   ☐ corresponding   ☐ overlapping

Rate how well you can _identify congruent overlapping triangles_.

5-1 Midsegments of Triangles

Vocabulary

● Review

Use the number line at the right for Exercises 1–3.

A   B   C   D   E

−4 −3 −2 −1   0   1   2   3   4

1. Point ▢ is the *midpoint* of $\overline{AE}$.

2. Point ▢ is the *midpoint* of $\overline{CE}$.

3. Point ▢ is the *midpoint* of $\overline{AC}$.

Use the graph at the right for Exercises 4–6. Name each *segment*.

4. a *segment* that lies on the *x*-axis

5. a *segment* that contains the point (0, 4)

6. a *segment* whose endpoints both have *x*-coordinate 3

● Vocabulary Builder

midsegment

midsegment (noun) MID **seg munt**

Related Words: midpoint, segment

Definition: A **midsegment** of a triangle is a segment connecting the midpoints of two sides of the triangle.

● Use Your Vocabulary

Circle the correct statement in each pair.

7. A *midsegment* connects the midpoints of two sides of a triangle.

     A *midsegment* connects a vertex of a triangle to the midpoint of the opposite side.

8. A triangle has exactly one *midsegment*.   A triangle has three *midsegments*.

Theorem 5-1 Triangle Midsegment Theorem

If a segment joins the midpoints of two sides of a triangle, then the segment is parallel to the third side and is half as long.

9. Use the triangle at the right to complete the table below.

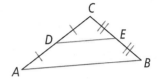

If	Then
☐ is the midpoint of $\overline{CA}$ and	☐ $\parallel \overline{AB}$
☐ is the midpoint of $\overline{CB}$	☐ $= \frac{1}{2} AB$

Use the graph at the right for Exercises 10–11.

10. Draw $\overline{RS}$. Then underline the correct word or number to complete each sentence below.

$\overline{RS}$ is a midsegment of / parallel to $\triangle ABC$.

$\overline{RS}$ is a midsegment of / parallel to $\overline{AC}$.

11. Use the Triangle Midsegment Theorem to complete.

$RS = $ ☐ AC

12. Draw $\overline{ST}$. What do you know about $\overline{ST}$?

_____

_____

✓ **Problem 1** **Identifying Parallel Segments**

Got It? In $\triangle XYZ$, A is the midpoint of $\overline{XY}$, B is the midpoint of $\overline{YZ}$, and C is the midpoint of $\overline{ZX}$. **What are the three pairs of parallel segments?**

13. Draw a diagram to illustrate the problem.

14. Write the segment parallel to each given segment.

$\overline{AB} \parallel$ ☐ $\overline{CB} \parallel$ ☐ $\overline{CA} \parallel$ ☐

Got It? In the figure below, $AD = 6$ and $DE = 7.5$. What are the lengths of $\overline{DC}$, $\overline{AC}$, $\overline{EF}$, and $\overline{AB}$?

15. Complete the problem-solving model below.

Know	Need	Plan
$AD = 6$ and $DE = 7.5$. $CE = EB, AD = DC$, $BF = \boxed{}$		Use the Triangle Midsegment Theorem to find DC, AC, EF, and $\boxed{}$.

16. The diagram shows that $\overline{EF}$ and $\overline{DE}$ join the midpoints of two sides of $\triangle\;\boxed{}$.

    By the Triangle Midsegment Theorem, $EF = \frac{1}{2} \cdot \boxed{}$ and $DE = \frac{1}{2} \cdot \boxed{}$.

Complete each statement.

17. $DC = AD = \boxed{}$

18. $AC = AD + \boxed{} = \boxed{} + \boxed{} = \boxed{}$

19. $EF = \boxed{} \cdot AC = \boxed{} \cdot \boxed{} = 6$

20. $CB = \boxed{} \cdot DE = \boxed{} \cdot \boxed{} = 15$

Got It? $\overline{CD}$ is a bridge being built over a lake, as shown in the figure at the right. What is the length of the bridge?

963 ft · Bridge · 2640 ft · 963 ft · C · D

21. Complete the flow chart to find the length of the bridge.

$\overline{CD}$ joins the __?__ of two sides of a triangle.

$\overline{CD}$ is parallel to a side that is $\boxed{}$ ft.

Use the Triangle __?__ Theorem.

$CD = \frac{1}{2} \cdot \boxed{}$

$CD = \boxed{}$

22. The length of the bridge is $\boxed{}$ ft.

Lesson Check • Do you know HOW?

If $JK = 5x + 20$ and $NO = 20$, what is the value of x?

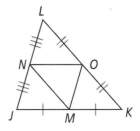

Complete each statement.

23. ▢ is the midpoint of $\overline{LJ}$.

24. ▢ is the midpoint of $\overline{LK}$.

25. $\overline{NO}$ is a ___?___ of $\triangle JKL$, so $NO = \frac{1}{2}JK$. _____

26. Substitute the given information into the equation in Exercise 25 and solve for x.

Lesson Check • Do you UNDERSTAND?

Reasoning If two noncollinear segments in the coordinate plane have slope 3, what can you conclude?

27. Place a ✓ in the box if the response is correct. Place an ✗ if it is incorrect.

   ▢ If two segments in a plane are parallel, then they have the same slope.

   ▢ If two segments lie on the same line, they are parallel.

28. Now answer the question.

   _____

   _____

Math Success

Check off the vocabulary words that you understand.

☐ midsegment   ☐ midpoint   ☐ segment

Rate how well you can *use properties of midsegments*.

| Need to review | 0   2   4   6   8   10 | Now I get it! |

Lesson 5-1

Vocabulary

● Review

Complete each statement with *bisector* or *bisects*.

1. $\overrightarrow{BD}$ is the __?__ of ∠ABC.

2. BD __?__ ∠ABC.

Write T for *true* or F for *false*.

_____ 3. Two *perpendicular* segments intersect to form four right angles.

_____ 4. You can draw more than one line *perpendicular* to a given line through a point not on the line.

● Vocabulary Builder

equidistant (adjective) **ee kwih DIS tunt**

Related Words: equal, distance

Definition: Equidistant means at an equal distance from a single point or object.

equidistant

● Use Your Vocabulary

Use to the number line at the right for Exercises 5 and 6.

5. Circle two points *equidistant* from zero.

6. Name points that are *equidistant* from point C.

[ ] and [ ]

Use to the diagram at the right for Exercises 7 and 8.

7. Circle two points *equidistant* from point Q.

8. Name four segments that are *equidistant* from the origin.

[ ]   [ ]   [ ]   [ ]

Theorem 5-2 Perpendicular Bisector Theorem

If a point is on the perpendicular bisector of a segment, **then** it is equidistant from the endpoints of the segment.

9. Use the diagrams below to complete the hypothesis and the conclusion.

If
$\overleftrightarrow{PM} \perp \overline{AB}$ and $AM = $ ☐

Then
$PA = $ ☐

Theorem 5-3 Converse of the Perpendicular Bisector Theorem

10. Complete the converse of Theorem 5-2.

If a point is equidistant from the endpoints of a segment, then it is on the _?_ of the segment.

11. Complete the diagram at the right to illustrate Theorem 5-3.

 Problem 1 Using the Perpendicular Bisector

Got It? Use the diagram at the right. What is the length of $\overline{QR}$?

12. Complete the reasoning model below.

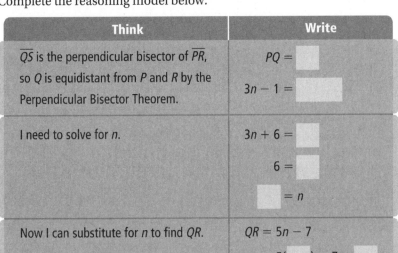

Think	Write
$\overline{QS}$ is the perpendicular bisector of $\overline{PR}$, so Q is equidistant from P and R by the Perpendicular Bisector Theorem.	$PQ = $ ☐ $3n - 1 = $ ☐
I need to solve for n.	$3n + 6 = $ ☐ $6 = $ ☐ ☐ $= n$
Now I can substitute for n to find QR.	$QR = 5n - 7$ $= 5($ ☐ $) - 7 = $ ☐

Lesson 5-2

Problem 2 Using a Perpendicular Bisector

Got It? If the director of the park at the right wants a T-shirt stand built at a point equidistant from the Spaceship Shoot and the Rollin' Coaster, by the Perpendicular Bisector Theorem he can place the stand anywhere along line ℓ. Suppose the park director wants the T-shirt stand to be equidistant from the paddle boats and the Spaceship Shoot. What are the possible locations?

13. On the diagram, draw $\overline{PS}$.

14. On the diagram, sketch the points that are equidistant from the paddle boats and the Spaceship Shoot. Describe these points.

_____

_____

Got It? Reasoning Can you place the T-shirt stand so that it is equidistant from the paddle boats, the Spaceship Shoot, and the Rollin' Coaster? Explain.

15. Does the line you drew in Exercise 14 intersect line ℓ?   Yes / No

16. Where should the T-shirt stand be placed so that it is equidistant from the paddle boats, the Spaceship Shoot, and the Rollin Coaster? Explain.

_____

_____

_____

The **distance from a point to a line** is the length of the perpendicular segment from the point to the line. This distance is also the length of the shortest segment from the point to the line.

Theorems 5-4 and 5-5

Angle Bisector Theorem

If a point is on the bisector of an angle, then the point is equisdistant from the sides of the angle.

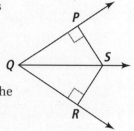

17. If point S is on the angle bisector of ∠ [ ], then SP = [ ].

Converse of the Angle Bisector Theorem

If a point in the interior of an angle is equidistant from the sides of the angle, then the point is on the angle bisector.

18. Point S is in the interior of ∠ [ ].

19. If SP = SR, then S is on the __?__ of ∠PQR.   _____

Problem 3 Using the Angle Bisector Theorem

Got It? What is the length of $\overline{FB}$?

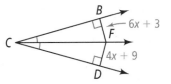

20. The problem is solved below. Justify each step.

$$FB = FD$$

$$6x + 3 = 4x + 9$$

$$6x = 4x + 6$$

$$2x = 6$$

$$x = 3$$

$$FB = 6x + 3$$

$$= 6(3) + 3 = 21$$

Lesson Check • Do you know HOW?

Use the figure at the right. What is the relationship between $\overline{AC}$ and $\overline{BD}$?

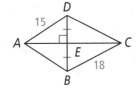

21. Underline the correct word or symbol to complete each sentence.

$\overline{AC}$ is parallel / perpendicular to $\overline{BD}$.

$\overline{AC}$ divides $\overline{BD}$ into two congruent / noncongruent segments.

$\overline{BD}$ divides $\overline{AC}$ into two congruent / noncongruent segments.

$\overline{AC}$ / $\overline{BD}$ is the perpendicular bisector of $\overline{AC}$ / $\overline{BD}$.

Math Success

Check off the vocabulary words that you understand.

☐ perpendicular bisector   ☐ equidistant   ☐ distance from a point to a line

Rate how well you can *understand bisectors*.

Lesson 5-2

5-3 Bisectors in Triangles

Vocabulary

● Review

Use the figure at the right. Write T for *true* or F for *false*.

_____ **1.** $\overline{AB}$ is the *perpendicular bisector* of $\overline{CD}$.

_____ **2.** $\overline{CD}$ is a *perpendicular bisector*, so it intersects $\overline{AB}$ at its midpoint.

_____ **3.** Any point on $\overleftrightarrow{CD}$ is *equidistant* from points A and B.

● Vocabulary Builder

concurrent lines

concurrent	(adjective)	**kun KUR unt**

Main Idea: **Concurrent** means occurring or existing at the same time.

Math Usage: When three or more lines intersect in one point, they are **concurrent**.

● Use Your Vocabulary

Complete each statement with *concurrency, concurrent,* or *concurrently*.

4. Two classes are __?__ when they meet at the same time.

5. The point of __?__ of three streets is the intersections of the streets.

6. A person may go to school and hold a job __?__ .

Label each diagram below *concurrent* or *not concurrent*.

7.

8.

9.

Theorem 5-6 Concurrency of Perpendicular Bisectors Theorem

The perpendicular bisectors of the sides of a triangle are concurrent at a point equidistant from the vertices.

Perpendicular bisectors $\overline{PX}$, $\overline{PY}$ and $\overline{PZ}$ are concurrent at P.

10. Mark $\triangle ABC$ to show all congruent segments.

Problem 1 Finding the Circumcenter of a Triangle

Got It? What are the coordinates of the circumcenter of the triangle with vertices $A(2, 7)$, $B(10, 7)$, and $C(10, 3)$?

11. Draw $\triangle ABC$ on the coordinate plane.

12. Label the coordinates the midpoint of $\overline{AB}$ and the midpoint of $\overline{BC}$.

13. Draw the perpendicular bisector of $\overline{AB}$.

14. Draw the perpendicular bisector of $\overline{BC}$.

15. Label the coordinates of the point of intersection of the bisectors.

16. The circumcenter of $\triangle ABC$ is (___ , ___).

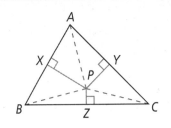

Problem 2 Using a Circumcenter

Got It? A town planner wants to place a bench equidistant from the three trees in the park. Where should he place the bench?

17. Complete the problem-solving model below.

Know	Need	Plan
The trees form the ___?___ of a triangle.	Find the point of concurrency of the ___?___ of the sides.	Find the ___?___ of the triangle, which is equidistant from the three trees.

18. How can the town planner determine where to place the bench? Explain.

Lesson 5-3

Theorem 5-7   Concurrency of Angle Bisectors Theorem

The bisectors of the angles of a triangle are concurrent at a point equidistant from the sides of the triangle.

Angle bisectors $\overline{AP}$, $\overline{BP}$, and $\overline{CP}$ are concurrent at P.

19. $PX = $ ☐ $=$ ☐

Complete each sentence with the appropriate word from the list.

incenter   inscribed   inside

20. The point of concurrency of the angle bisectors of a triangle is the __?__ of the triangle.

21. The point of concurrency of the angle bisectors of a triangle is always __?__ the triangle.

22. The circle is __?__ in △ABC.

 Identifying and Using the Incenter

Got It? $QN = 5x + 36$ and $QM = 2x + 51$. What is QO?

23. Complete the reasoning model below.

Think	Write
I know that Q is the point of concurrency of the angle bisectors.	Q is the incenter / midpoint of △JKL.
And I know that	the distance from Q to each side of △JKL is equal / unequal .
I can write an equation and solve for x.	$QO = $ ☐ $5x + 36 = $ ☐ $5x = $ ☐ $3x = $ ☐ $x = $ ☐

24. Use your answer to Exercise 23 to find QO.

Got It? Reasoning Is it possible for QP to equal 50? Explain.

25. Drawn an inscribed circle in the diagram at the right.

26. ☐ and ☐ are two segments that have the same length as $\overline{QO}$.

27. Circle the correct relationship between QO and QP.

$QO < QP$ $\qquad\qquad$ $QO = QP$ $\qquad\qquad$ $QO > QP$

28. Given your answer to Exercise 27, is it possible for QP to equal 50? Explain.

_____

_____

✓ Lesson Check • Do you UNDERSTAND?

Vocabulary A triangle's circumcenter is outside the triangle. What type of triangle is it?

29. Draw an example of each type of triangle on a coordinate plane below.

acute $\qquad\qquad$ obtuse $\qquad\qquad$ right

30. Circle the phrase that describes the circumcenter of a triangle.

the point of concurrency of the angle bisectors $\qquad$ the point of concurrency of the perpendicular bisectors of the sides

31. Underline the correct word to complete the sentence.

When a triangle's circumcenter is outside the triangle, the triangle is acute / obtuse / right .

✓ Math Success

Check off the vocabulary words that you understand.

☐ concurrent ☐ circumscribed about ☐ incenter ☐ inscribed in ☐ bisector

Rate how well you can *use bisectors in triangles.*

| Need to review | 0 | 2 | 4 | 6 | 8 | 10 | Now I get it! |

Lesson 5-3

Vocabulary

● Review

1. Are three diameters of a circle *concurrent*?   Yes / No

2. Are two diagonals of a rectangle *concurrent*?   Yes / No

3. Is point *C* at the right a point of *concurrency*?   Yes / No

● Vocabulary Builder

median (noun) MEE **dee un**

Related Words: median (adjective), middle (noun), midpoint (noun)

Definition: A **median** of a triangle is a segment whose endpoints are a vertex and the midpoint of the opposite side.

● Use Your Vocabulary

Write T for *true* or F for *false*.

_____ 4. The *median* of a triangle is a segment that connects the midpoint of one side to the midpoint of an adjacent side.

_____ 5. The point of concurrency of the *medians* of a triangle is where they intersect.

_____ 6. A triangle has one median.

7. Circle the drawing that shows *median* $\overline{AD}$ of $\triangle ABC$.

Theorem 5-8 Concurrency of Medians Theorem

The medians of a triangle are concurrent at a point (the centroid of the triangle) that is two thirds the distance from each vertex to the midpoint of the opposite side.

For any triangle, the centroid is always inside the triangle.

8. Complete each equation.

$DC = \frac{2}{3}$ [   ] $EC = \frac{2}{3}$ [   ] $FC =$ [   ]

Problem 1 Finding the Length of a Median

Got It? In the diagram at the right, $ZA = 9$. What is the length of $\overline{ZC}$?

9. Point [   ] is the centroid of $\triangle XYZ$.

10. Use the justifications at the right to solve for ZC.

$ZA = $ [   ] $\cdot ZC$ Concurrency of Medians Theorem

[   ] $=$ [   ] $\cdot ZC$ Substitute for ZA.

[   ] $=$ [   ] $\cdot ZC$ Multiply each side by $\frac{3}{2}$.

[   ] $= ZC$ Simplify.

11. ZC is [   ], or [   ].

An *altitude* of a triangle is the perpendicular segment from a vertex of the triangle to the line containing the opposite side.

Problem 2 Identifying Medians and Altitudes

Got It? For $\triangle ABC$, is each segment, $\overline{AD}$, $\overline{EG}$, and $\overline{CF}$, a *median*, an *altitude*, or *neither*? Explain.

12. Read each statement. Then cross out the words that do NOT describe $\overline{AD}$.

$\overline{AD}$ is a segment that extends from vertex A to $\overline{CB}$, which is opposite A.

$\overline{AD}$ meets $\overline{CB}$ at point D, which is the midpoint of $\overline{CB}$ since $\overline{CD} \cong \overline{DB}$.

$\overline{AD}$ is not perpendicular to $\overline{CB}$.

altitude	median	neither altitude nor median

13. Circle the correct statement below.

$\overline{AD}$ is a median.	$\overline{AD}$ is an altitude.	$\overline{AD}$ is neither a median nor an altitude.

14. Read the statement. Then circle the correct description of $\overline{EG}$.

$\overline{EG}$ does not extend from a vertex.

$\overline{EG}$ is a median.	$\overline{EG}$ is an altitude.	$\overline{EG}$ is neither a median nor an altitude.

15. Read each statement. Then circle the correct description of $\overline{CF}$.

$\overline{CF}$ is a segment that extends from vertex C to $\overline{AB}$, which opposite C.

$\overline{CF} \perp \overline{AB}$

| $\overline{CF}$ is median. | $\overline{CF}$ is an altitude. | $\overline{CF}$ is neither a median nor an altitude. |

Theorem 5-9   Concurrency of Altitudes Theorem

The lines that contain the altitudes of a triangle are concurrent.

The point of concurrency is the *orthocenter of the triangle*. The orthocenter of a triangle can be inside, on, or outside the triangle.

16. Draw an example of each type of triangle on a coordinate plane below.

acute   obtuse   right

Draw a line from the type of triangle in Column A to the location of its orthocenter in Column B.

Column A

17. acute

18. right

19. obtuse

Column B

outside the triangle

inside the triangle

at a vertex of the triangle

Problem 3 **Finding the Orthocenter**

Got It? $\triangle DEF$ has vertices $D(1, 2)$, $E(1, 6)$, and $F(4, 2)$. What are the coordinates of the orthocenter of $\triangle DEF$?

20. Graph $\triangle DEF$ on the coordinate plane.

Underline the correct word to complete each sentence.

21. $\triangle DEF$ is a(n) acute / right triangle, so the

orthocenter is at vertex D.

22. The altitude to $\overline{DF}$ is horizontal / vertical .

23. The altitude to $\overline{DE}$ is horizontal / vertical .

24. The coordinates of the orthocenter

of $\triangle DEF$ are ([ ] , [ ]).

Concept Summary Special Segments and Lines in Triangles

25. Use the words *altitudes, angle bisectors, medians,* and *perpendicular bisectors* to describe the intersecting lines in each triangle below.

Incenter   Orthocenter   Centroid   Circumcenter

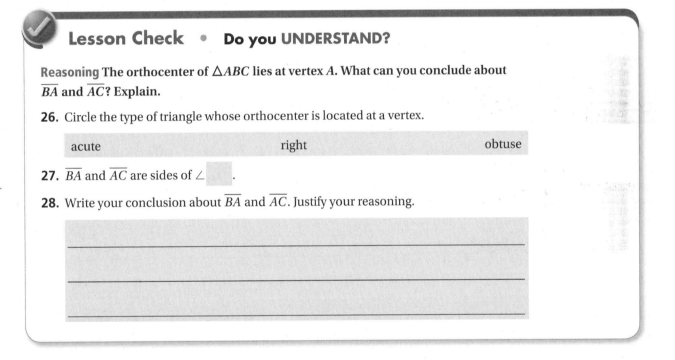

Lesson Check • Do you UNDERSTAND?

Reasoning The orthocenter of $\triangle ABC$ lies at vertex A. What can you conclude about $\overline{BA}$ and $\overline{AC}$? Explain.

26. Circle the type of triangle whose orthocenter is located at a vertex.

acute	right	obtuse

27. $\overline{BA}$ and $\overline{AC}$ are sides of $\angle$ ____ .

28. Write your conclusion about $\overline{BA}$ and $\overline{AC}$. Justify your reasoning.

Math Success

Check off the vocabulary words that you understand.

☐ median of a triangle   ☐ altitude of a triangle   ☐ orthocenter of a triangle

Rate how well you can *understand medians and altitudes.*

Need to review   0   2   4   6   8   10   Now I get it!

Vocabulary

● Review

Draw a line from each statement in Column A to one or more pictures that contradict it in Column B.

Column A	Column B

1. $x < y$

A

y   *x*

C   *B*

2. $x = y$

◯— ≅ ◯—

Radius = x   Radius = y

3. $x > y$

Ordered pair (3, 3)

● Vocabulary Builder

indirect (adjective)   **in duh** REKT

Definition: **Indirect** means not direct in course or action, taking a roundabout route to get to a point or idea.

Math Usage: In **indirect** reasoning, all possibilities are considered and then all but one are proved false. The remaining possibility must be true.

● Use Your Vocabulary

Write *indirect* or *indirectly* to complete each sentence.

4. The __?__ way home from school takes a lot more time.

_____

5. By finding the negation of a statement false, you __?__ prove the statement true.

_____

Key Concept Writing an Indirect Proof

Step 1
State as a temporary assumption the opposite (negation) of what you want to prove.

Step 2
Show that this temporary assumption leads to a contradiction.

Step 3
Conclude that the temporary assumption must be false and what you want to prove must be true.

 Problem 1 Writing the First Step of an Indirect Proof

Got It? Suppose you want to write an indirect proof of the statement. As the first step of the proof, what would you assume?

△*BOX* is not acute.

6. What do you want to prove?

7. What is the opposite of what you want to prove?

8. The first step in the indirect proof is to write the following:

Assume temporarily that △*BOX* is _?_ .

Got It? Suppose you want to write an indirect proof of the statement. As the first step of the proof, what would you assume?

At least one of the items costs more than $25.

9. What do you want to prove?

For Exercises 10–11, use <, >, ≤, ≥, or = to complete each statement.
Let *n* = the cost of at least one of the items.

10. What do you want to prove?
    n ☐ 25

11. What is the opposite of what you want to prove?
    n ☐ 25

12. The first step in the indirect proof is to write the following:

Assume temporarily that at least one of the items costs _?_ $25.

Write the first step of the indirect proof of each statement.

13. Prove: *AB* = *CD*

14. Prove: The sun is shining.

Lesson 5-5

Problem 2 Identifying Contradictions

Got It? Which two statements contradict each other?

    I. △XYZ is acute.   **II.** △XYZ is scalene   **III.** △XYZ is equiangular

15. Use the words in the box at the right to complete the flow chart below.

16. In the first row of the flow chart above, circle the two statements that contradict one another.

Problem 3 Writing an Indirect Proof

Got It? Given: $7(x + y) = 70$ and $x \neq 4$.

      Prove: $y \neq 6$

17. Give the reason for each statement of the proof.

Statements	Reasons
1) Assume $y = 6$.	1)
2) $7(x + y) = 70$	2)
3) $7(x + 6) = 70$	3)
4) $7x + 42 = 70$	4)
5) $\quad\quad 7x = 28$	5)
6) $\quad\quad\quad x = 4$	6)
7) $\quad\quad\quad x \neq 4$	7)
8) $\quad\quad\quad y \neq 6$	8)

Lesson Check • Do you know HOW?

Suppose you want to write an indirect proof of the following statement. As the first step of the proof, what would you assume?

> Quadrilateral *ABCD* has four right angles.

18. Place a ✓ if the statement is the correct assumption to make as the first step in the indirect proof. Place an ✗ if it is not.

☐ Quadrilateral *ABCD* is a rectangle.

☐ Quadrilateral *ABCD* has four non-right angles.

☐ Quadrilateral *ABCD* does *not* have four right angles.

Lesson Check • Do you UNDERSTAND?

Error Analysis A classmate began an indirect proof as shown at the right. Explain and correct your classmate's error.

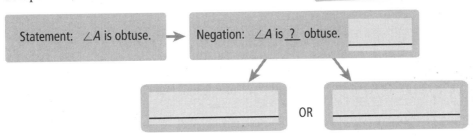

Given: △ABC
Prove: ∠A is obtuse.
~~Assume temporarily that ∠A is acute.~~

19. Complete the flow chart.

Statement: ∠A is obtuse. → Negation: ∠A is _?_ obtuse. ☐_____

☐_____ OR ☐_____

20. Underline the correct words to complete the sentence.

The indirect proof has an incorrect conclusion / assumption because the opposite of

"∠A is obtuse" is "∠A is acute / not obtuse / right."

Math Success

Check off the vocabulary words that you understand.

☐ indirect reasoning ☐ indirect proof ☐ contradiction

Rate how well you can *use indirect reasoning.*

Lesson 5-5

5-6 Inequalities in One Triangle

Vocabulary

● Review

1. Circle the labeled *exterior angle*.

2. Write the *Exterior Angle* Theorem as it relates to the diagram.

$$m\angle \boxed{} = m\angle \boxed{} + m\angle \boxed{}$$

3. Draw an *exterior angle* adjacent to $\angle 1$ and label it $\angle 5$.

Circle the statement that represents an *inequality* in each pair below.

4. $x \neq 32$

   $x = 32$

5. The number of votes is equal to 10,000.

   The number of votes is greater than 10,000.

Complete each statement with an inequality symbol.

6. y is less than or equal to z.

   $y \boxed{} z$

7. The temperature t is at least 80 degrees.

   $t \boxed{} 80°$

● Vocabulary Builder

> There are more letters in the word *comparison* than in the word *compare*.

compare (verb) **kum** PEHR

Other Word Form: comparison (noun)

Definition: To **compare** is to examine two or more items, noting similarities and differences.

Math Usage: Use inequalities to **compare** amounts.

● Use Your Vocabulary

8. Complete each statement with the appropriate form of the word *compare*.

   NOUN   By _?_, a spider has more legs than a beetle.

   VERB   You can _?_ products before deciding which to buy.

   VERB   To _?_ quantities, you can write an equation or an inequality.

take note

Property   Comparison Property of Inequality

If $a = b + c$ and $c > 0$, then $a > b$.

9. Circle the group of values that satisfies the Comparison Property of Inequality.

$a = 5, b = 5,$ and $c = 0$ $a = 5, b = 2,$ and $c = 3$ $a = 8, b = 6,$ and $c = 1$

take note

Corollary   Corollary to the Triangle Exterior Angle Theorem

The measure of an exterior angle of a triangle is greater than the measure of each of its remote interior angles.

10. Circle the angles whose measures are always less than the measure of $\angle 1$.

Problem 1   **Applying the Corollary**

Got It? Use the figure at the right. Why is $m\angle 5 > m\angle C$?

Write the justification for each statement.

11. $\angle 5$ is an exterior angle of $\triangle ADC$.

_____

_____

12. $m\angle 5 > m\angle C$

_____

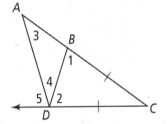

You can use the Corollary to the Triangle Exterior Angle Theorem to prove the following theorem.

take note

Theorem 5-10 and Theorem 5-11

Theorem 5-10

If two sides of a triangle are not congruent, then the larger angle lies opposite the longer side.

If $XZ > XY$, then $m\angle Y > m\angle Z$.

13. Theorem 5-11 is related to Theorem 5-10. Write the text of Theorem 5-11 by exchanging the words "larger angle" and "longer side."

Theorem 5-11 If two sides of a triangle are not congruent, then

.

Lesson 5-6

Got It? Reasoning In the figure at the right, $m\angle S = 24$ and $m\angle O = 130$. Which side of $\triangle SOX$ is the shortest side? Explain your reasoning.

14. By the Triangle Angle-Sum Theorem, $m\angle S + m\angle O + m\angle X = 180$, so $m\angle X = \boxed{} - m\angle S - m\angle O$.

15. Use the given angle measures and the equation you wrote in Exercise 14 to find $m\angle X$.

$m\angle X = \boxed{} - \boxed{} - \boxed{} = \boxed{}$

16. Complete the table below.

angle			
angle measure	130	26	24
opposite side			

17. Which is the shortest side? Explain.

The shortest side is $\boxed{}$ because it is opposite the smallest angle, $\angle \boxed{}$.

 take note

Theorem 5-12 Triangle Inequality Theorem

The sum of the lengths of any two sides of a triangle is greater than the length of the third side.

18. Complete each inequality.

$XY + YZ > \boxed{}$ $YZ + ZX > \boxed{}$ $ZX + XY > \boxed{}$

Problem 4 Using the Triangle Inequality Theorem

Got It? Can a triangle have sides with lengths 2 m, 6 m, and 9 m? Explain.

19. Complete the reasoning model below.

Think	Write
The sum of the lengths of any two sides must be greater than the length of the third side.	$2 + 6 = 8$ $6 + 9 = 15$ $2 + 9 = 11$
I need to write three sums and three inequalities.	$8 \boxed{} 9$ $15 \boxed{} 2$ $11 \boxed{} 6$
One of those sums is greater / not greater than the length of the third side.	It is / is not possible for a triangle to have sides with lengths 2 m, 6 m, and 9 m.

Problem 5 Finding Possible Side Lengths

Got It? A triangle has side lengths of 4 in. and 7 in. What is the range of possible lengths for the third side?

20. Let x = the length of the third side. Use the Triangle Inequality Theorem to write and solve three inequalities.

$x + 4 > \boxed{}$ $x + 7 > \boxed{}$ $7 + 4 > \boxed{}$

$x > \boxed{}$ $x > \boxed{}$ $11 > \boxed{}$

21. Underline the correct word to complete each sentence.

    Length is always / sometimes / never positive.

    The first / second / third inequality pair is invalid in this situation.

22. Write the remaining inequalities as the compound inequality $\boxed{} < x < \boxed{}$.

23. The third side must be longer than $\boxed{}$ in. and shorter than $\boxed{}$ in.

Lesson Check • Do you UNDERSTAND?

Error Analysis A friend tells you that she drew a triangle with perimeter 16 and one side of length 8. How do you know she made an error in her drawing?

24. If one side length is 8 and the perimeter is 16, then the sum of the lengths of the two remaining sides must be $16 - 8 = \boxed{}$.

25. Underline the correct words or number to complete each sentence.

    By the Triangle Inequality Theorem, the sum of the lengths of two sides of a triangle must be equal to / greater than / less than the length of the third side.

    By the Triangle Inequality Theorem, the sum of the lengths of the two unknown sides must be equal to / greater than / less than the length 8 / 16 .

    But 8 is *not* equal to / greater than 8, so there must be an error in the drawing.

Math Success

Check off the vocabulary words that you understand.

☐ exterior angle   ☐ comparison property of inequality

Rate how well you can *use the Triangle Inequality Theorem.*

Need to review   0   2   4   6   8   10   Now I get it!

Lesson 5-6

5-7 Inequalities in Two Triangles

Vocabulary

● Review

Circle the *included angles* in each diagram.

1.

2.

In Exercises 3–5, cross out the group of values that does not satisfy the *Comparison Property of Inequality.*

3. $a = 3, b = 3, c = 0$

$a = 6, b = 4, c = 2$

4. $a = 11, b = 3, c = 8$

$a = 1, b = 2, c = 3$

5. $a = 8, b = 3, c = 5$

$a = 8, b = 5, c = 4$

Write a number so that each group satisfies the *Comparison Property of Inequality.*

6. $a = \boxed{}, b = 0, c = 2$

7. $a = 9, b = \boxed{}, c = 1$

8. $a = 3, b = \boxed{}, c = 2$

● Vocabulary Builder

hinge (noun, verb) <u>hinj</u>

Definition (noun): A **hinge** is a device on which something else depends or turns.

Definition (verb): To **hinge** upon means to depend on.

● Use Your Vocabulary

Circle the correct form of the word *hinge.*

9. Everything *hinges* on his decision.

Noun / Verb

10. The *hinge* on a gate allows it to swing open or closed.

Noun / Verb

11. Your plan *hinges* on your teacher's approval.

Noun / Verb

12. The lid was attached to the jewelry box by two *hinges.*

Noun / Verb

Theorems 5-13 and 5-14 The Hinge Theorem and its Converse

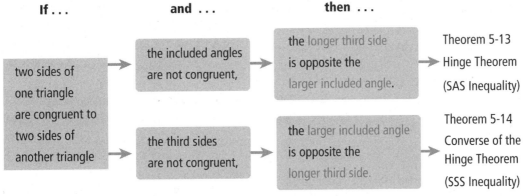

	If . . .		and . . .		then . . .	
two sides of one triangle are congruent to two sides of another triangle	→	the included angles are not congruent,	→	the longer third side is opposite the larger included angle.	→	Theorem 5-13 Hinge Theorem (SAS Inequality)
		the third sides are not congruent,	→	the larger included angle is opposite the longer third side.	→	Theorem 5-14 Converse of the Hinge Theorem (SSS Inequality)

13. Use the triangles at the right to complete the table.

Theorem	If...	Then...
5-13: Hinge Theorem	$m\angle A > m\angle X$	BC [ ] YZ
5-14: Converse of the Hinge Theorem	$BC >$ [ ]	$m\angle A >$ [ ]

14. Explain why Theorems 5-13 and 5-14 are also called the SAS and SSS Inequality Theorems.

Problem 1 Using the Hinge Theorem

Got It? What inequality relates *LN* and *OQ* in the figure at the right?

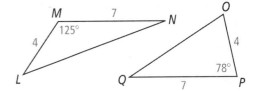

15. Use information in the diagram to complete each statement.

The included angle in $\triangle LMN$ is $\angle$ [ ] .

The included angle in $\triangle OPQ$ is $\angle$ [ ] .

16. Circle the side opposite the included angle in $\triangle LMN$. Underline the side opposite the included angle in $\triangle OPQ$.

$\overline{LM}$	$\overline{LN}$	$\overline{MN}$
$\overline{QO}$	$\overline{QP}$	$\overline{OP}$

17. Use the Hinge Theorem to complete the statement below

$m\angle$ [ ] $> m\angle$ [ ] , so $LN >$ [ ] .

Lesson 5-7

Problem 3 Using the Converse of the Hinge Theorem

Got It? What is the range of possible values for x in the figure at the right?

18. From the diagram you know that the triangles have two pairs of congruent corresponding sides, that

$LM < $ [ ] , and that $m\angle N = $ [ ] .

Complete the steps and justifications to find upper and lower limits on x.

19. $m\angle K < $ [ ]   Converse of the Hinge Theorem

$3x + 18 < $ [ ]   Substitute.

$3x < $ [ ]   Subtract [ ] from each side.

$x < $ [ ]   Divide each side by [ ] .

20. $m\angle K > $ [ ]   The measure of an angle of a triangle is greater than 0.

$3x + 18 > $ [ ]   Substitute.

$3x > $ [ ]   Subtract [ ] from each side.

$x > $ [ ]   Divide each side by [ ] .

21. Write the two inequalities as the compound inequality [ ] $< x < $ [ ] .

  Problem 4 Proving Relationships in Triangles

Got It? Given: $m\angle MON = 80$; O is the midpoint of $\overline{LN}$.

   Prove: $LM > MN$

22. Write a justification for each statement.

Statements	Reasons
1) $m\angle MON = 80$	1) _____
2) $m\angle MON + m\angle MOL = 180$	2) _____
3) $80 + m\angle MOL = 180$	3) _____
4) $m\angle MOL = 100$	4) _____
5) $\overline{LO} \cong \overline{ON}$	5) _____
6) $\overline{MO} \cong \overline{MO}$	6) _____
7) $m\angle MOL > m\angle MON$	7) _____
8) $LM > MN$	8) _____

Chapter 5   144

Lesson Check • Do you know HOW?

Write an inequality relating *FD* and *BC*.

In Exercises 23–26, circle the correct statement in each pair.

23. $\overline{AC} \cong \overline{EF}$ $AC > EF$ **24.** $AB > ED$ $\overline{AB} \cong \overline{ED}$

25. $m\angle BAC > m\angle FED$ $m\angle BAC < m\angle FED$

26. By the Hinge Theorem, you can relate *FD* and *BC*.

By the Converse of Hinge Theorem, you can relate *FD* and *BC*.

27. Write an inequality relating *FD* and *BC*.

FD ☐ BC

Lesson Check • Do you UNDERSTAND?

Error Analysis From the figure at the right, your friend concludes that $m\angle BAD > m\angle BCD$. How would you correct your friend's mistake?

Write T for *true* or F for *false*.

____ **28.** $AB = CD$ ____ **29.** $AD = CB$ ____ **30.** $BD = BD$

31. Your friend should compare ☐ and ☐.

32. The longer of the two sides your friend should compare is ☐.

33. How would you correct your friend's mistake? Explain.

_____

_____

Math Success

Check off the vocabulary words that you understand.

☐ exterior angle   ☐ comparison property of inequality   ☐ Hinge Theorem

Rate how well you can *use triangle inequalities*.

Need to review   0   2   4   6   8   10   Now I get it!

Lesson 5-7

Vocabulary

● Review

1. Underline the correct word to complete the sentence.

In a *convex* polygon, no point on the lines containing the sides of the polygon is in the
interior / exterior of the polygon.

2. Cross out the polygon that is NOT *convex*.

● Vocabulary Builder

regular polygon (noun) REG yuh lur PAHL ih gahn

Definition: A **regular polygon** is a polygon that is both equilateral and equiangular.

Example: An equilateral triangle is a **regular polygon** with three congruent sides
and three congruent angles.

● Use Your Vocabulary

Underline the correct word(s) to complete each sentence.

3. The sides of a *regular polygon* are congruent / scalene .

4. A right triangle is / is not a *regular polygon*.

5. An isosceles triangle is / is not always a *regular polygon*.

Write *equiangular, equilateral,* or *regular* to identify each hexagon. Use each
word once.

6.

7.

8.

Theorem 6-1   Polygon Angle-Sum Theorem and Corollary

Theorem 6-1 The sum of the measures of the interior angles of an *n*-gon is $(n - 2)180$.

Corollary The measure of each interior angle of a regular *n*-gon is $\frac{(n - 2)180}{n}$.

9. When $n - 2 = 1$, the polygon is a(n) __?__.

10. When $n - 2 = 2$, the polygon is a(n) __?__.

Problem 1   Finding a Polygon Angle Sum

Got It? What is the sum of the interior angle measures of a 17-gon?

11. Use the justifications below to find the sum.

$$\text{sum} = \left(\boxed{} - 2\right)180 \qquad \text{Polygon Angle-Sum Theorem}$$

$$= \left(\boxed{} - 2\right)180 \qquad \text{Substitute for } n.$$

$$= \boxed{} \cdot 180 \qquad \text{Subtract.}$$

$$= \boxed{} \qquad \text{Simplify.}$$

13. The sum of the interior angle measures of a 17-gon is $\boxed{}$.

12. Draw diagonals from vertex *A* to check your answer.

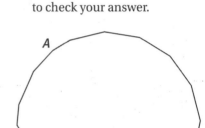

Problem 2   Using the Polygon Angle-Sum Theorem

Got It? What is the measure of each interior angle in a regular nonagon?

Underline the correct word or number to complete each sentence.

14. The interior angles in a regular polygon are congruent / different .

15. A regular nonagon has 7 / 8 / 9 congruent sides.

16. Use the Corollary to the Polygon Angle-Sum Theorem to find the measure of each interior angle in a regular nonagon.

$$\text{Measure of an angle} = \frac{\left(\boxed{} - 2\right)180}{\boxed{}}$$

$$= \frac{\left(\boxed{}\right)180}{\boxed{}}$$

$$= \boxed{}$$

17. The measure of each interior angle in a regular nonagon is $\boxed{}$.

Problem 3 Using the Polygon Angle-Sum Theorem

Got It? What is $m\angle G$ in quadrilateral *EFGH*?

18. Use the Polygon Angle-Sum Theorem to find $m\angle G$ for $n = 4$.

$$m\angle E + m\angle F + m\angle G + m\angle H = (n - 2)180$$

$$m\angle E + m\angle F + m\angle G + m\angle H = \left(\boxed{} - 2\right)180$$

$$\boxed{} + \boxed{} + \boxed{} + \boxed{} = \boxed{} \cdot 180$$

$$m\angle G + \boxed{} = \boxed{}$$

$$m\angle G = \boxed{}$$

19. $m\angle G$ in quadrilateral *EFGH* is $\boxed{}$.

take note

Theorem 6-2 Polygon Exterior Angle-Sum Theorem

The sum of the measures of the exterior angles of a polygon, one at each vertex, is 360.

20. In the pentagon below, $m\angle 1 + m\angle 2 + m\angle 3 + m\angle 4 + m\angle 5 = \boxed{}$.

Use the Polygon Exterior Angle-Sum Theorem to find each measure.

21.

$$120 + 81 + \boxed{} + 87 = 360$$

22.

$$90 + \boxed{} + 75 + 73 + 66 = \boxed{}$$

 Problem 4 Finding an Exterior Angle Measure

Got It? What is the measure of an exterior angle of a regular nonagon?

Underline the correct number or word to complete each sentence.

23. Since the nonagon is regular, its interior angles are congruent / right .

24. The exterior angles are complements / supplements of the interior angles.

25. Since the nonagon is regular, its exterior angles are congruent / right .

26. The sum of the measures of the exterior angles of a polygon is 180 / 360 .

27. A regular nonagon has 7 / 9 / 12 sides.

28. What is the measure of an exterior angle of a regular nonagon? Explain.

_____

_____

_____

Lesson Check • Do you UNDERSTAND?

Error Analysis Your friend says that she measured an interior angle of a regular polygon as 130. Explain why this result is impossible.

29. Use indirect reasoning to find a contradiction.

Assume temporarily that a regular n-gon has a $130°$ interior angle.

angle sum = ☐ · n		A regular n-gon has n congruent angles.
angle sum = (☐) 180		Polygon Angle-Sum Theorem
☐ = (☐) 180		Use the Transitive Property of Equality.
☐ = ☐ − ☐		Use the Distributive Property.
☐ = ☐		Subtract $180n$ from each side.
n = ☐		Divide each side by -50.
$n \neq$ ☐		The number of sides in a polygon is a whole number ≥ 3.

30. Explain why your friend's result is impossible.

_____

_____

_____

_____

Math Success

Check off the vocabulary words that you understand.

☐ equilateral polygon ☐ equiangular polygon ☐ regular polygon

Rate how well you can *find angle measures of polygons.*

Need to review   0   2   4   6   8   10   Now I get it!

Lesson 6-1

6-2 Properties of Parallelograms

Vocabulary

● Review

1. Supplementary angles are two angles whose measures sum to [ ] .

2. Suppose $\angle X$ and $\angle Y$ are *supplementary*. If $m\angle X = 75$, then $m\angle Y =$ [ ] .

Underline the correct word to complete each sentence.

3. A linear pair is complementary / *supplementary* .

4. $\angle AFB$ and $\angle EFD$ at the right are complementary / *supplementary* .

● Vocabulary Builder

> **consecutive** (adjective) **kun SEK yoo tiv**
>
> **Definition:** **Consecutive** items follow one after another in uninterrupted order.
>
> **Math Usage:** **Consecutive** angles of a polygon share a common side.
>
> **Examples:** The numbers $-3, -2, -1, 0, 1, 2, 3, \ldots$ are **consecutive** integers.
>
> **Non-Example:** The letters A, B, C, F, P, . . . are NOT **consecutive** letters of the alphabet.

● Use Your Vocabulary

Use the diagram at the right. Draw a line from each angle in Column A to a *consecutive* angle in Column B.

Column A	Column B
5. $\angle A$	$\angle F$
6. $\angle C$	$\angle E$
7. $\angle D$	$\angle D$

Write the next two *consecutive* months in each sequence.

8. January, February, March, April, _____ , _____

9. December, November, October, September, _____ , _____

take note

Theorems 6-3, 6-4, 6-5, 6-6

Theorem 6-3 If a quadrilateral is a parallelogram, then its opposite sides are congruent.

Theorem 6-4 If a quadrilateral is a parallelogram, then its consecutive angles are supplementary.

Theorem 6-5 If a quadrilateral is a parallelogram, then its opposite angles are congruent.

Theorem 6-6 If a quadrilateral is a parallelogram, then its diagonals bisect each other.

Use the diagram at the right for Exercises 10–12.

10. Mark parallelogram *ABCD* to model Theorem 6-3 and Theorem 6-5.

11. $\overline{AE} \cong$ ⬚

12. $\overline{BE} \cong$ ⬚

✓ **Problem 1** **Using Consecutive Angles**

Got It? Suppose you adjust the lamp so that $m\angle S$ is 86. What is $m\angle R$ in $\square PQRS$?

Underline the correct word or number to complete each statement.

13. $\angle R$ and $\angle S$ are adjacent / consecutive angles, so they are supplementary.

14. $m\angle R + m\angle S =$ 90 / 180

15. Now find $m\angle R$.

16. $m\angle R =$ ⬚ .

✓ **Problem 2** **Using Properties of Parallelograms in a Proof**

Got It? Use the diagram at the right.

   Given: $\square ABCD$, $\overline{AK} \cong \overline{MK}$ **Prove:** $\angle BCD \cong \angle CMD$

17. Circle the classification of $\triangle AKM$.

   equilateral   isosceles   right

18. Complete the proof. The reasons are given.

Statements	Reasons
1) $\overline{AK} \cong$ ⬚	1) Given
2) $\angle DAB \cong$ ⬚	2) Angles opposite congruent sides of a triangle are congruent.
3) $\angle BCD \cong$ ⬚	3) Opposite angles of a parallelogram are congruent.
4) $\angle BCD \cong$ ⬚	4) Transitive Property of Congruence

Problem 3 **Using Algebra to Find Lengths**

Got It? Find the values of *x* and *y* in □*PQRS* at the right. What are *PR* and *SQ*?

19. Circle the reason $\overline{PT} \cong \overline{TR}$ and $\overline{ST} \cong \overline{TQ}$.

Diagonals of a parallelogram bisect each other.	Opposite sides of a parallelogram are congruent.	$\overline{PR}$ is the perpendicular bisector of $\overline{QS}$.

20. Cross out the equation that is NOT true.

$$3(x + 1) - 7 = 2x \qquad y = x + 1 \qquad 3y - 7 = x + 1 \qquad 3y - 7 = 2x$$

21. Find the value of *x*.

22. Find the value of *y*.

23. Find *PT*.

$$PT = 3\boxed{} - 7$$

$$PT = \boxed{} - 7$$

$$PT = \boxed{}$$

24. Find *ST*.

$$ST = \boxed{} + 1$$

$$ST = \boxed{}$$

25. Find *PR*.

$$PR = 2(\boxed{})$$

$$PR = \boxed{}$$

26. Find *SQ*.

$$SQ = 2(\boxed{})$$

$$SQ = \boxed{}$$

27. Explain why you do not need to find *TR* and *TQ* after finding *PT* and *ST*.

_____

_____

Theorem 6-7

If three (or more) parallel lines cut off congruent segments on one transversal, then they cut off congruent segments on every transversal.

Use the diagram at the right for Exercises 28 and 29.

28. If $\overleftrightarrow{AB} \parallel \overleftrightarrow{CD} \parallel \overleftrightarrow{EF}$ and $\overline{AC} \cong \overline{CE}$, then $\overline{BD} \cong \boxed{}$.

29. Mark the diagram to show your answer to Exercise 28.

Problem 4 **Using Parallel lines and Transversals**

Got It? In the figure at the right, $\overleftrightarrow{AE} \parallel \overleftrightarrow{BF} \parallel \overleftrightarrow{CG} \parallel \overleftrightarrow{DH}$. If $EF = FG = GH = 6$ and $AD = 15$, what is CD?

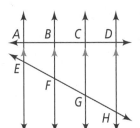

30. You know that the parallel lines cut off congruent segments on transversal ⬚.

31. By Theorem 6-7, the parallel lines also cut off congruent segments on ⬚.

32. $AD = AB + BC +$ ⬚ by the Segment Addition Postulate.

33. $AB =$ ⬚ $= CD$, so $AD =$ ⬚ $\cdot CD$. Then $CD =$ ⬚ $\cdot AD$.

34. You know that $AD = 15$, so $CD =$ ⬚ $\cdot 15 =$ ⬚.

 Lesson Check • **Do you UNDERSTAND?**

Error Analysis Your classmate says that $QV = 10$. Explain why the statement may not be correct.

35. Place a ✓ in the box if you are given the information. Place an ✗ if you are not given the information.

⬚ three lines cut by two transversals

⬚ three parallel lines cut by two transversals

⬚ congruent segments on one transversal

36. What needs to be true for QV to equal 10?

_____

37. Explain why your classmate's statement may not be correct.

_____

 Math Success

Check off the vocabulary words that you understand.

☐ parallelogram   ☐ opposite sides   ☐ opposite angles   ☐ consecutive angles

Rate how well you *understand parallelograms*.

Lesson 6-2

Proving That a Quadrilateral Is a Parallelogram

Vocabulary

● **Review**

1. Does a pentagon have *opposite sides*? | Yes / No |

2. Does an *n*-gon have *opposite sides* if *n* is an odd number? | Yes / No |

Draw a line from each side in Column A to the *opposite side* in Column B.

Column A	Column B
3. $\overline{AB}$	$\overline{BC}$
4. $\overline{AD}$	$\overline{DC}$

● **Vocabulary Builder**

parallelogram (noun) **pa ruh** LEL **uh gram**

Definition: A **parallelogram** is a quadrilateral with two pairs of opposite sides parallel. Opposite sides may include arrows to show the sides are parallel.

Related Words: square, rectangle, rhombus

parallelogram

● **Use Your Vocabulary**

Write P if the statement describes a *parallelogram* or NP if it does not.

_____ 5. octagon   _____ 6. five congruent sides   _____ 7. regular quadrilateral

Write P if the figure appears to be a *parallelogram* or NP if it does not.

_____ 8.   _____ 9.   _____ 10.

take note

Theorems 6-8 through 6-12

Theorem 6-8 If both pairs of opposite sides of a quadrilateral are congruent, then the quadrilateral is a parallelogram.

Theorem 6-9 If an angle of a quadrilateral is supplementary to both of its consecutive angles, then the quadrilateral is a parallelogram.

Theorem 6-10 If both pairs of opposite angles of a quadrilateral are congruent, then the quadrilateral is a parallelogram.

Theorem 6-11 If the diagonals of a quadrilateral bisect each other, then the quadrilateral is a parallelogram.

Theorem 6-12 If one pair of opposite sides of a quadrilateral is both congruent and parallel, then the quadrilateral is a parallelogram.

Use the diagram at the right and Theorems 6-8 through 6–12 for Exercises 11–16.

11. If $\overline{AB} \cong$ ⬜ , and $\overline{BC} \cong$ ⬜ , then $ABCD$ is a ▱.

12. If $m\angle A + m\angle B =$ ⬜ and $m\angle$ ⬜ $+ m\angle D = 180$, then $ABCD$ is a ▱.

13. If $\angle A \cong \angle$ ⬜ and $\angle$ ⬜ $\cong \angle D$, then $ABCD$ is a ▱.

14. If $\overline{AE} \cong$ ⬜ and $\overline{BE} \cong$ ⬜ , then $ABCD$ is a ▱.

15. If $\overline{BC} \cong$ ⬜ and $\overline{BC} \parallel$ ⬜ , then $ABCD$ is a ▱.

16. If $\overline{CD} \cong$ ⬜ and $\overline{CD} \parallel$ ⬜ , then $ABCD$ is a ▱.

✓ **Problem 1** **Finding Values for Parallelograms**

Got It? Use the diagram at the right. For what values of x and y must $EFGH$ be a parallelogram?

17. Circle the equation you can use to find the value of y. Underline the equation you can use to find the value of x.

$y + 10 = 3y - 2$	$y + 10 = 4x + 13$	$(y + 10) + (3y - 2) = 180$

18. Find y.

19. Find x.

20. What equation could you use to find the value of x first?

21. $EFGH$ must be a parallelogram for $x =$ ⬜ and $y =$ ⬜ .

155

Lesson 6-3

Problem 2 Deciding Whether a Quadrilateral Is a Parallelogram

Got It? Can you prove that the quadrilateral is a parallelogram based on the given information? Explain.

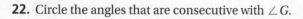

Given: $\overline{EF} \cong \overline{GD}$, $\overline{DE} \parallel \overline{FG}$

Prove: *DEFG* is a parallelogram.

22. Circle the angles that are consecutive with $\angle G$.

$\angle D$	$\angle E$	$\angle F$

23. Underline the correct word to complete the sentence.

Same-side interior angles formed by parallel lines cut by a transversal are

complementary / congruent / supplementary .

24. Circle the interior angles on the same side of transversal $\overline{DG}$. Underline the interior angles on the same side of transversal $\overline{EF}$.

$\angle D$	$\angle E$	$\angle F$	$\angle G$

25. Can you prove *DEFG* is a parallelogram? Explain.

_____

_____

Problem 3 Identifying Parallelograms

Got It? **Reasoning** A truck sits on the platform of a vehicle lift. Two moving arms raise the platform. What is the maximum height that the vehicle lift can elevate the truck? Explain.

26. Do the lengths of the opposite sides change as the truck is lifted?   Yes / No

27. The least and greatest possible angle measures for $\angle P$ and $\angle Q$ are ____ and ____ .

28. The greatest possible height is when $m\angle P$ and $m\angle Q$ are ____ .

29. What is the maximum height that the vehicle lift can elevate the truck? Explain.

_____

_____

Lesson Check • Do you UNDERSTAND?

Compare and Contrast How is Theorem 6-11 in this lesson different from Theorem 6-6 in the previous lesson? In what situations should you use each theorem? Explain.

For each theorem, circle the hypothesis and underline the conclusion.

30. Theorem 6-6

If a quadrilateral is a parallelogram, then its diagonals bisect each other.

31. Theorem 6-11

If the diagonals of a quadrilateral bisect each other, then the quadrilateral is a parallelogram.

Draw a line from each statement in Column A to the corresponding diagram in Column B.

Column A

32. A quadrilateral is a parallelogram.

33. The diagonals of a quadrilateral bisect each other.

Column B

34. Circle the word that describes how Theorem 6-6 and Theorem 6-11 are related.

contrapositive   converse   inverse

35. In which situations should you use each theorem? Explain.

_____

_____

_____

Math Success

Check off the vocabulary words that you understand.

☐ diagonal   ☐ parallelogram   ☐ quadrilateral

Rate how well you can *prove that a quadrilateral is a parallelogram.*

Need to review   0   2   4   6   8   10   Now I get it!

Lesson 6-3

6-4 Properties of Rhombuses, Rectangles, and Squares

Vocabulary

● Review

1. Circle the segments that are *diagonals*.

$\overline{AG}$	$\overline{AC}$	$\overline{HD}$	$\overline{GC}$
$\overline{BF}$	$\overline{AE}$	$\overline{EG}$	$\overline{EF}$

[diagram of rectangle with vertices labeled A, B, C across top, H and D on sides, G, F, E across bottom, with diagonals drawn]

2. Is a *diagonal* ever a line or a ray?   Yes / No

3. The *diagonals* of quadrilateral *JKLM* are ▢ and ▢.

● Vocabulary Builder

rhombus

rhombus (noun) RAHM **bus**

Definition: A **rhombus** is a parallelogram with four congruent sides.

Main Idea: A **rhombus** has four congruent sides but not necessarily four right angles.

Examples: diamond, square

● Use Your Vocabulary

Complete each statement with *always, sometimes,* or *never.*

4. A *rhombus* is _?_ a parallelogram.

5. A parallelogram is _?_ a *rhombus.*

6. A rectangle is _?_ a *rhombus.*

7. A square is _?_ a *rhombus.*

8. A *rhombus* is _?_ a square.

9. A *rhombus* is _?_ a hexagon.

Chapter 6

158

Copyright © by Pearson Education, Inc. or its affiliates. All Rights Reserved.

Key Concept Special Parallelograms

A *rhombus* is a parallelogram with four congruent sides.

A *rectangle* is a parallelogram with four right angles.

A *square* is a parallelogram with four congruent sides and four right angles.

10. Write the words *rectangles, rhombuses,* and *squares* in the Venn diagram below to show that one special parallelogram has the properties of the other two.

Special Parallelograms

Problem 1 Classifying Special Parallelograms

Got It? Is ▱*EFGH* a *rhombus*, a *rectangle*, or a *square*? Explain.

11. Circle the number of sides marked congruent in the diagram.

| 1 | 2 | 3 | 4 |

12. Are any of the angles right angles?   Yes / No

13. Is ▱*EFGH* a rhombus, a rectangle, or a square? Explain.

_____

_____

Theorems 6-13 and 6-14

Theorem 6-13 If a parallelogram is a rhombus, then its diagonals are perpendicular.

Theorem 6-14 If a parallelogram is a rhombus, then each diagonal bisects a pair of opposite angles.

Use the diagram at the right for Exercises 14–18.

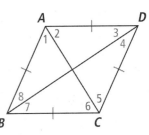

14. If *ABCD* is a rhombus, then $\overline{AC}$ ⊥ ▢.

15. If *ABCD* is a rhombus, then $\overline{AC}$ bisects ∠▢ and ∠▢.

16. If *ABCD* is a rhombus, then ∠1 ≅ ∠2 ≅ ∠▢ ≅ ∠▢.

17. If *ABCD* is a rhombus, then $\overline{BD}$ bisects ∠▢ and ∠▢.

18. If *ABCD* is a rhombus, then ∠3 ≅ ∠▢ ≅ ∠▢ ≅ ∠▢.

Lesson 6-4

Problem 2   Finding Angle Measures

Got It? What are the measures of the numbered angles in rhombus *PQRS*?

Diagram: rhombus *PQRS* with diagonal from *P* to *R*. Angle at *Q* is 104°. Numbered angles 3 and 4 near *R*, angles 1 and 2 near *P*.

19. Circle the word that describes △*PQR* and △*RSP*.

> equilateral   isosceles   right

20. Circle the congruent angles in △*PQR*. Underline the congruent angles in △*RSP*.

> ∠1   ∠2   ∠3   ∠4   ∠Q   ∠S

21. $m\angle 1 + m\angle 2 + 104 =$ ☐   **22.** $m\angle 1 + m\angle 2 =$ ☐   **23.** $m\angle 1 =$ ☐

24. Each diagonal of a rhombus __?__ a pair of opposite angles. _____

25. Circle the angles in rhombus *PQRS* that are congruent.

> ∠1   ∠2   ∠3   ∠4

26. $m\angle 1 =$ ☐ , $m\angle 2 =$ ☐ , $m\angle 3 =$ ☐ , and $m\angle 4 =$ ☐ .

---

take note

Theorem 6-15

Theorem 6-15 If a parallelogram is a rectangle, then its diagonals are congruent.

27. If *RSTU* is a rectangle, then $\overline{RT} \cong$ ☐ .

Problem 3   Finding Diagonal Length

Got It? If $LN = 4x - 17$ and $MO = 2x + 13$, what are the lengths of the diagonals of rectangle *LMNO*?

Diagram: rectangle *LMNO* with diagonals intersecting at *P*.

Underline the correct word to complete each sentence.

28. *LMNO* is a   rectangle / rhombus .

29. The diagonals of this figure are   congruent / parallel .

30. Complete.

     $LN =$ ☐ , so $4x - 17 =$ ☐ .

31. Write and solve an equation to find the value of *x*.

32. Use the value of *x* to find the length of $\overline{LN}$.

33. The diagonals of a rectangle are congruent, so the length of each diagonal is ☐ .

Lesson Check • Do you UNDERSTAND?

Error Analysis Your class needs to find the value of x for which $\square DEFG$ is a rectangle. A classmate's work is shown below. What is the error? Explain.

Write T for *true* or F for *false*.

_____ **34.** If a parallelogram is a rectangle, then each diagonal bisects a pair of opposite angles.

_____ **35.** If a parallelogram is a rhombus, then each diagonal bisects a pair of opposite angles.

36. If *DEFG* is a rectangle, $m\angle D = m\angle \boxed{} = m\angle \boxed{} = m\angle \boxed{}$.

37. $m\angle F = \boxed{}$.

38. What is the error? Explain.

_____

_____

39. Find the value of x for which $\square DEFG$ is a rectangle.

40. The value of x for which $\square DEFG$ is a rectangle is $\boxed{}$.

Math Success

Check off the vocabulary words that you understand.

☐ parallelogram ☐ rhombus ☐ rectangle ☐ square ☐ diagonal

Rate how well you can *find angles and diagonals of special parallelograms.*

Lesson 6-4

6-5 Conditions for Rhombuses, Rectangles, and Squares

Vocabulary

● Review

1. A *quadrilateral* is a polygon with ⬚ sides.

2. Cross out the figure that is NOT a *quadrilateral*.

● Vocabulary Builder

diagonal (noun) **dy AG uh nul**

Definition: A **diagonal** is a segment with endpoints at two nonadjacent vertices of a polygon.

Word Origin: The word **diagonal** comes from the Greek prefix *dia-*, which means "through," and *gonia*, which means "angle" or "corner."

diagonals

● Use Your Vocabulary

3. Circle the polygon that has no *diagonal*.

| triangle | quadrilateral | pentagon | hexagon |

4. Circle the polygon that has two *diagonals*.

| triangle | quadrilateral | pentagon | hexagon |

5. Draw the *diagonals* from one vertex in each figure.

6. Write the number of diagonals you drew in each of the figures above.

pentagon: ⬚   hexagon: ⬚   heptagon: ⬚

Chapter 6
162

Theorems 6-16, 6-17, and 6-18

Theorem 6-16 If the diagonals of a parallelogram are perpendicular, then the parallelogram is a rhombus.

Theorem 6-17 If one diagonal of a parallelogram bisects a pair of opposite angles, then the parallelogram is a rhombus.

7. Insert a right angle symbol in the parallelogram at the right to illustrate Theorem 6-16. Insert congruent marks to illustrate Theorem 6-17.

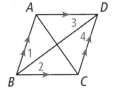

Use the diagram from Exercise 7 to complete Exercises 8 and 9.

8. If *ABCD* is a parallelogram and $\overline{AC} \perp$ ▢ , then *ABCD* is a rhombus.

9. If *ABCD* is a parallelogram, $\angle 1 \cong$ ▢ , and $\angle 3 \cong$ ▢ , then *ABCD* is a rhombus.

Theorem 6-18 If the diagonals of a parallelogram are congruent, then the parallelogram is a rectangle.

10. Insert congruent marks and right angle symbols in the parallelogram to the right to illustrate Theorem 6-18.

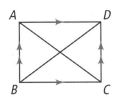

11. Use the diagram from Exercise 10 to complete the statement.

If *ABCD* is a parallelogram, and $\overline{BD} \cong$ ▢ then *ABCD* is a rectangle.

12. Circle the parallelogram that has diagonals that are both perpendicular and congruent.

parallelogram	rectangle	rhombus	square

✓ **Problem 1** **Identifying Special Parallelograms**

Got It? A parallelogram has angle measures of 20, 160, 20, and 160. Can you conclude that it is a rhombus, a rectangle, or a square? Explain.

13. Draw a parallelogram in the box below. Label the angles with their measures. Use a protractor to help you make accurate angle measurements.

Lesson 6-5

Underline the correct word or words to complete each sentence.

14. You do / do not know the lengths of the sides of the parallelogram.

15. You do / do not know the lengths of the diagonals.

16. The angles of a rectangle are all acute / obtuse / right angles.

17. The angles of a square are all acute / obtuse / right angles.

18. Can you conclude that the parallelogram is a rhombus, a rectangle, or a square? Explain.

_____

_____

_____

Problem 2   Using Properties of Special Parallelograms

Got It? For what value of y is $\square DEFG$ a rectangle?

19. For $\square DEFG$ to be a parallelogram, the diagonals must __?__ each other.

20. $EG = 2 ($ _____ $)$ **21.** $DF = 2 ($ _____ $)$

   $=$ _____ $=$ _____

22. For $\square DEFG$ to be a rectangle, the diagonals must be __?__.

23. Now write an equation and solve for y.

24. $\square DEFG$ is a rectangle for $y =$ _____ .

Problem 3   Using Properties of Parallelograms

Got It? Suppose you are on the volunteer building team at the right. You are helping to lay out a square play area. How can you use properties of diagonals to locate the four corners?

25. You can cut two pieces of rope that will be the diagonals of the square play area. Cut them the same length because a parallelogram is a __?__ if the diagonals are congruent.

26. You join the two pieces of rope at their midpoints because a quadrilateral is a __?__ if the diagonals bisect each other.

27. You move so the diagonals are perpendicular because a parallelogram is a __?__ if the diagonals are perpendicular.

28. Explain why the polygon is a square when you pull the ropes taut.

Lesson Check • Do you UNDERSTAND?

Name all of the special parallelograms that have each property.

A. Diagonals are perpendicular.　　**B.** Diagonals are congruent.　　**C.** Diagonals are angle bisectors.

D. Diagonals bisect each other.　　**E.** Diagonals are perpendicular bisectors of each other.

29. Place a ✓ in the box if the parallelogram has the property. Place an ✗ if it does not.

Property	Rectangle	Rhombus	Square
A	☐	☐	☐
B	☐	☐	☐
C	☐	☐	☐
D	☐	☐	☐
E	☐	☐	☐

Math Success

Check off the vocabulary words that you understand.

☐ rhombus　　☐ rectangle　　☐ square　　☐ diagonal

Rate how well you can *use properties of parallelograms*.

Lesson 6-5

6-6   Trapezoids and Kites

Vocabulary

● Review

Underline the correct word to complete each sentence.

1. An *isosceles* triangle always has two / three congruent sides.

2. An equilateral triangle is also a(n) *isosceles* / right triangle.

3. Cross out the length(s) that can NOT be side lengths of an *isosceles* triangle.

     3, 4, 5   8, 8, 10   3.6, 5, 3.6   7, 11, 11

● Vocabulary Builder

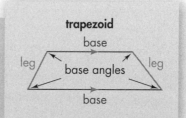

trapezoid (noun) TRAP ih zoyd

Related Words: base, leg

Definition: A **trapezoid** is a quadrilateral with exactly one pair of parallel sides.

Main Idea: The parallel sides of a **trapezoid** are called *bases*. The nonparallel sides are called *legs*. The two angles that share a base of a **trapezoid** are called *base angles*.

● Use Your Vocabulary

4. Cross out the figure that is NOT a *trapezoid*.

5. Circle the figure(s) than can be divided into two *trapezoids*. Then divide each figure that you circled into two *trapezoids*.

Theorems 6-19, 6-20, and 6-21

Theorem 6-19 If a quadrilateral is an isosceles trapezoid, then each pair of base angles is congruent.

Theorem 6-20 If a quadrilateral is an isosceles trapezoid, then its diagonals are congruent.

6. If *TRAP* is an isosceles trapezoid with bases $\overline{RA}$ and $\overline{TP}$, then $\angle T \cong \angle$ [ ] and $\angle R \cong \angle$ [ ].

7. Use Theorem 6-19 and your answers to Exercise 6 to draw congruence marks on the trapezoid at the right.

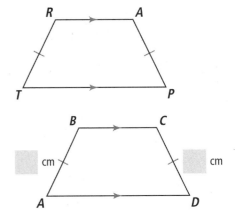

8. If *ABCD* is an isosceles trapezoid, then $\overline{AC} \cong$ [ ].

9. If *ABCD* is an isosceles trapezoid and $AB = 5$ cm, then $CD =$ [ ] cm.

10. Use Theorem 6-20 and your answer to Exercises 8 and 9 to label the diagram at the right.

Theorem 6-21 Trapezoid Midsegment Theorem If a quadrilateral is a trapezoid, then

(1) the midsegment is parallel to the bases, and

(2) the length of the midsegment is half the sum of the lengths of the bases.

11. If *TRAP* is a trapezoid with midsegment $\overline{MN}$, then

(1) $\overline{MN} \parallel$ [ ] $\parallel$ [ ]   (2) $MN = \frac{1}{2} \left(\boxed{\ } + \boxed{\ } \right)$

Problem 2 **Finding Angle Measures in Isosceles Trapezoids**

Got It? A fan has 15 angles meeting at the center. What are the measures of the base angles of the congruent isosceles trapezoids in its second ring?

Use the diagram at the right for Exercises 12–16.

12. Circle the number of isosceles triangles in each wedge. Underline the number of isosceles trapezoids in each wedge.

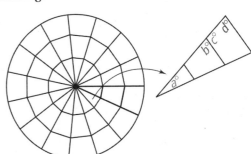

one	two	three	four

13. $a = 360 \div$ [ ] = [ ]

14. $b = \dfrac{180 - \boxed{\ }}{2} =$ [ ]

15. $c = 180 -$ [ ] = [ ]

16. $d = 180 -$ [ ] = [ ]

17. The measures of the base angles of the isosceles trapezoids are [ ] and [ ].

Lesson 6-6

Got It? Algebra $\overline{MN}$ is the midsegment of trapezoid *PQRS*. What is *x*? What is *MN*?

18. The value of *x* is found below. Write a reason for each step.

$$MN = \tfrac{1}{2}(QR + PS)$$

$$2x + 11 = \tfrac{1}{2}[10 + (8x - 12)]$$

$$2x + 11 = \tfrac{1}{2}(8x - 2)$$

$$2x + 11 = 4x - 1$$

$$2x + 12 = 4x$$

$$12 = 2x$$

$$6 = x$$

19. Use the value of *x* to find *MN*.

A *kite* is a quadrilateral with two pairs of consecutive sides congruent and no opposite sides congruent.

take note

Theorem 6-22

Theorem 6-22 If a quadrilateral is a kite, then its diagonals are perpendicular.

20. If *ABCD* is a kite, then $\overline{AC} \perp$ ☐.

21. Use Theorem 6-22 and Exercise 20 to draw congruence marks and right angle symbol(s) on the kite at the right.

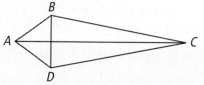

Got It? Quadrilateral *KLMN* is a kite. What are $m\angle 1$, $m\angle 2$, and $m\angle 3$?

22. Diagonals of a kite are perpendicular, so $m\angle 1 =$ ☐.

23. $\triangle KNM \cong \triangle KLM$ by SSS, so $m\angle 3 = m\angle NKM =$ ☐.

24. $m\angle 2 = m\angle 1 - m\angle$ ☐ by the Triangle Exterior Angle Theorem.

25. Solve for $m\angle 2$.

Lesson Check • **Do you UNDERSTAND?**

Compare and Contrast How is a kite similar to a rhombus? How is it different? Explain.

26. Place a ✓ in the box if the description fits the figure. Place an ✗ if it does not.

Kite	Description	Rhombus
☐	Quadrilateral	☐
☐	Perpendicular diagonals	☐
☐	Each diagonal bisects a pair of opposite angles.	☐
☐	Congruent opposite sides	☐
☐	Two pairs of congruent consecutive sides	☐
☐	Two pairs of congruent opposite angles	☐
☐	Supplementary consecutive angles	☐

27. How is a kite similar to a rhombus? How is it different? Explain.

_____

_____

_____

_____

 Math Success

Check off the vocabulary words that you understand.

☐ trapezoid   ☐ kite   ☐ base   ☐ leg   ☐ midsegment

Rate how well you can use *properties of trapezoids and kites*.

Lesson 6-6

Vocabulary

● Review

1. Draw a line from each item in Column A to the corresponding part of the *coordinate plane* in Column B.

Column A

origin

Quadrant I

Quadrant II

Quadrant III

Quadrant IV

x-axis

y-axis

Column B

● Vocabulary Builder

classify (verb) KLAS uh fy

Definition: To **classify** is to organize by category or type.

Math Usage: You can **classify** figures by their properties.

Related Words: classification (noun), classified (adjective)

Example: Rectangles, squares, and rhombuses are **classified** as parallelograms.

● Use Your Vocabulary

Complete each statement with the correct word from the list. Use each word only once.

    classification   classified   classify

2. Trapezoids are __?__ as quadrilaterals.

3. Taxonomy is a system of __?__ in biology.

4. Schools __?__ children by age.

Key Concept   Formulas on the Coordinate Plane

	Distance Formula	Midpoint Formula	Slope Formula
Formula	$d = \sqrt{(x_2 - x_1)^2 + (y_2 - y_1)^2}$	$M = \left(\dfrac{x_1 + x_2}{2}, \dfrac{y_1 + y_2}{2}\right)$	$m = \dfrac{y_2 - y_1}{x_2 - x_1}$
When to Use It	To determine whether • sides are congruent • diagonals are congruent	To determine • the coordinates of the midpoint of a side • whether diagonals bisect each other	To determine whether • opposite sides are parallel • diagonals are perpendicular • sides are perpendicular

Decide when to use each formula. Write D for *Distance Formula*,
M for *Midpoint Formula,* or S for *Slope Formula.*

_____ **5.** You want to know whether diagonals bisect each other.

_____ **6.** You want to find whether opposite sides of a quadrilateral are parallel.

_____ **7.** You want to know whether sides of a polygon are congruent.

Problem 1   Classifying a Triangle

Got It? $\triangle DEF$ has vertices $D(0, 0)$, $E(1, 4)$, and $F(5, 2)$. Is $\triangle DEF$ *scalene, isosceles,* or *equilateral*?

8. Graph $\triangle DEF$ on the coordinate plane at the right.

Use the Distance Formula to find the length of each side.

9. $EF = \sqrt{\left(5 - \boxed{}\right)^2 + \left(2 - \boxed{}\right)^2}$

$= \sqrt{\boxed{} + \boxed{}}$

$= \sqrt{\boxed{}}$

10. $DE = \sqrt{\left(1 - \boxed{}\right)^2 + \left(4 - \boxed{}\right)^2}$

$= \sqrt{\boxed{} + \boxed{}}$

$= \sqrt{\boxed{}}$

11. $DF = \sqrt{\left(5 - \boxed{}\right)^2 + \left(2 - \boxed{}\right)^2}$

$= \sqrt{\boxed{} + \boxed{}}$

$= \sqrt{\boxed{}}$

12. What type of triangle is $\triangle DEF$? Explain.

_____

Lesson 6-7

Problem 2 Classifying a Parallelogram

Got It? □*MNPQ* has vertices *M*(0, 1), *N*(−1, 4), *P*(2, 5), and *Q*(3, 2). Is □*MNPQ* a rectangle? Explain.

13. Find *MP* and *NQ* to determine whether the diagonals $\overline{MP}$ and $\overline{NQ}$ are congruent.

$$MP = \sqrt{\left(2 - \boxed{}\right)^2 + \left(5 - \boxed{}\right)^2} \qquad NQ = \sqrt{\left(3 - \boxed{}\right)^2 + \left(2 - \boxed{}\right)^2}$$

$$= \sqrt{\boxed{} + \boxed{}} \qquad\qquad\qquad = \sqrt{\boxed{} + \boxed{}}$$

$$= \sqrt{\boxed{}} \qquad\qquad\qquad\qquad = \sqrt{\boxed{}}$$

14. Is □*MNPQ* a rectangle? Explain.

_____

Problem 3 Classifying a Quadrilateral

Got It? An isosceles trapezoid has vertices *A*(0, 0), *B*(2, 4), *C*(6, 4), and *D*(8, 0). What special quadrilateral is formed by connecting the midpoints of the sides of *ABCD*?

15. Draw the trapezoid on the coordinate plane at the right.

16. Find the coordinates of the midpoints of each side.

$\overline{AB}$

$$\left(\frac{0 + \boxed{}}{2}, \frac{0 + \boxed{}}{2}\right) = \left(\boxed{}, \boxed{}\right)$$

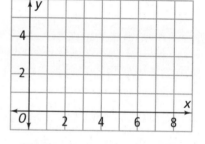

$\overline{CD}$ $\overline{BC}$ $\overline{AD}$

17. Draw the midpoints on the trapezoid and connect them. Judging by appearance, what type of special quadrilateral did you draw? Circle the most precise answer.

    kite   parallelogram   rhombus   trapezoid

18. To verify your answer to Exercise 17, find the slopes of the segments.

    connecting midpoints of $\overline{AB}$ and $\overline{BC}$:   connecting midpoints of $\overline{BC}$ and $\overline{CD}$:

    connecting midpoints of $\overline{CD}$ and $\overline{AD}$:   connecting midpoints of $\overline{AD}$ and $\overline{AB}$:

19. Are the slopes of opposite segments equal?   Yes / No

20. Are consecutive segments perpendicular?   Yes / No

21. The special quadrilateral is a ___?___ .

Lesson Check • Do you UNDERSTAND?

Error Analysis A student says that the quadrilateral with vertices $D(1, 2)$, $E(0, 7)$, $F(5, 6)$, and $G(7, 0)$ is a rhombus because its diagonals are perpendicular. What is the student's error?

22. Draw *DEFG* on the coordinate plane at the right.

23. Underline the correct words to complete Theorem 6-16.

If the diagonals of a parallelogram / polygon are perpendicular,

then the parallelogram / polygon is a rhombus.

24. Check whether *DEFG* is a parallelogram.

slope of $\overline{DE}$: $\dfrac{7 - \boxed{}}{0 - \boxed{}} = \boxed{}$

slope of $\overline{FG}$: $\dfrac{0 - \boxed{}}{7 - \boxed{}} = \boxed{}$

slope of $\overline{DG}$: $\dfrac{0 - \boxed{}}{7 - \boxed{}} = \boxed{}$

slope of $\overline{EF}$: $\dfrac{6 - \boxed{}}{5 - \boxed{}} = \boxed{}$

25. Are both pairs of opposite sides parallel?   Yes / No

26. Find the slope of diagonal $\overline{DF}$.

27. Find the slope of diagonal $\overline{EG}$.

28. Are the diagonals perpendicular?   Yes / No

29. Explain the student's error.

_____

_____

Math Success

Check off the vocabulary words that you understand.

☐ distance   ☐ midpoint   ☐ slope

Rate how well you can *classify quadrilaterals in the coordinate plane*.

Need to review   0   2   4   6   8   10   Now I get it!

Lesson 6-7

Applying Coordinate Geometry

Vocabulary

● Review

Write T for *true* or F for *false*.

____ **1.** The *vertex* of an angle is the endpoint of two rays.

____ **2.** When you name angles using three points, the *vertex* gets named first.

____ **3.** A polygon has the same number of sides and *vertices*.

4. Circle the *vertex* of the largest angle in △*ABC* at the right.

5. Circle the figure that has the greatest number of *vertices*.

| hexagon | kite | rectangle | trapezoid |

● Vocabulary Builder

coordinates (noun) **koh AWR din its**

Definition: *Coordinates* are numbers or letters that specify the location of an object.

Math Usage: The *coordinates* of a point on a plane are an ordered pair of numbers.

Main Idea: The first *coordinate* of an ordered pair is the *x-coordinate*. The second is the *y-coordinate*.

> **coordinates**
>
> (–1, 3)
>
> x-coordinate   y-coordinate

● Use Your Vocabulary

Draw a line from each point in Column A to its *coordinates* in Column B.

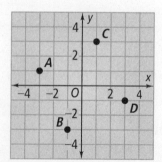

Column A	Column B
6. *A*	(−1, −3)
7. *B*	(1, 3)
8. *C*	(3, −1)
9. *D*	(−3, 1)

Got It? *RECT* is a rectangle with height *a* and length 2*b*. The *y*-axis bisects $\overline{EC}$ and $\overline{RT}$. What are the coordinates of the vertices of *RECT*?

10. Use the information in the problem to mark all segments that are congruent to $\overline{OT}$.

11. Rectangle *RECT* has length [ ],

so *RT* = [ ] and *RO* = *OT* = [ ].

12. The coordinates of *O* are ([ ], 0), so the coordinates of *T* are ([ ], 0), and the coordinates of *R* are (− [ ], 0).

13. Rectangle *RECT* has height *a*, so *TC* = *RE* = [ ].

14. The coordinates of *C* are ([ ], [ ]), so the coordinates of *E* are ([ ], [ ]).

15. Why is it helpful that one side of rectangle *RECT* is on the *x*-axis and the figure is centered on the *y*-axis.

_____

_____

 Problem 2 **Using Variable Coordinates**

Got It? **Reasoning** The diagram at the right shows a general parallelogram with a vertex at the origin and one side along the *x*-axis. Explain why the *x*-coordinate of *B* is the sum of 2*a* and 2*b*.

16. Complete the diagram.

17. Complete the reasoning model below.

Think	Write
Opposite sides of a parallelogram are congruent.	*OA* = [ ] = [ ]
The *x*-coordinate is the sum of the lengths in the brackets.	The *x*-coordinate of *B* is [ ] + [ ] = [ ].

18. Explain why the *x*-coordinate of *B* is the sum of 2*a* + 2*b*.

_____

_____

Lesson 6-8

You can use coordinate geometry and algebra to prove theorems in geometry. This kind of proof is called a *coordinate proof*.

 Problem 3 **Planning a Coordinate Proof**

Got It? Plan a coordinate proof of the Triangle Midsegment Theorem (Theorem 5-1).

19. Underline the correct words to complete Theorem 5-1.

If a segment joins the vertices / midpoints of two sides of a triangle, then the

segment is perpendicular / parallel to the third side, and is half its length.

20. Write the coordinates of the vertices of △ABC on the grid below. Use multiples of 2 to name the coordinates.

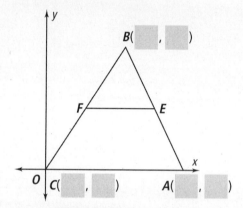

21. Reasoning Why should you make the coordinates of A and B multiples of 2?

22. Complete the *Given* and *Prove*.

Given: E is the __?__ of $\overline{AB}$ and F is the __?__ of $\overline{BC}$.

Prove: $\overline{EF} \parallel \overline{AC}$, and $EF = \frac{1}{2}AC$

23. Circle the formula you need to use to prove $\overline{EF} \parallel \overline{AC}$. Underline the formula you need to use to prove $EF = \frac{1}{2}AC$.

| Distance Formula | Midpoint Formula | Slope Formula |

Underline the correct word to complete each sentence.

24. If the slopes of $\overline{EF}$ and $\overline{AC}$ are equal, then $\overline{EF}$ and $\overline{AC}$ are congruent / parallel .

25. If you know the lengths of $\overline{EF}$ and $\overline{AC}$, then you can add / compare them.

26. Write three steps you must do before writing the plan for a coordinate proof.

Lesson Check • Do you UNDERSTAND?

Error Analysis A classmate says the endpoints of the midsegment of the trapezoid at the right are $\left(\frac{b}{2}, \frac{c}{2}\right)$ and $\left(\frac{d+a}{2}, \frac{c}{2}\right)$. What is your classmate's error? Explain.

27. What is the Midpoint Formula?

$$M = \left(\frac{x_1 + x_2}{\boxed{}}, \frac{y_1 + y_2}{\boxed{}}\right)$$

28. Find the midpoint of each segment to find the endpoints of $\overline{MN}$.

$\overline{OR}$

$\overline{AP}$

29. The endpoints of the midsegment are (☐ , ☐) and (☐ , ☐).

30. How are the endpoints that your classmate found different from the endpoints that you found in Exercise 28?

_____

_____

31. What is your classmate's error? Explain.

_____

_____

_____

Math Success

Check off the vocabulary words that you understand.

☐ coordinate geometry   ☐ coordinate proof   ☐ variable coordinates

Rate how well you can *use properties of special figures.*

177

Lesson 6-8

6-9 Proofs Using Coordinate Geometry

Vocabulary

● Review

1. Circle the *Midpoint Formula* for a segment in the coordinate plane. Underline the *Distance Formula* for a segment in the coordinate plane.

$$M = \left(\frac{x_1 + x_2}{2}, \frac{y_1 + y_2}{2}\right) \qquad d = \sqrt{(x_2 - x_1)^2 + (y_2 - y_1)^2} \qquad m = \frac{y_2 - y_1}{x_2 - x_1}$$

2. Circle the *Midpoint Formula* for a segment on a number line. Underline the *Distance Formula* for a segment on a number line.

$$M = \frac{x_1 + x_2}{2} \qquad d = |x_1 - x_2| \qquad m = \frac{x_1 - x_2}{2}$$

● Vocabulary Builder

variable (noun) VEHR ee uh bul

x and *y* are often used as **variables**.

Related Words: vary (verb), variable (adjective)

Definition: A **variable** is a symbol (usually a letter) that represents one or more numbers.

Math Usage: A **variable** represents an unknown number in equations and inequalities.

● Use Your Vocabulary

Underline the correct word to complete each sentence.

3. An interest rate that can change is a *variable* / vary interest rate.

4. You can *variable* / vary your appearance by changing your hair color.

5. The amount of daylight *variables* / varies from summer to winter.

6. Circle the *variable(s)* in each expression below.

$3n$ $4 + x$ $p^2 - 2p$ $\frac{4}{y}$

7. Cross out the expressions that do NOT contain a *variable*.

$2 + m$ $36 \div (2 \cdot 3)$ $9a^2 - 4a$ $8 - (15 \div 3)$

Chapter 6   178   Copyright © by Pearson Education, Inc. or its affiliates. All Rights Reserved.

Got It? Reasoning You want to prove that the midpoint of the hypotenuse of a right triangle is equidistant from the three vertices. What is the advantage of using coordinates $O(0, 0)$, $E(0, 2b)$, and $F(2a, 0)$ rather than $O(0, 0)$, $E(0, b)$, and $F(a, 0)$?

8. Label each triangle.

   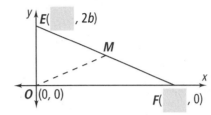

9. Use the Midpoint Formula $M = \left(\dfrac{x_1 + x_2}{2}, \dfrac{y_1 + y_2}{2} \right)$ to find the coordinates of M in each triangle.

Fisrt Triangle

$$\left(\frac{a + 0}{2}, \frac{\boxed{} + \boxed{}}{2} \right) = \left(\frac{a}{2}, \frac{\boxed{}}{2} \right)$$

Second Triangle

$$\left(\frac{\boxed{} + \boxed{}}{2}, \frac{0 + 2b}{2} \right) = (\boxed{}, b)$$

10. Use the Distance Formula, $d = \sqrt{(x_2 - x_1)^2 + (y_2 - y_1)^2}$ and your answers to Exercise 9 to verify that $EM = FM = OM$ for the first triangle.

EM	*FM*	*OM*

11. Use the Distance Formula, $d = \sqrt{(x_2 - x_1)^2 + (y_2 - y_1)^2}$ and your answers to Exercise 9 to verify that $EM = FM = OM$ for the second triangle.

EM	*FM*	*OM*

12. Which set of coordinates is easier to use? Explain.

Lesson 6-9

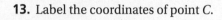

Problem 2 Writing a Coordinate Proof

Got It? Write a coordinate proof of the Triangle Midsegment Theorem (Theorem 5-1).

Given: E is the midpoint of $\overline{AB}$ and

　　　F is the midpoint of $\overline{BC}$

Prove: $\overline{EF} \parallel \overline{AC}$, $EF = \frac{1}{2}AC$

Use the diagram at the right.

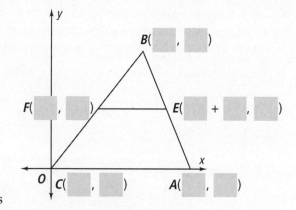

13. Label the coordinates of point C.

14. Reasoning Why should you make the coordinates of A and B multiples of 2?

15. Label the coordinates of A and B in the diagram.

16. Use the Midpoint Formula to find the coordinates of E and F. Label the coordinates in the diagram.

coordinates of E　　　　　　　　　　　coordinates of F

$$\left(\frac{\boxed{} + \boxed{}}{2}, \frac{\boxed{} + \boxed{}}{2} \right) = \left(\boxed{}, \boxed{} \right) \qquad \left(\frac{\boxed{} + \boxed{}}{2}, \frac{\boxed{} + \boxed{}}{2} \right) = \left(\boxed{}, \boxed{} \right)$$

17. Use the Slope Formula to determine whether $\overline{EF} \parallel \overline{AC}$.

$$\text{slope of } \overline{EF} = \frac{\boxed{} - \boxed{}}{\boxed{} - \boxed{}} = \boxed{}$$

$$\text{slope of } \overline{AC} = \frac{\boxed{} - \boxed{}}{\boxed{} - \boxed{}} = \boxed{}$$

18. Is $\overline{EF} \parallel \overline{AC}$? Explain.

19. Use the Distance Formula to determine whether $EF = \frac{1}{2}AC$.

$$EF = \sqrt{(\boxed{} - \boxed{})^2 + (\boxed{} - \boxed{})^2} = \sqrt{(a)^2 + (0)^2} = \boxed{}$$

$$AC = \sqrt{(\boxed{} - \boxed{})^2 + (\boxed{} - \boxed{})^2} = \sqrt{(2a)^2 + (0)^2} = \boxed{}$$

20. $\frac{1}{2}AC = \frac{1}{2} \cdot \boxed{} = \boxed{} = EF$

Lesson Check • Do you know HOW?

Use coordinate geometry to prove that the diagonals of a rectangle are congruent.

21. Draw rectangle *PQRS* with *P* at (0, 0).

22. Label *Q(a,* ____), *R(* ____ , *b),* and *S(* ____ , ____).

23. Complete the *Given* and *Prove* statements.

Given: *PQRS* is a _____ .   Prove: $\overline{PR} \cong$ ____

24. Use the Distance Formula to find the length of eatch diagonal.

$$PR = \sqrt{(\boxed{} - \boxed{})^2 + (\boxed{} - \boxed{})^2} = \boxed{}$$

$$QS = \sqrt{(\boxed{} - \boxed{})^2 + (\boxed{} - \boxed{})^2} = \boxed{}$$

25. $PR = $ ____ , so $\overline{PR} \cong$ ____ .

Lesson Check • Do you UNDERSTAND?

Error Analysis Your classmate places a trapezoid on the coordinate plane. What is the error?

26. Check whether the coordinates are for an isosceles trapezoid.

$$OP = \sqrt{(b - \boxed{})^2 + (c - \boxed{})^2} = \boxed{}$$

$$QR = \sqrt{(a - \boxed{})^2 + (0 - \boxed{})^2} = \boxed{}$$

P(b, c) Q(a − b, c)

R(a, 0)

27. Does the trapezoid look like an isosceles triangle?   Yes / No

28. Describe your classmate's error.

_____

_____

Math Success

Check off the vocabulary words that you understand.

☐ proof   ☐ theorem   ☐ coordinate plane   ☐ coordinate geometry

Rate how well you can *prove theorems using coordinate geometry.*

Lesson 6-9

Vocabulary

● Review

1. Write a *ratio* to compare 9 red marbles to 16 blue marbles in three ways.

9 to ☐   ☐ : ☐

In simplest form, write the *ratio* of vowels to consonants in each word below.

2. comparison   **3.** geometry   **4.** ratio

          to ☐

5. Cross out the *ratio* that is NOT equivalent to 12 to 8.

6 : 2   9 to 6 $\frac{24}{16}$ 48 : 32

● Vocabulary Builder

> A **proportion** always includes an **equal** sign, =.

proportion (noun) **pruh PAWR shun**

Other Word Form: proportional (adjective)

Definition: A **proportion** is an equation stating that two ratios are equal.

Examples: $\frac{2}{3} = \frac{8}{12}$ and $\frac{1}{2} = \frac{5}{10}$ are **proportions.**

● Use Your Vocabulary

6. Write 3 or 6 to make each *proportion* true.

$\frac{2}{3} = \frac{\boxed{}}{9}$ $\frac{\boxed{}}{4} = \frac{6}{8}$ $\frac{1}{3} = \frac{2}{\boxed{}}$ $\frac{5}{\boxed{}} = \frac{10}{6}$

Underline the correct word to complete each sentence.

7. Distance on a map is proportion / proportional to the actual distance.

8. The number of ounces in 3 lb is in proportion / proportional to the number of ounces in 1 lb.

Key Concept   Properties of Proportions

Cross Products Property In a proportion $\frac{a}{b} = \frac{c}{d}$, where $b \neq 0$ and $d \neq 0$, the product of the extremes a and d equals the product of the means b and c.

$$\frac{a}{b} = \frac{c}{d}$$

$$a \cdot d = b \cdot \boxed{}$$

$$\boxed{} = \boxed{}$$

Equivalent Forms of Proportions

Property 1	Property 2	Property 3
$\frac{a}{b} = \frac{c}{d}$ is equivalent to	$\frac{a}{b} = \frac{c}{d}$ is equivalent to	$\frac{a}{b} = \frac{c}{d}$ is equivalent to
$\frac{b}{a} = \frac{d}{c}$.	$\frac{a}{c} = \frac{b}{d}$.	$\frac{a + b}{b} = \frac{c + d}{d}$.

9. Identify the *means* and *extremes* in the proportion $\frac{2}{3} = \frac{4}{x}$.

   Means $\boxed{}$ and $\boxed{}$ **Extremes** $\boxed{}$ and $\boxed{}$

Identify the *Property of Proportions* each statement illustrates.

10. If $\frac{3}{12} = \frac{1}{4}$, then $\frac{3}{1} = \frac{12}{4}$.

11. If $\frac{4}{5} = \frac{8}{10}$, then $4(10) = 5(8)$.

12. If $\frac{1}{3} = \frac{3}{9}$, then $\frac{3}{1} = \frac{9}{3}$.

13. If $\frac{3}{4} = \frac{x}{y}$, then $\frac{7}{4} = \frac{x + y}{y}$.

Problem 1   Writing a Ratio

Got It? A bonsai tree is 18 in. wide and stands 2 ft tall. What is the ratio of the width of the bonsai to its height?

14. The bonsai is $\boxed{}$ in. wide and $\boxed{}$ in. tall.

15. Write the same ratio three different ways.

width of bonsai to height of bonsai

Write using the word "to."	Write as a fraction.	Write using a colon.
$\boxed{}$ to $\boxed{}$	$\frac{\boxed{}}{\boxed{}}$	$\boxed{}$: $\boxed{}$

Lesson 7-1

Problem 3 Using an Extended Ratio

Got It? The lengths of the sides of a triangle are in the extended ratio $4:7:9$. The perimeter is 60 cm. What are the lengths of the sides?

16. Label the triangle at the right. Use the extended ratio to write an expression for each side length.

17. Complete the model to write an equation.

Relate   the sum of the side lengths   is   the perimeter

perimeter = ⬚

Write $4x +$ ⬚ $+$ ⬚ $=$ 60

18. Use the justifications below to find the value of x.

$4x +$ ⬚ $+$ ⬚ $= 60$ Write the equation.

⬚ $\cdot x = 60$ Combine like terms.

$\dfrac{⬚ \cdot x}{⬚} = \dfrac{60}{⬚}$ Divide each side by ⬚.

$x =$ ⬚   Simplify.

19. Use the value of x to find each side length.

$4x = 4 \cdot$ ⬚ 7 ⬚ $= 7 \cdot$ ⬚   ⬚ $=$ ⬚ $\cdot$ ⬚

$=$ ⬚ $=$ ⬚ $=$ ⬚

20. The lengths of the sides of the triangle are ⬚ cm, ⬚ cm, and ⬚ cm.

Problem 4 Solving a Proportion

Got It? **Algebra** What is the solution of the proportion $\frac{9}{2} = \frac{a}{14}$?

21. Write a justification for each statement below.

$$\frac{9}{2} = \frac{a}{14}$$

$$9(14) = 2a$$

$$126 = 2a$$

$$\frac{126}{2} = \frac{2a}{2}$$

$$a = 63$$

Chapter 7

184

Problem 5 Writing Equivalent Proportions

Got It? Use the proportion $\frac{x}{6} = \frac{y}{7}$. What ratio completes the equivalent proportion $\frac{6}{x} = \frac{\blacksquare}{\blacksquare}$? Justify your answer.

22. Use the diagram at the right. Draw arrows from the x and the 6 in the original proportion to the x and the 6 in the new proportion.

$$\frac{x}{6} = \frac{y}{7} \qquad \frac{6}{x} = \frac{\blacksquare}{\blacksquare}$$

23. Circle the proportion equivalent to $\frac{a}{b} = \frac{c}{d}$ that you can use.

 $\frac{b}{a} = \frac{d}{c}$ $\qquad\qquad$ $\frac{a}{c} = \frac{b}{d}$ $\qquad\qquad$ $\frac{a+b}{b} = \frac{c+d}{d}$

24. Complete: $\frac{x}{6} = \frac{y}{7}$ is equivalent to $\frac{6}{x} = \dfrac{\boxed{}}{\boxed{}}$.

Lesson Check • Do you UNDERSTAND?

Error Analysis What is the error in the solution of the proportion at the right?

25. Circle the means of the proportion. Then underline the extremes.

3	4	7	x

26. Write each product.

Means ⬜ · ⬜ = ⬜ $\qquad$ **Extremes** ⬜ · ⬜ = ⬜

27. What is the error in the solution of the proportion?

_____

28. Now solve the proportion correctly.

$$\frac{7}{3} = \frac{4}{x}$$
$$28 = 3x$$
$$\frac{28}{3} = x$$

Math Success

Check off the vocabulary words that you understand.

⬜ proportion $\qquad$ ⬜ means $\qquad$ ⬜ extremes $\qquad$ ⬜ Cross Products Property

Rate how well you can *solve proportions*.

Vocabulary

● **Review**

1. What does it mean when two segments are *congruent*?

2. What does it mean when two angles are *congruent*?

3. Measure each segment. Then circle the congruent segments.

● **Vocabulary Builder**

The symbol for similar is ~.

similar (adjective) SIM uh lur

Other Word Forms: similarity (noun), similarly (adverb)

Definition: Things that are **similar** are alike, but not identical.

Math Usage: Figures that have the same shape but not necessarily the same size are **similar.**

● **Use Your Vocabulary**

4. How are the two squares at the right *similar*?

5. How are the two squares NOT *similar*?

Key Concept Similar Polygons

Two polygons are **similar polygons** if corresponding angles are congruent and if the lengths of corresponding sides are proportional.

$ABCD \sim GHIJ$. **Draw a line from each angle in Column A to its corresponding angle in Column B.**

Column A	Column B
6. $\angle A$	$\angle H$
7. $\angle B$	$\angle J$
8. $\angle C$	$\angle G$
9. $\angle D$	$\angle I$

10. Complete the extended proportion to show that corresponding sides of $ABCD$ and $GHIJ$ are proportional.

$$\frac{AB}{GH} = \frac{BC}{\boxed{}} = \frac{\boxed{}}{IJ} = \frac{AD}{\boxed{}}$$

Problem 1 Understanding Similarity

Got It? $DEFG \sim HJKL$. **What are the pairs of congruent angles? What is the extended proportion for the ratios of the lengths of corresponding sides?**

11. Complete each congruence statement.

$\angle D \cong \angle \boxed{}$

$\angle E \cong \angle \boxed{}$

$\angle K \cong \angle \boxed{}$

$\angle L \cong \angle \boxed{}$

12. Complete the extended proportion.

$$\frac{DE}{HJ} = \frac{EF}{\boxed{}} = \frac{\boxed{}}{KL} = \frac{\boxed{}}{\boxed{}}$$

A *scale factor* is the ratio of the lengths of corresponding sides of similar triangles.

Problem 2 Determining Similarity

Got It? Are the polygons similar? If they are, write a similarity statement and give the scale factor.

13. Circle the short sides of each rectangle. Underline the long sides.

$\overline{KL}$	$\overline{LM}$	$\overline{MN}$	$\overline{NK}$
$\overline{WX}$	$\overline{XY}$	$\overline{YZ}$	$\overline{ZW}$

14. Write the ratios of corresponding sides in simplest form.

$\dfrac{KL}{XY} = \dfrac{10}{15} = \dfrac{\boxed{}}{\boxed{}}$ $\dfrac{LM}{YZ} = \dfrac{15}{\boxed{}} = \dfrac{\boxed{}}{\boxed{}}$ $\dfrac{MN}{ZW} = \dfrac{\boxed{}}{15} = \dfrac{\boxed{}}{\boxed{}}$ $\dfrac{NK}{WX} = \dfrac{\boxed{}}{\boxed{}} = \dfrac{\boxed{}}{\boxed{}}$

Lesson 7-2

15. Place a ✓ in the box if the statement is correct. Place an ✗ if it is incorrect.

☐ $KLMN \sim XYZW$ and the scale factor is $\frac{2}{3}$.

☐ $KLMN \sim XYZW$ and the scale factor is $\frac{3}{4}$.

☐   The polygons are not similar.

Problem 3   Using Similar Polygons

Got It? $ABCD \sim EFGD$. **What is the value of** y?

16. Circle the side of $ABCD$ that corresponds to $\overline{EF}$.

$\overline{AB}$	$\overline{BC}$	$\overline{CD}$	$\overline{AD}$

17. Use the justifications at the right to find the value of y.

$\dfrac{EF}{\boxed{}} = \dfrac{ED}{AD}$ Corresponding sides of similar polygons are proportional.

$\dfrac{y}{\boxed{}} = \dfrac{6}{9}$ Substitute.

$9y = \boxed{}$ Cross Products Property

$y = \boxed{}$ Divide each side by 9.

Problem 4   Using Similarity

Got It? A rectangular poster's design is 6 in. high by 10 in. wide. What are the dimensions of the largest complete poster that will fit in a space 3 ft high by 4 ft wide?

18. Determine how many times the design can be enlarged.

Height: 3 ft = ☐ in.   **Width:** 4 ft = ☐ in.

☐ in. ÷ 6 in. = 6   ☐ in. ÷ 10 in. = 4.8

The design can be enlarged at most ☐ times.

19. Let x represent the height of the poster. Write a proportion and solve for x.

20. The largest complete poster that will fit is ☐ in. by ☐ in.

Problem 5 Using a Scale Drawing

Got It? Use the scale drawing of the bridge. What is the actual height of the towers above the roadway?

21. Use a centimeter ruler to measure the height of the towers above the roadway in the scale drawing. Label the drawing with the height.

cm

Scale 1 cm : 200 m

22. Identify the variable.

Let h = the __?__ of the towers.

23. Use the information on the scale drawing to write a proportion. Then solve to find the value of the variable.

$$\left(Hint: \frac{1}{200} = \frac{\text{tower height in drawing (cm)}}{\text{actual height (m)}} \right)$$

24. The actual height of the towers above the roadway is ☐ m.

Lesson Check • Do you UNDERSTAND?

The triangles at the right are similar. What are three similarity statements for the triangles?

25. The triangles are △ ☐ and △ ☐ .

26. $\angle A \cong \angle$ ☐ $\angle B \cong \angle$ ☐ $\angle S \cong \angle$ ☐

27. $\triangle ABS \sim$ ☐ $\triangle BSA \sim$ ☐ $\triangle SAB \sim$ ☐

Math Success

Check off the vocabulary words that you understand.

☐ similar   ☐ extended proportion   ☐ scale factor   ☐ scale drawing

Rate how well you can *identify and apply similar polygons.*

Need to review   0   2   4   6   8   10   Now I get it!

Lesson 7-2

Vocabulary

● **Review**

Write the converse of each *theorem*.

1. If the diagonals of a parallelogram are perpendicular, then the parallelogram is a rhombus.

If _____ ,

then _____ .

2. If a point is on the perpendicular bisector of a segment, then it is equidistant from the endpoints of the segment.

If _____ ,

then _____ .

● **Vocabulary Builder**

verify (verb) VEHR **uh fy**

Related Word: proof (noun)

Definition: To **verify** something means to find the truth or accuracy of it.

Math Usage: A proof is a way to **verify** a conjecture or statement.

● **Use Your Vocabulary**

Write T for *true* or F for *false*.

_____ **3.** You can *verify* that two triangles are similar by showing that corresponding angles are proportional.

_____ **4.** You can use properties, postulates, and previously proven *theorems* to *verify* steps in a proof.

Key Concept   Postulate 7–1, Theorem 7–1, Theorem 7–2

Postulate 7-1 Angle-Angle Similarity (AA ~) Postulate If two angles of one triangle are congruent to two angles of another triangle, then the triangles are similar.

Theorem 7-1 Side-Angle-Side Similarity (SAS ~) Theorem If an angle of one triangle is congruent to an angle of a second triangle, and the sides that include the two angles are proportional, then the triangles are similar.

Theorem 7-2 Side-Side-Side Similarity (SSS ~) Theorem If the corresponding sides of two triangles are proportional, then the triangles are similar.

5. Write the postulate or theorem that proves the triangles similar.

_____

 Problem 1 Using the AA~Postulate

Got It? Are the two triangles similar? How do you know?

6. Complete the diagram.

7. Are the triangles similar? Explain.

_____

_____

Problem 2 Verifying Triangle Similarity

Got It? Are the triangles similar? If so, write a similarity statement for the triangles and explain how you know the triangles are similar.

 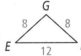

8. Write ratios for each pair of corresponding sides.

9. Circle the postulate or theorem you can use to verify that the triangles are similar.

AA ~ Postulate   SAS ~ Theorem   SSS ~ Theorem

10. Complete the similarity statement.

$\triangle ABC \sim \triangle$ ▢

Proving Triangles Similar

Got It? Given: $\overline{AC} \parallel \overline{MP}$ Prove: $\triangle ABC \sim \triangle PBM$

11. The proof is shown below. Write a reason from the box for each statement.

> AA ~ Postulate
>
> Given
>
> Vertical angles are
> congruent.

Statements	Reasons
1) $\overline{AC} \parallel \overline{MP}$	1) _____
2) $\angle A \cong \angle P$	2) If parallel lines are cut by a transversal, alternate interior angles are congruent.
3) $\angle ABC \cong \angle PBM$	3) _____
4) $\triangle ABC \sim \triangle PBM$	4) _____

Problem 4 **Finding Lengths in Similar Triangles**

Got It? **Reasoning** Why is it important that the ground be flat to use the method of indirect measurement illustrated in the problem below? Explain.

Before rock climbing, Darius wants to know how high he will climb. He places a mirror on the ground and walks backward until he can see the top of the cliff in the mirror.

12. If the ground is NOT flat, will $\angle HTV$ and $\angle JSV$ be right angles?   Yes / No

13. If the ground is NOT flat, will you be able to find congruent angles?   Yes / No

14. Why is it important that the ground be flat? Explain.

_____

_____

Lesson Check • Do you UNDERSTAND?

Error Analysis Which solution for the value of x in the figure at the right is *not* correct? Explain.

A.

$$\frac{4}{8} = \frac{8}{x}$$

$$4x = 72$$

$$x = 18$$

B.

$$\frac{8}{x} = \frac{4}{6}$$

$$48 = 4x$$

$$12 = x$$

15. Write the side lengths of the triangles.

Triangle	Shortest Side	Longest Side	Third Side
Larger	6		
Smaller			

16. Write ratios to compare the lengths of the corresponding sides.

shortest sides: longest sides: third sides:

17. Cross out the proportion that does NOT show ratios of corresponding sides.

$$\frac{9}{6} = \frac{6}{4} \qquad\qquad \frac{9}{4} = \frac{x}{8} \qquad\qquad \frac{x}{8} = \frac{6}{4} \qquad\qquad \frac{x}{8} = \frac{9}{6}$$

18. Cross out the solution that does NOT show ratios of corresponding sides.

Solution A   Solution B

19. Explain why the solution you crossed out does NOT show the correct value of x.

_____

Math Success

Check off the vocabulary words that you understand.

☐ indirect measurement   ☐ similar triangles

Rate how well you can *prove triangles similar*.

Need to review   0   2   4   6   8   10   Now I get it!

7-4 | Similarity in Right Triangles

Vocabulary

● Review

Underline the correct word to complete the sentence.

1. The *altitude* of a triangle is a segment from a vertex to the opposite side that is parallel / perpendicular to the opposite side.

2. In an isosceles triangle, the *altitude* to the base divides the triangle into two congruent / isosceles triangles.

3. Circle the *altitude* of $\triangle ABC$.

| $\overline{AB}$ | $\overline{AC}$ | $\overline{BC}$ | $\overline{CD}$ |

● Vocabulary Builder

geometric mean (noun) jee uh MEH trik meen

Definition: For any two positive numbers a and b, the **geometric mean** of a and b is the positive number x such that $\frac{a}{x} = \frac{x}{b}$.

Example: The **geometric mean** of 4 and 10 is the value of x in $\frac{4}{x} = \frac{x}{10}$, or $x = 2\sqrt{10}$.

● Use Your Vocabulary

4. Multiple Choice Which proportion can you use to find the *geometric mean* of 5 and 15?

  Ⓐ $\frac{x}{5} = \frac{x}{15}$ Ⓑ $\frac{5}{x} = \frac{15}{x}$ Ⓒ $\frac{5}{x} = \frac{x}{15}$ Ⓓ $\frac{5}{15} = \frac{x}{x}$

Underline the correct equation to complete each sentence.

5. The *geometric mean* x of a and b is $x = \sqrt{ab}$ / $x = ab$.

6. The *geometric mean* x of 3 and 7 is $x = \sqrt{21}$ / $x = 21$.

7. Circle the geometric mean of $\sqrt{3}$ and $\sqrt{3}$.

| $\sqrt{3}$ | 3 | $3\sqrt{3}$ | $\sqrt{33}$ |

Theorem 7-3 The altitude to the hypotenuse of a right triangle divides the triangle into two triangles that are similar to the original triangle and to each other.

If . . .

$\triangle ABC$ is a right triangle with right $\angle ACB$, and $\overline{CD}$ is the altitude to the hypotenuse

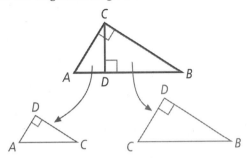

Then . . .

$\triangle ABC \sim \triangle ACD$

$\triangle ABC \sim \triangle CBD$

$\triangle ACD \sim \triangle CBD$

Corollary 1 to Theorem 7-3

The length of the altitude to the hypotenuse of a right triangle is the geometric mean of the lengths of the segments of the hypotenuse.

If . . .

Then . . .

$\dfrac{AD}{CD} = \dfrac{CD}{DB}$

Corollary 2 to Theorem 7-3

The altitude to the hypotenuse of a right triangle separates the hypotenuse so that the length of each leg of the triangle is the geometric mean of the length of the hypotenuse and the length of the segment of the hypotenuse adjacent to the leg.

If . . .

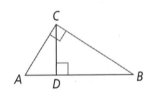

Then . . .

$\dfrac{AB}{AC} = \dfrac{AC}{AD}$

$\dfrac{AB}{CB} = \dfrac{CB}{DB}$

8. $\triangle LMN$ is a right triangle with right $\angle LMN$. $\overline{NP}$ is the altitude to the hypotenuse. Complete the similarity statements.

$\triangle LMN \sim \triangle$ ▢

$\triangle LMN \sim \triangle$ ▢

$\triangle LNP \sim \triangle$ ▢

Use the triangle at the right. Write *Corollary 1* or *Corollary 2* for each proportion.

9. $\dfrac{c}{a} = \dfrac{a}{x}$ _____

10. $\dfrac{x}{m} = \dfrac{m}{y}$ _____

11. $\dfrac{c}{b} = \dfrac{b}{y}$ _____

Problem 1 Identifying Similar Triangles

Got It? What similarity statement can you write relating the
three triangles in the diagram?

12. Write the names of the triangles.

△RPQ   △   △

13. Write the three right angles.

∠RPQ   ∠ ____   ∠ ____

14. Write the three smallest angles.

∠QRP   ∠ ____   ∠ ____

15. Use your answers to Exercises 13 and 14 to write three similarity statements
beginning with the vertex of the smallest angle in each triangle and ending with
the vertex of the right angle.

△RQP ~ △ ____   △RQP ~ △ ____   △ ____ ~ △ ____

Problem 2 Finding the Geometric Mean

Got It? What is the geometric mean of 4 and 18?

16. Use the justifications below to find the geometric mean.

$\dfrac{4}{x} = \dfrac{x}{\boxed{}}$ Definition of geometric mean

$x^2 = \boxed{}$ Cross Products Property

$x = \sqrt{\boxed{}}$ Take the positive square root of each side.

$x = \boxed{}\sqrt{\boxed{}}$ Write in simplest radical form.

Problem 3 Using the Corollaries

Got It? What are the values of x and y?

Underline the correct word to complete each sentence.

17. x is the length of a leg of the largest
triangle, so use Corollary 1 / Corollary 2
to find the value of x.

18. y is the length of the altitude of the largest
triangle, so use Corollary 1 / Corollary 2
to find the value of y.

19. The values of x and y are found below. Write a justification for each step.

$\dfrac{4}{x} = \dfrac{x}{4 + 5}$ ____

$x^2 = 36$ ____

$x = \sqrt{36}$ ____

$x = 6$ ____

$\dfrac{4}{y} = \dfrac{y}{5}$

$y^2 = 20$

$y = \sqrt{20}$

$y = 2\sqrt{5}$

Got It? Points A, B, and C are located so that $AB = 20$ in., and $\overline{AB} \perp \overline{BC}$. Point D is located on $\overline{AC}$ so that $\overline{BD} \perp \overline{AC}$ and $DC = 9$ in. You program a robot to move from A to D and to pick up a plastic bottle at D. From point D, the robot must turn right and move to point B to put the bottle in a recycling bin. How far does the robot travel from D to B?

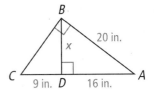

20. Place a ✓ in the box if the statement is correct. Place an ✗ if it is incorrect.

I know the length of the hypotenuse of $\triangle ABC$.

I know the lengths of the segments of the hypotenuse of $\triangle ABC$.

I know the length of the altitude of $\triangle ABC$.

I can use Corollary 1 to solve the problem.

21. Find the length of $\overline{BD}$.

22. The robot travels ____ in. from D to B.

Lesson Check • **Do you UNDERSTAND?**

Vocabulary Identify the following in $\triangle RST$.

23. The hypotenuse is ____ .

24. The segments of the hypotenuse are ____ and ____ .

25. The segment of the hypotenuse adjacent to leg $\overline{ST}$ is ____ .

Math Success

Check off the vocabulary words that you understand.

☐ geometric mean   ☐ altitude   ☐ similarity

Rate how well you understand *similar right triangles*.

| Need to review | 0 | 2 | 4 | 6 | 8 | 10 | Now I get it! |

Vocabulary

● **Review**

1. Circle the model that can form a *proportion* with $\frac{10}{15}$.

  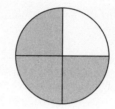

2. Circle the ratios that you can use to form a *proportion*.

$\frac{1}{2}$ $\frac{3}{4}$ $\frac{25}{100}$ $\frac{75}{100}$

3. Cross out the *proportion* that does NOT have the same solution as the others.

$\frac{12}{17} = \frac{n}{20}$ $\frac{12}{n} = \frac{17}{20}$ $\frac{n}{17} = \frac{20}{12}$ $\frac{20}{n} = \frac{17}{12}$

● **Vocabulary Builder**

> **bisector** (noun) BY **sek tur**
>
> **Other Word Form:** bisect (verb)
>
> **Definition:** A **bisector** divides a whole into two equal parts.
>
> **Math Usage:** A **bisector** is a point, segment, ray, or line that divides an angle or a segment into two congruent angles or segments.

● **Use Your Vocabulary**

Use the diagram at the right. Complete each statement with the correct word from the list below. Use each word only once.

   bisects   bisector   bisected

4. $\overrightarrow{BD}$ is the __?__ of $\angle ABC$.

5. $\angle ABC$ is __?__ by $\overrightarrow{BD}$.

6. $\overrightarrow{BD}$ __?__ $\angle ABC$.

Theorem 7-4 Side-Splitter Theorem and Its Corollary

Side-Splitter Theorem

If a line is parallel to one side of a triangle and intersects the other two sides, then it divides those sides proportionally.

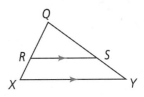

If $\overleftrightarrow{RS} \parallel \overleftrightarrow{XY}$, then $\dfrac{XR}{RQ} = \dfrac{\boxed{}}{SQ}$.

7. If $XR = 4$, $RQ = 4$, and $YS = 5$, then $SQ = \boxed{}$.

8. If $XR = 3$, $RQ = 6$, and $YS = 4$, then $SQ = \boxed{}$.

Corollary to the Side-Splitter Theorem

If three parallel lines intersect two transversals, then the segments intercepted on the transversals are proportional.

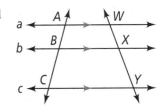

If $a \parallel b \parallel c$, then $\dfrac{AB}{BC} = \dfrac{WX}{XY}$.

Complete each proportion.

9. $\dfrac{BC}{AB} = \dfrac{XY}{\boxed{}}$

10. $\dfrac{\boxed{}}{BA} = \dfrac{YX}{XW}$

11. $\dfrac{AC}{AB} = \dfrac{\boxed{}}{WX}$

Problem 1 **Using the Side-Splitter Theorem**

Got It? What is the value of a in the diagram at the right?

12. The value of a is found below. Use one of the reasons in the box to justify each step.

> Cross Products Property
> Side-Splitter Theorem
> Subtract 12a from each side.
>
> Divide each side by 6.
> Simplify.

$\dfrac{a}{a+4} = \dfrac{12}{18}$ _____

$18a = 12a + 48$ _____

$18a - 12a = 12a - 12a + 48$ _____

$6a = 48$ _____

$\dfrac{6a}{6} = \dfrac{48}{6}$ _____

$a = 8$ _____

Lesson 7-5

Problem 2 Finding a Length

Got It? **Camping** Three campsites are shown in the diagram. What is the length of Site C along the road?

13. Let y be the length of Site C along the road. Use the justifications at the right to find the value of y.

$$\frac{y}{7.2} = \frac{6.4}{\boxed{}}$$ Corollary to Side-Splitter Theorem

$$\boxed{} \cdot y = 46.08$$ Cross Products Property

$$\frac{\boxed{} \cdot y}{\boxed{}} = \frac{46.08}{\boxed{}}$$ Divide each side by the coefficient of y.

$$y = \boxed{}$$ Simplify.

14. The length of Site C along the road is $\boxed{}$ yd.

---

take note

Theorem 7-5 Triangle-Angle-Bisector Theorem

Triangle-Angle-Bisector Theorem

If a ray bisects an angle of a triangle, then it divides the opposite side into two segments that are proportional to the other two sides of the triangle.

If $\overrightarrow{AD}$ bisects $\angle CAB$, then $\frac{CD}{DB} = \frac{CA}{BA}$.

Problem 3 Using the Triangle-Angle-Bisector Theorem

Got It? What is the value of y in the diagram at the right?

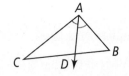

15. Complete the reasoning model below.

Think	Write
I can use the Triangle-Angle-Bisector Theorem to write a proportion.	$\dfrac{9.6}{16} = \dfrac{y}{\boxed{}}$
Then I can use the Cross-Products Property.	$\boxed{} = 16y$
Now I divide each side by $\boxed{}$ and simplify.	$\dfrac{\boxed{}}{16} = \dfrac{16}{16}y$ $\quad y = \boxed{}$

16. The value of y is $\boxed{}$.

Chapter 7

200

Lesson Check • Do you know HOW?

What is the value of *x* in the figure at the right?

17. Circle the proportion you can use to solve the problem.

$$\frac{10}{30} = \frac{x}{45} \qquad \frac{x}{10} = \frac{30}{45} \qquad \frac{x}{x+10} = \frac{30}{45} \qquad \frac{10}{x+10} = \frac{30}{45}$$

18. Solve the proportion.

Lesson Check • Do you UNDERSTAND?

Error Analysis A classmate says you can use the Side-Splitter Theorem to find both *x* and *y* in the diagram. Explain what is wrong with your classmate's statement.

19. Cross out the lengths that are NOT parts of the sides intersected by the parallel line.

2	2.4	3	7	*x*	*y*

20. Can you use the Side-Splitter Theorem to find *x*?   Yes / No

21. Can you use the Side-Splitter Theorem to find *y*?   Yes / No

22. Explain what is wrong with your classmate's statement.

_____

_____

Math Success

Check off the vocabulary words that you understand.

☐ bisector   ☐ proportion   ☐ Side-Splitter Theorem

Rate how well you understand *side and angle bisectors*.

Lesson 7-5

The Pythagorean Theorem and Its Converse

Vocabulary

● **Review**

1. Write the *square* and the positive *square root* of each number.

Number	Square	Positive Square Root
9		
$\frac{1}{4}$	$\frac{1}{16}$	___

● **Vocabulary Builder**

leg (noun) **leg**

Related Word: hypotenuse

Definition: In a right triangle, the sides that form the right angle are the **legs**.

Main Idea: The **legs** of a right triangle are perpendicular. The hypotenuse is the side opposite the right angle.

● **Use Your Vocabulary**

2. Underline the correct word to complete the sentence.

The *hypotenuse* is the longest / shortest side in a right triangle.

Write T for *true* or F for *false*.

_____ **3.** The *hypotenuse* of a right triangle can be any one of the three sides.

_____ **4.** One *leg* of the triangle at the right has length 9 cm.

_____ **5.** The *hypotenuse* of the triangle at the right has length 15 cm.

12 cm

9 cm

15 cm

Theorems 8-1 and 8-2 Pythagorean Theorem and Its Converse

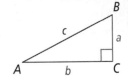

Pythagorean Theorem If a triangle is a right triangle, then the sum of the squares of the lengths of the legs is equal to the square of the length of the hypotenuse.

If $\triangle ABC$ is a right triangle, then $a^2 + b^2 = c^2$.

Converse of the Pythagorean Theorem If the sum of the squares of the lengths of two sides of a triangle is equal to the square of the length of the third side, then the triangle is a right triangle.

If $a^2 + b^2 = c^2$, then $\triangle ABC$ is a right triangle.

6. Circle the equation that shows the correct relationship among the lengths of the legs and the hypotenuse of a right triangle.

$$13^2 + 5^2 = 12^2 \qquad\qquad 5^2 + 12^2 = 13^2 \qquad\qquad 12^2 + 13^2 = 5^2$$

Underline the correct words to complete each sentence.

7. A triangle with side lengths 3, 4, and 5 is / is not a right triangle because $3^2 + 4^2$ is equal / not equal to 5^2.

8. A triangle with side lengths 4, 5, and 6 is / is not a right triangle because $4^2 + 5^2$ is equal / not equal to 6^2.

 Problem 1 Finding the Length of the Hypotenuse

Got It? The legs of a right triangle have lengths 10 and 24. What is the length of the hypotenuse?

9. Label the triangle at the right.

10. Use the justifications below to find the length of the hypotenuse.

$a^2 + b^2 = c^2$	Pythagorean Theorem
$\boxed{}^2 + \boxed{}^2 = c^2$	Substitute for a and b.
$\boxed{} + \boxed{} = c^2$	Simplify.
$\boxed{} = c^2$	Add.
$\boxed{} = c$	Take the positive square root.

11. The length of the hypotenuse is $\boxed{}$.

12. One Pythagorean triple is 5, 12, and 13. If you multiply each number by 2, what numbers result? How do the numbers that result compare to the lengths of the sides of the triangle in Exercises 9–11?

_____

_____

_____

Lesson 8-1

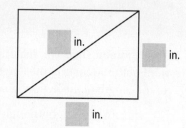

Problem 3 · Finding Distance

Got It? The size of a computer monitor is the length of its diagonal. You want to buy a 19-in. monitor that has a height of 11 in. What is the width of the monitor? Round to the nearest tenth of an inch.

13. Label the diagram of the computer monitor at the right.

14. The equation is solved below. Write a justification for each step.

$$a^2 + b^2 = c^2$$

$$11^2 + b^2 = 19^2$$

$$121 + b^2 = 361$$

$$121 - 121 + b^2 = 361 - 121$$

$$b^2 = 240$$

$$b = \sqrt{240}$$

$$b \approx 15.49193338$$

15. To the nearest tenth of an inch, the width of the monitor is [ ] in.

Problem 4 · Identifying a Right Triangle

Got It? A triangle has side lengths 16, 48, and 50. Is the triangle a right triangle? Explain.

16. Circle the equation you will use to determine whether the triangle is a right triangle.

$$16^2 + 48^2 \stackrel{?}{=} 50^2 \qquad\qquad 16^2 + 50^2 \stackrel{?}{=} 48^2 \qquad\qquad 48^2 + 50^2 \stackrel{?}{=} 16^2$$

17. Simplify your equation from Exercise 16.

18. Underline the correct words to complete the sentence.

The equation is true / false , so the triangle is / is not a right triangle.

A *Pythagorean triple* is a set of nonzero whole numbers a, b, and c that satisfy the equation $a^2 + b^2 = c^2$. If you multiply each number in a Pythagorean triple by the same whole number, the three numbers that result also form a Pythagorean triple.

Theorems 8-3 and 8-4 Pythagorean Inequality Theorems

Theorem 8-3 If the square of the length of the longest side of a triangle is greater than the sum of the squares of the lengths of the other two sides, then the triangle is obtuse.

Theorem 8-4 If the square of the length of the longest side of a triangle is less than the sum of the squares of the lengths of the other two sides, then the triangle is acute.

Use the figures at the right. Complete each sentence with *acute* or *obtuse*.

19. In $\triangle ABC$, $c^2 > a^2 + b^2$, so $\triangle ABC$ is __?__.

20. In $\triangle RST$, $s^2 < r^2 + t^2$, so $\triangle RST$ is __?__.

Lesson Check • Do you UNDERSTAND?

Error Analysis A triangle has side lengths 16, 34, and 30. Your friend says it is not a right triangle. Look at your friend's work and describe the error.

$$16^2 + 34^2 \overset{?}{=} 30^2$$
$$256 + 1156 \overset{?}{=} 900$$
$$1412 \neq 900$$

21. Underline the length that your friend used as the longest side. Circle the length of the longest side of the triangle.

| 16 | 30 | 34 |

22. Write the comparison that your friend should have used to determine whether the triangle is a right triangle.

23. Describe the error in your friend's work.

Math Success

Check off the vocabulary words that you understand.

☐ hypotenuse ☐ leg ☐ Pythagorean Theorem ☐ Pythagorean triple

Rate how well you can *use the Pythagorean Theorem and its converse*.

Need to review 0 2 4 6 8 10 Now I get it!

Vocabulary

● Review

1. Circle the segment that is a *diagonal* of square *ABCD*.

$$\overline{AB} \qquad \overline{AC} \qquad \overline{AD} \qquad \overline{BC} \qquad \overline{CD}$$

2. Underline the correct word to complete the sentence.

A *diagonal* is a line segment that joins two sides / vertices of a polygon.

● Vocabulary Builder

complement (noun) KAHM **pluh munt**

Other Word Form: complementary (adjective)

Math Usage: When the measures of two angles have a sum of 90, each angle is a **complement** of the other.

Nonexample: Two angles whose measures sum to 180 are supplementary.

● Use Your Vocabulary

Complete each statement with the word *complement* or *complementary*.

3. If $m\angle A = 40$ and $m\angle B = 50$, the angles are ? .

4. If $m\angle A = 30$ and $m\angle B = 60$, $\angle B$ is the ? of $\angle A$.

5. $\angle P$ and $\angle Q$ are ? because the sum of their measures is 90.

Complete.

6. If $\angle R$ has a measure of 35, then the *complement* of $\angle R$ has a measure of ____.

7. If $\angle X$ has a measure of 22, then the *complement* of $\angle X$ has a measure of ____.

8. If $\angle C$ has a measure of 65, then the *complement* of $\angle C$ has a measure of ____.

9. Circle the *complementary* angles.

  60°   40°   50°   120°

Theorem 8-5   45°-45°-90° Triangle Theorem

In a 45°-45°-90° triangle, both legs are congruent and the length of the hypotenuse is $\sqrt{2}$ times the length of a leg.

Complete each statement for a 45° −45° −90° triangle.

10. hypotenuse = ☐ · leg

11. If leg = 10, then hypotenuse = ☐ · ☐ .

Problem 1 Finding the Length of the Hypotenuse

Got It? What is the length of the hypotenuse of a 45°-45°-90° triangle with leg length $5\sqrt{3}$?

12. Use the justifications to find the length of the hypotenuse.

hypotenuse = ☐ · leg	45°-45°-90° Triangle Theorem
$= \sqrt{2} \cdot$ ☐	Substitute.
$=$ ☐ $\cdot$ ☐	Commutative Property of Multiplication.
$=$ ☐	Simplify.

Problem 2 Finding the Length of a Leg

Got It? The length of the hypotenuse of a 45°-45°-90° triangle is 10. What is the length of one leg?

13. Will the length of the leg be *greater than* or *less than* 10? Explain.

14. Use the justifications to find the length of one leg.

hypotenuse $= \sqrt{2} \cdot$ leg	45°-45°-90° Triangle Theorem
☐ $= \sqrt{2} \cdot$ leg	Substitute.
$\dfrac{☐}{\sqrt{2}} = \dfrac{\sqrt{2}}{\sqrt{2}} \cdot$ leg	Divide each side by $\sqrt{2}$.
leg $= \dfrac{☐}{\sqrt{2}}$	Simplify.
leg $= \dfrac{☐}{\sqrt{2}} \cdot \dfrac{☐}{\sqrt{2}}$	Multiply by a form of 1 to rationalize the denominator.
leg $= \dfrac{☐}{2}$	Simplify.
leg $=$ ☐	Divide by 2.

Lesson 8-2

Problem 3 Finding Distance

Got It? You plan to build a path along one diagonal of a 100 ft-by-100 ft square garden. To the nearest foot, how long will the path be?

15. Use the words *path, height,* and *width* to complete the diagram.

16. Write L for *leg* or H for *hypotenuse* to identify each part of the right triangle in the diagram.

⬚ path   ⬚ height   ⬚ width

17. Substitute for hypotenuse and leg. Let h = the length of the hypotenuse.

$$\text{hypotenuse} = \sqrt{2} \cdot \text{leg}$$

$$\boxed{} = \sqrt{2} \cdot \boxed{}$$

18. Solve the equation. Use a calculator to find the length of the path.

19. To the nearest foot, the length of the path will be ⬚ feet.

Theorem 8-6 30°-60°-90° Triangle Theorem

In a 30°-60°-90° triangle, the length of the hypotenuse is twice the length of the shorter leg. The length of the longer leg is $\sqrt{3}$ times the length of the shorter leg.

Complete each statement for a 30°-60°-90° triangle.

20. hypotenuse = ⬚ · shorter leg

21. longer leg = ⬚ · shorter leg

Problem 4 Using the Length of One Side

Got It? What is the value of f in simplest radical form?

22. Complete the reasoning model below.

Think	Write
f is the length of the hypotenuse. I can write an equation relating the hypotenuse and the shorter leg $\dfrac{5\sqrt{3}}{3}$ of the 30°-60°-90° triangle.	hypotenuse = ⬚ · shorter leg $f = \boxed{} \cdot \dfrac{\boxed{}}{\boxed{}}$
Now I can solve for f.	$f = \dfrac{\boxed{}}{\boxed{}}$

Problem 5 Applying the 30°-60°-90° Triangle Theorem

Got It? Jewelry Making An artisan makes pendants in the shape of equilateral triangles. Suppose the sides of a pendant are 18 mm long. What is the height of the pendant to the nearest tenth of a millimeter?

18 mm   18 mm

18 mm

23. Circle the formula you can use to find the height of the pendant.

hypotenuse = 2 · shorter leg   longer leg = $\sqrt{3}$ · shorter leg

24. Find the height of the pendant.

25. To the nearest tenth of a millimeter, the height of the pendant is [ ] mm.

 Lesson Check • Do you UNDERSTAND?

Reasoning A test question asks you to find two side lengths of a 45°-45°-90° triangle. You know that the length of one leg is 6, but you forgot the special formula for 45°-45°-90° triangles. Explain how you can still determine the other side lengths. What are the other side lengths?

26. Underline the correct word(s) to complete the sentence. In a 45°-45°-90° triangle, the lengths of the legs are different / the same .

27. Use the Pythagorean Theorem to find the length of the longest side.

28. The other two side lengths are [ ] and [ ] .

 Math Success

Check off the vocabulary words that you understand.

☐ leg   ☐ hypotenuse   ☐ right triangle   ☐ Pythagorean Theorem

Rate how well you can *use the properties of special right triangles*.

Need to review   0   2   4   6   8   10   Now I get it!

Lesson 8-2

8-3 Trigonometry

Vocabulary

● Review

The Venn diagram at the right shows the relationship between *similar* and congruent figures. Write T for *true* or F for *false*.

Similar Figures

_____ **1.** All *similar* figures are congruent figures.

_____ **2.** All congruent figures are *similar* figures.

_____ **3.** Some *similar* figures are congruent figures.

4. Circle the postulate or theorem you can use to verify that the triangles at the right are *similar*.

| AA ~ Postulate | SAS ~ Theorem | SSS ~ Theorem |

● Vocabulary Builder

ratio (noun) RAY **shee oh**

Related Words: rate, rational

Definition: A **ratio** is the comparison of two quantities by division.

Example: If there are 6 triangles and 5 squares, the **ratio** of triangles to squares is $\frac{6}{5}$ and the **ratio** of squares to triangles is $\frac{5}{6}$.

● Use Your Vocabulary

Use the triangle at the right for Exercises 5–7.

5. Circle the *ratio* of the length of the longer leg to the length of the shorter leg.

$$\frac{5}{13} \qquad \frac{5}{12} \qquad \frac{12}{13} \qquad \frac{13}{12} \qquad \frac{12}{5} \qquad \frac{13}{5}$$

6. Circle the *ratio* of the length of the shorter leg to the length of the hypotenuse.

$$\frac{5}{13} \qquad \frac{5}{12} \qquad \frac{12}{13} \qquad \frac{13}{12} \qquad \frac{12}{5} \qquad \frac{13}{5}$$

7. Circle the *ratio* of the length of the longer leg to the length of the hypotenuse.

$$\frac{5}{13} \qquad \frac{5}{12} \qquad \frac{12}{13} \qquad \frac{13}{12} \qquad \frac{12}{5} \qquad \frac{13}{5}$$

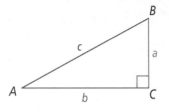

Key Concept   The Trigonometric Ratios

$$\textbf{sine of } \angle A = \frac{\text{length of leg opposite} \angle A}{\text{length of hypotenuse}} = \frac{a}{c}$$

$$\textbf{cosine of } \angle A = \frac{\text{length of leg adjacent to} \angle A}{\text{length of hypotenuse}} = \frac{\boxed{}}{c}$$

$$\textbf{tangent of } \angle A = \frac{\text{length of leg opposite} \angle A}{\text{length of leg adjacent to} \angle A} = \frac{\boxed{}}{\boxed{}}$$

Draw a line from each trigonometric ratio in Column A to its corresponding ratio in Column B.

Column A	Column B
8. $\sin B$	$\frac{a}{c}$
9. $\cos B$	$\frac{b}{a}$
10. $\tan B$	$\frac{b}{c}$

11. Reasoning Suppose $\triangle ABC$ is a right isosceles triangle. What would the tangent of $\angle B$ equal? Explain.

Problem 1   Writing Trigonometric Ratios

Got It? What are the sine, cosine, and tangent ratios for $\angle G$?

12. Circle the measure of the leg opposite $\angle G$.

8	15	17

13. Circle the measure of the hypotenuse.

8	15	17

14. Circle the measure of the leg adjacent to $\angle G$.

8	15	17

15. Write each trigonometric ratio.

$$\sin G = \frac{\text{opposite}}{\text{hypotenuse}} = \frac{\boxed{}}{\boxed{}}$$

$$\cos G = \frac{\text{adjacent}}{\text{hypotenuse}} = \frac{\boxed{}}{\boxed{}}$$

$$\tan G = \frac{\text{opposite}}{\text{adjacent}} = \frac{\boxed{}}{\boxed{}}$$

Lesson 8-3

Problem 2 Using a Trigonometric Ratio to Find Distance

Got It? Find the value of w to the nearest tenth.

Below is one student's solution.

$$\cos 54° = \frac{w}{17}$$
$$\cos 54°(17) = w$$
$$9.992349289 \approx w$$
$$10 \approx w$$

16. Circle the trigonometric ratio that uses sides w and 17.

| sin 54° | cos 54° | tan 54° |

17. What error did the student make?

_____

_____

18. Find the value of w correctly.

19. The value of w to the nearest tenth is ☐.

Problem 3 Using Inverses

Got It? Use the figure below. What is $m\angle Y$ to the nearest degree?

20. Circle the lengths that you know.

| hypotenuse | side adjacent to $\angle Y$ | side opposite $\angle Y$ |

21. Cross out the ratios that you will NOT use to find $m\angle Y$.

| sine | cosine | tangent |

22. Underline the correct word to complete the statement.

If you know the sine, cosine, or tangent ratio of an angle, you can use the

inverse / ratio to find the measure of the angle.

Chapter 8

212

23. Follow the steps to find $m\angle Y$.

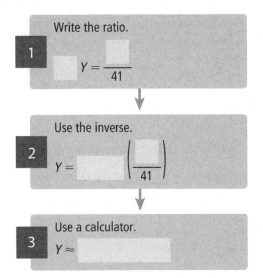

24. To the nearest degree, $m\angle Y \approx \boxed{}$.

Lesson Check • Do you UNDERSTAND?

Error Analysis A student states that $\sin A > \sin X$ because the lengths of the sides of $\triangle ABC$ are greater than the lengths of the sides of $\triangle XYZ$. What is the student's error? Explain.

Underline the correct word(s) to complete each sentence.

25. $\triangle ABC$ and $\triangle XYZ$ are / are not similar.

26. $\angle A$ and $\angle X$ are / are not congruent, so $\sin 35°$ is / is not equal to $\sin 35°$.

27. What is the student's error? Explain.

_____

_____

_____

Math Success

Check off the vocabulary words that you understand.

☐ trigonometric ratios   ☐ sine   ☐ cosine   ☐ tangent

Rate how well you can *use trigonometric ratios*.

Lesson 8-3

Angles of Elevation and Depression

Vocabulary

● Review

Underline the correct word(s) or number to complete each sentence.

1. The measure of a *right angle* is greater / less than the measure of an acute angle
   and greater / less than the measure of an obtuse angle.

2. A *right angle* has a measure of 45 / 90 /180 .

3. Lines that intersect to form four *right angles* are parallel / perpendicular lines.

4. Circle the *right angle*(s) in the figure.

∠ACB	∠ADB	∠BAC
∠BAD	∠CBA	∠DBA

● Vocabulary Builder

elevation (noun) **el uh VAY shun**

Related Word: depression

Definition: The **elevation** of an object is its height above a given level, such as eye
level or sea level.

Math Usage: Angles of **elevation** and **depression** are acute angles of right triangles
formed by a horizontal distance and a vertical height.

● Use Your Vocabulary

**Complete each statement with the correct word from the list below. Use each word
only once.**

elevate   elevated   elevation

5. John __?__ his feet on a footstool.

6. The __?__ of Mt McKinley is 20,320 ft.

7. You __?__ an object by raising it to a higher position.

Problem 1 Identifying Angles of Elevation and Depression

Got It? What is a description of ∠2 as it relates to the situation shown?

Write T for *true* or F for *false*.

_____ **8.** ∠2 is above the horizontal line.

_____ **9.** ∠2 is the *angle of elevation* from the person in the hot-air balloon to the bird.

_____ **10.** ∠2 is the *angle of depression* from the person in the hot-air balloon to the bird.

_____ **11.** ∠2 is the *angle of elevation* from the top of the mountain to the person in the hot-air balloon.

12. Describe ∠2 as it relates to the situation shown.

_____

_____

Problem 2 Using the Angle of Elevation

Got It? You sight a rock climber on a cliff at a 32° angle of elevation. Your eye level is 6 ft above the ground and you are 1000 feet from the base of the cliff. What is the approximate height of the rock climber from the ground?

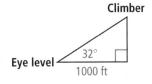

13. Use the information in the problem to complete the problem-solving model below.

Know	Need	Plan
Angle of elevation is [ ] °. Distance to the cliff is [ ] ft. Eye level is [ ] ft above the ground.	Height of climber from the ground	Find the length of the leg opposite 32° by using tan [ ] °. Then add [ ] ft.

215

Lesson 8-4

14. Explain why you use tan 32° and not sin 32° or cos 32°.

_____

_____

15. The problem is solved below. Use one of the reasons from the list at the right to justify each step.

$$\tan 32° = \frac{d}{1000}$$

_____

$$(\tan 32°)\,1000 = d$$

_____

$$d \approx 624.8693519$$

_____

> Solve for *d*.
> Use a calculator.
> Write the equation.

16. The height from your eye level to the climber is about ▢ ft.

17. The height of the rock climber from the ground is about ▢ ft.

✓ **Problem 3** **Using the Angle of Depression**

Got It? An airplane pilot sights a life raft at a 26° angle of depression. The airplane's altitude is 3 km. What is the airplane's horizontal distance *d* from the raft?

18. Label the diagram below.

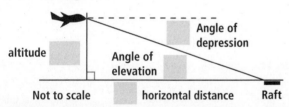

altitude ▢   Angle of elevation ▢   Angle of depression ▢

Not to scale   ▢ horizontal distance   Raft

19. Circle the equation you could use to find the horizontal distance *d*.

$$\sin 26° = \frac{3}{d} \qquad\qquad \cos 26° = \frac{3}{d} \qquad\qquad \tan 26° = \frac{3}{d}$$

20. Solve your equation from Exercise 19.

21. To the nearest tenth, the airplane's horizontal distance from the raft is ▢ km.

Chapter 8   216

Lesson Check • Do you UNDERSTAND?

Vocabulary How is an angle of elevation formed?

Underline the correct word(s) to complete each sentence.

22. The angle of elevation is formed above / below a horizontal line.

23. The angle of depression is formed above / below a horizontal line.

24. The measure of an angle of elevation is equal to / greater than / less than the measure of the angle of depression.

Lesson Check • Do you UNDERSTAND?

Error Analysis A homework question says that the angle of depression from the bottom of a house window to a ball on the ground is 20°. At the right is your friend's sketch of the situation. Describe your friend's error.

25. Is the angle that your friend identified as the angle of depression formed by the horizontal and the line

of sight?   Yes / No

26. Is the correct angle of depression *adjacent to* or *opposite* the angle identified by your friend?

adjacent to / opposite

27. Describe your friend's error.

Math Success

Check off the vocabulary words that you understand.

☐ angle of elevation   ☐ angle of depression   ☐ trigonometric ratios

Rate how well you can *use angles of elevation and depression.*

8-5   Law of Sines

Vocabulary

● **Review**

1. Draw a line segment from each angle of the triangle to its *opposite* side.

2. Circle the correct word.

A *ratio* is the comparison of two quantities by

addition	subtraction	multiplication	division

● **Vocabulary Builder**

sine (noun) **syn**

Related Words: triangle, side length, angle measure, opposite, cosine

Definition: In a right triangle, **sine** is the ratio of the side opposite a given acute angle to the hypotenuse.

Example: If you know the measure of an acute angle of a right triangle and the length of the opposite side, you can use the **sine** ratio to find the length of the hypotenuse.

● **Use Your Vocabulary**

3. A triangle has a given acute angle. Circle its sine ratio.

$\dfrac{\text{hypotenuse}}{\text{opposite}}$	$\dfrac{\text{adjacent}}{\text{hypotenuse}}$	$\dfrac{\text{opposite}}{\text{hypotenuse}}$	$\dfrac{\text{opposite}}{\text{adjacent}}$

4. A right triangle has one acute angle measuring 36.9°. The length of the side adjacent to this angle is 4 units, and the length of the side opposite this angle is 3 units. The length of the hypotenuse is 5 units. Circle the sine ratio of the 36.9° angle.

$$\frac{4}{3} \qquad \frac{3}{5} \qquad \frac{4}{5} \qquad \frac{5}{4} \qquad \frac{5}{3}$$

take note

Law of Sines

For any $\triangle ABC$, let the lengths of the sides opposite angles A, B, and C be a, b, and c, respectively.

Then the **Law of Sines** relates the sine of each angle to the length of its opposite side.

$$\frac{\sin A}{a} = \frac{\sin B}{b} = \frac{\sin C}{c}$$

5. If you know 2 angles and 1 side of a triangle, can you find all of the missing measures? Explain.

✓ **Problem 1** Using the Law of Sines (AAS)

Got It? In $\triangle ABC$, $m\angle A = 48$, $m\angle B = 93$, and $AC = 15$. What is AB to the nearest tenth?

6. Find and label $m\angle C$. $180° = 48° + 93° + \boxed{}$

7. Label side lengths a, b, and c. Which side is the length of AB? _____

8. Circle the equation which can be used to solve this problem. Explain your reasoning.

$$\frac{\sin C}{c} = \frac{\sin A}{a} \qquad \frac{\sin C}{c} = \frac{\sin B}{b} \qquad \frac{\sin B}{b} = \frac{\sin A}{a}$$

9. Replace the variables in the equation with values from $\triangle ABC$.

$$\frac{\sin \boxed{}}{\boxed{}} = \frac{\boxed{}}{\boxed{}}$$

10. Find the sine values of the given angles, cross multiply, then solve for c.

$$c \approx \frac{(\boxed{}) \cdot (\boxed{})}{(\boxed{})} \approx \boxed{}$$

11. The length of $\overline{AB}$ is about $\boxed{}$ units.

✓ **Problem 2** Using the Law of Sines (SSA)

Got It? In $\triangle KLM$, $LM = 9$, $KM = 14$, and $m\angle L = 105$. To the nearest tenth, what is $m\angle K$?

12. Label the triangle with information from the problem and the length of the sides as k, l, m.

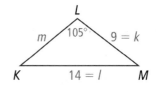

Lesson 8-5

13. Use the letter that represents the length of $\overline{KM}$ to write a pair of ratios using some of the letters k, l, m, K, L and M.

$$\frac{\sin \boxed{}}{\boxed{}} = \frac{\sin \boxed{}}{\boxed{}}$$

14. Fill in the values in the equation from Exercise 13 and solve for $\sin K$.

$\sin K \approx \boxed{}$

15. Use your calculator and take the inverse sine of both sides of the equation to find $m\angle K$.

$\sin^{-1}(\sin K) \approx \sin^{-1} \boxed{}$, therefore $m\angle K \approx \boxed{}$

Problem 3 Using the Law of Sines to Solve a Problem

Got It? The right-fielder fields a softball between first base and second base as shown in the figure. If the right-fielder throws the ball to second base, how far does she throw the ball?

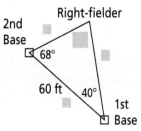

2nd Base Right-fielder
68°
60 ft 40°
1st Base

16. Underline the correct word to complete each sentence.

In this problem, the solution is a side / angle .

To find the solution, I need to *first* find a missing side / angle .

17. In order to use the Law of Sines what information will you need that is missing and why?

_____

_____

_____

18. Circle the equation you could use to solve for the missing solution.

$\dfrac{\sin 72°}{60} = \dfrac{\sin 40°}{c}$ $\dfrac{\sin 72°}{60} = \dfrac{\sin 68°}{a}$ $\dfrac{\sin 68°}{60} = \dfrac{\sin 72°}{b}$

19. Fill in the blanks to complete the equation. Then solve the equation and find the solution.

$$\frac{\sin \boxed{}}{\boxed{}} = \frac{\sin \boxed{}}{\boxed{}}$$

$$\frac{0.9511}{\boxed{}} = \frac{\boxed{}}{\boxed{}} \qquad \boxed{}(0.9511) \approx \boxed{} \qquad c \approx \boxed{}$$

Kimmy throws the ball about $\boxed{}$ feet.

Lesson Check • Do you UNDERSTAND?

Reasoning If you know the three side lengths of a triangle, can you use the Law of Sines to find the missing angle measures? Explain.

20. What do AAS, ASA, and SSA stand for? Match each term with its definition. Then tell what the three terms have in common.

AAS   Side-Side-Angle

ASA   Angle-Angle-Side

SSA   Angle-Side-Angle

_____

21. If you know only the three side lengths of a triangle, can you use the Law of Sines to find the missing angle measures? Explain.

_____

_____

Error Analysis In $\triangle PQR$, $PQ = 4$ cm, $QR = 3$ cm, and $m\angle R = 75$.

Your friend uses the Law of Sines to write $\dfrac{\sin 75°}{3} = \dfrac{\sin x°}{4}$ to find $m\angle Q$. Explain the error.

22. Label the diagram with the given information. Did your friend correctly match the angles and the sides?

_____

_____

Math Success

Check off the vocabulary words that you understand.

☐ Law of Sines   ☐ ratio   ☐ adjacent   ☐ inverse sine

Rate how well you can *use the Law of Sines.*

Lesson 8-5

Vocabulary

● **Review**

Look at △*ABC*.

1. Name the sides that are *adjacent* to angle *A*. _____

2. Which side is *opposite* of angle *B*? _____

3. Identify each *angle* measure as *acute, right,* or *obtuse.*

45° _____   100° _____   90° _____

● **Vocabulary Builder**

Cosine (noun) **KOH syn**

Related Word: triangle, side length, angle measure, opposite, sine

Definition: In a right triangle, **cosine** is the ratio of the side adjacent to a given acute angle to the hypotenuse.

Example: If you know the measure of an acute angle of a right triangle and the length of the adjacent side, you can use the **cosine** ratio to find the length of the hypotenuse.

● **Use Your Vocabulary**

4. A triangle has a given acute angle. Circle its cosine ratio.

$\dfrac{\text{hypotenuse}}{\text{adjacent}}$	$\dfrac{\text{adjacent}}{\text{hypotenuse}}$	$\dfrac{\text{opposite}}{\text{hypotenuse}}$	$\dfrac{\text{adjacent}}{\text{opposite}}$

5. A right triangle has one acute angle measuring 53.1°, the length of the side adjacent to this angle is 9 units, and the length of the side opposite this angle is 12 units. The length of the hypotenuse is 15 units. Circle the cosine ratio of the 53.1° angle.

$\dfrac{9}{12}$ $\dfrac{12}{15}$ $\dfrac{9}{15}$ $\dfrac{15}{9}$ $\dfrac{15}{12}$

Law of Cosines

take note

For any $\triangle ABC$ with side lengths a, b, and c opposite angles A, B, and C, respectively, the **Law of Cosines** relates the measures of the triangles according to the following equations.

$$a^2 = b^2 + c^2 - 2bc \cos A$$

$$b^2 = a^2 + c^2 - 2ac \cos B$$

$$c^2 = a^2 + b^2 - 2ab \cos C$$

6. Circle the equation that is true for $\triangle DEF$.

$$d^2 = f^2 + e^2 - 2de \cos D$$

$$f^2 = d^2 + e^2 - 2de \cos F$$

$$e^2 = d^2 + f^2 - df \cos E$$

Problem 1 Using the Law of Cosines (SAS)

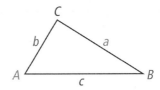

Got It? In $\triangle LMN$, $m\angle L = 104°$, $LM = 48$, and $LN = 29$. Find MN to the nearest tenth.

7. Label the sides of $\triangle LMN$ with the letters l, m, and n.

8. Use the information in the problem to complete the problem-solving model below.

Know	Need	Plan
LM is opposite $\angle$ ☐ $LM = 48 =$ letter ☐ LN is opposite $\angle$ ☐ $LN = 29 =$ letter ☐	$MN =$ letter ☐ An equation using letters l, m, n, and $\angle L$.	Because you know $m\angle$ ☐ and need MN, substitute the angle measure and the two side lengths into the equation and solve for l.

9. Find MN by solving for l.

a. ☐$^2 =$ ☐$^2 +$ ☐$^2 - 2($☐$)($☐$) \cos \angle L$ a. Write an equation using l, m, n, and $\angle L$.

b. $l^2 =$ ☐$^2 +$ ☐$^2 - 2($☐$)($☐$) \cos$ ☐   b. Substitute the values from the triangle.

c. l^2 ☐   c. Use the Order of Operations and
   l^2 ☐   solve for l^2.
   $l^2 \approx$ ☐

d. $l \approx$ ☐ $= MN$ d. Take the square root of both sides.

Lesson 8-6

T

4.4 / 6.7

U / 7.1 / V

Problem 2 Using the Law of Cosines (SSS)

Got It? In △*TUV* above, find $m\angle T$ to the nearest tenth of a degree.

10. Label the sides of the triangle with *t, u,* and *r*.

11. Solve for $m\angle T$ following the given STEPS.

$$\boxed{}^2 = \boxed{}^2 + \boxed{}^2 - 2(\boxed{})(\boxed{})\cos\boxed{}$$

Write an equation using the Law of Cosines.

$$\boxed{}^2 = \boxed{}^2 + \boxed{}^2 - 2(\boxed{})(\boxed{})\cos\boxed{}$$

Substitute the values from the triangle.

$$\boxed{} = \boxed{} + \boxed{} - \boxed{}\cos\boxed{}$$

Simplify by squaring and multiplying.

$$\boxed{} = \boxed{} - \boxed{}\cos\boxed{}$$

Add the first two numbers.

$$\boxed{} - \boxed{} = -\boxed{}\cos\boxed{}$$

Get coefficient of cos T and cos T alone.

$$\frac{\boxed{}}{\boxed{}} = \cos T$$

Divide by the coefficient of cos T.

$$\cos^{-1}\boxed{} \approx T$$

Take the inverse cosine of both sides of the equation.

$$m\angle T \approx \boxed{}$$

Problem 3 Using the Law of Cosines to Solve a Problem

Got It? You and a friend hike 1.4 miles due west from a campsite. At the same time two other friends hike 1.9 miles at a heading of S 11°W (11°west of south) from the campsite. To the nearest tenth of a mile, how far apart are the two groups?

12. Label the model with information from the problem and letter the angles and sides.

West

campsite

11° South

13. Find the measure of the angle that is the complement of the 11°angle.

$$90° - 11° = \boxed{}$$

14. Write and solve an equation for finding the distance between the two groups.

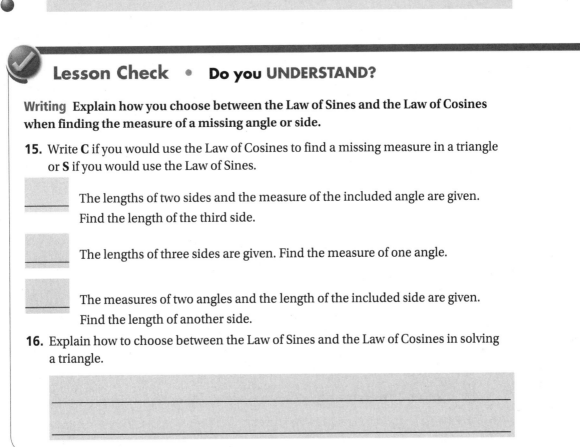

Lesson Check • Do you UNDERSTAND?

Writing Explain how you choose between the Law of Sines and the Law of Cosines when finding the measure of a missing angle or side.

15. Write **C** if you would use the Law of Cosines to find a missing measure in a triangle or **S** if you would use the Law of Sines.

_____ The lengths of two sides and the measure of the included angle are given. Find the length of the third side.

_____ The lengths of three sides are given. Find the measure of one angle.

_____ The measures of two angles and the length of the included side are given. Find the length of another side.

16. Explain how to choose between the Law of Sines and the Law of Cosines in solving a triangle.

_____

_____

Math Success

Check off the vocabulary words that you understand.

☐ Law of Cosines   ☐ Law of Sines   ☐ trigonometry

Rate how well you can *use the Law of Cosines.*

Lesson 8-6

9-1 Translations

Vocabulary

● Review

1. Underline the correct word to complete the sentence.

   If two triangles are *congruent*, corresponding angle measures are the same/ different and corresponding side lengths are the same/ different .

2. A *transformation* is a change in form or appearance.
   Which picture does not show a transformation of the soccer ball?

A.   **B.**   **C.**

● Vocabulary Builder

translation   (noun)   **truh anz lay shuh n**

Related Words: transformation, slide, preimage, image

Main Idea: A **translation** describes how a figure in a coordinate plane is slid from one place to another.

Example: Each point in $\triangle DEF$ was moved 5 units to the right. $\triangle D'E'F'$ is a **translation** of $\triangle DEF$.

● Use Your Vocabulary

3. Tell whether the pair of figures shows a translation. Write *yes* or *no*.

4. In what direction is the translation of figure *ABCD*? _____

5. How many units has figure *ABCD* been translated? _____

Key Concept   Translation

A **translation** is a transformation that maps all points of a figure the same distance in the same direction.

You write the translation that maps △ABC onto △A'B'C' as T(△ABC) = △A'B'C'. A translation is a **rigid motion** with the following properties:

If T(△ABC) = △A'B'C', then
  • AA' = BB' = CC'
  • AB = A'B', BC = B'C', AC = A'C'
  • m∠A = m∠A', m∠B = m∠B', m∠C = m∠C'

Circle the correct word in each statement.

7. Translations move some / all points in a figure the same distance, in the same direction.

8. Translations change / preserve side lengths of the figure.

9. Translations change / preserve angle measures of the figure.

Problem 1 Identifying a Rigid Motion

Transformation A

Transformation B

Got It? Does the transformation appear to be a rigid motion?

10. Compare the corresponding sides of the preimage and image. Are they equal in length?

   Transformation A: yes no   Transformation B: yes no

11. Compare the corresponding angles of the preimage and image. Are they equal in measure?

   Transformation A: yes no   Transformation B: yes no

12. A rigid motion preserves side lengths and angles measures of the preimage.

   Transformation A: is / is not a rigid motion.

   Transformation A: is / is not a rigid motion.

227

Lesson 9-1

Problem 2 Naming Images and Corresponding Parts

In the diagram, $\triangle NID \rightarrow SUP$.

Got It? What are the images of $\angle I$ and point D?
What are the pairs of corresponding sides?

13. Use the position of the letters in the
transformation statement $\triangle NID \rightarrow SUP$.

    a. Angle I is in the 2nd position in $\triangle NID$. The angle in the 2nd position for $\triangle SUP$ is $\angle \underline{}$.

    b. Point D is in the 3rd position in $\triangle NID$. The point in the 3rd position for $\triangle SUP$ is point $\underline{}$.

14. Name the three pairs of corresponding sides using $\triangle NID \rightarrow \triangle SUP$.

    $\overline{NI}$ and $\boxed{}$ $\overline{ID}$ and $\boxed{}$ $\overline{ND}$ and $\boxed{}$

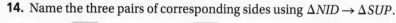 **Problem 3** Finding the Image of a Translation

Got It? What are the images of the vertices of $T_{<1, -4>}(\triangle ABC)$?
Graph the image of $\triangle ABC$.

15. Identify the coordinates of the vertices of $\triangle ABC$.

    $A(\boxed{}, \boxed{})$ $B(\boxed{}, \boxed{})$ $C(\boxed{}, \boxed{})$

16. Describe the translation rule, $T_{<1, -4>}$.

    Add $\boxed{}$ to each x-value.

    Subtract $\boxed{}$ from each y-value.

17. Use the rule to find the coordinates of the vertices of the image.

    $T_{<1, -4>}(A) = (\boxed{} + 1, \boxed{} - 4)$, or $A'(\boxed{}, \boxed{})$.

    $T_{<1, -4>}(B) = (\boxed{} + 1, \boxed{} - 4)$, or $B'(\boxed{}, \boxed{})$.

    $T_{<1, -4>}(C) = (\boxed{} + 1, \boxed{} - 4)$, or $C'(\boxed{}, \boxed{})$.

18. Plot the points A', B', and C.
Connect the points to form $\triangle A'B'C'$.

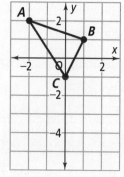

Got It? The translation image of △*LMN* is △*L'M'N'* with *L'*(1, −2), *M'*(3, −4), and *N'*(6, −2). What is a rule that describes the translation?

19. Choose a pair of corresponding vertices.

L([ ] , [ ])   *L'*(1, −2)

20. Find the horizontal change and the vertical change.

$1 - (\boxed{}) = \boxed{} \rightarrow x + 7$

$-2 - (\boxed{}) = \boxed{} \rightarrow y - 1$

21. The translation maps (*x*, *y*) to ([ ] , [ ]). The translation rule is $T_{< \boxed{} , \boxed{} >}(LMN)$.

Lesson Check • **Do you UNDERSTAND?**

Error Analysis Your friend says the transformation △*ABC* → △*PQR* is a translation. Explain and correct her error.

22. Identify the corresponding vertices in the statement △*ABC* → △*PQR*.

A and [ ]   *B* and [ ]   *C* and [ ]

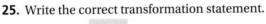

23. Identify the corresponding vertices from the diagram.

A and [ ]   *B* and [ ]   *C* and [ ]

24. What was your friend's error? Explain.

_____

_____

25. Write the correct transformation statement.

△*ABC* → △ [ ]

Math Success

Check off the vocabulary words that you understand.

 ☐ rigid motion   ☐ preimage   ☐ image   ☐ translation

Rate how well you can use the properties of reflections.

Lesson 9-1

9-2 Reflections

Vocabulary

● Review

1. △*ABC* is congruent to △*RST*. Name the side that *corresponds* to $\overline{BC}$.

2. In the diagram, *r* is the _____ of $\overline{AB}$.

● Vocabulary Builder

reflection (noun) **ri flek shuh n**

Related Words: transformation, mirror image, flip, pre-image, image

Main Idea: A reflection is a transformation which flips a figure over a line of reflection resulting in a mirror image of the original figure. The orientation of the figure reverses.

Example: Figure *ABCD* was reflected over the *y*-axis to form figure *LMNO*. Figure *LMNO* is a reflection of figure *ABCD*.

● Use Your Vocabulary

3. Tell whether the pair of figures shows a reflection. Write *yes* or *no*.

4. Reflect △*ABC* over the line. Draw and label its reflection.

Key Concept Reflection Across a Line

Reflection across a line m, called the **line of reflection,** is a transformation with these two properties:

- If a point A is on line m, then the image of A is itself (that is, $A' = A$).

- If a point B is not on line m, then m is the perpendicular bisector of $\overline{BB'}$.

- You write the reflection across m that takes P to P' as $R_m(P) = P'$.

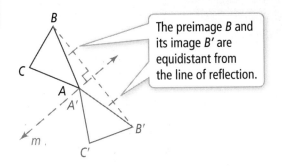

The preimage B and its image B' are equidistant from the line of reflection.

Reflections preserve distance and angle measures.

5. If $R_m(A) = A'$, and $R_m(B) = B'$, then $AB = \boxed{}$.

6. If $R_m(\angle ABC) = \angle A'B'C'$, then $m\angle \boxed{} = m\angle \boxed{}$

7. If $AC = 3$ units, $A'C' = \boxed{}$ units.

8. If $m\angle \boxed{} = 55°$, $m\angle \boxed{} = \boxed{}$

Problem 1 Reflecting a Point Across a Line

Point P has coordinates $(3, 4)$.

Got It? $R_{x=1}(P) = P'$. **What are the coordinates of the image P'?**

9. Graph point P and the line of reflection $x = 1$.

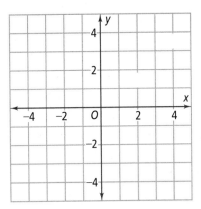

10. Describe point P in relation to the line of reflection.

Point P is $\boxed{}$ units to the right/left of the line of reflection $x = 1$.

11. Describe image P' in relation to the line of reflection.

Point P and image P' are the same distance from the line of reflection but in opposite directions, so image P' is $\boxed{}$ units to the right/left of the line of reflection $x = 1$.

12. Graph image P'. Write its coordinates.

Lesson 9-2

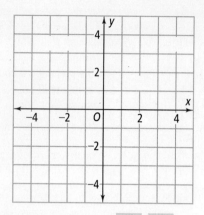

- Move left along the line through P that is perpendicular to the line of reflection.

- Stop when the distances of P and P' to the line of reflection are the same.

 The coordinates of P' are (⬜, ⬜).

Problem 2 Graphing a Reflection Image

Got It? Graph $\triangle ABC$, where $A(-3, 4)$, $B(0, 1)$, and $C(4, 2)$. Graph and label $R_{x\text{-axis}}(\triangle A'B'C')$.

13. Graph $\triangle ABC$.
Show the x-axis as the dashed line of reflection.

14. Draw $\triangle A'B'C'$ following the given STEPS.

Step 1: Draw a line perpendicular to the line of reflection that passes through point A.

Step 2: Locate A' so that the x-axis is the perpendicular bisector of $\overline{AA'}$.

Step 3: Repeat steps 1 and 2 for points B and C.

Step 4: Connect points A', B', and C' to form $\triangle A'B'C'$

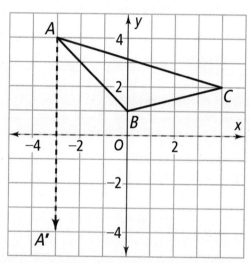

Problem 4 Using Properties of Reflections

In the diagram, $R_t(G) = G$, $R_t(H) = J$, and $R_t(D) = D$.

Got It? Can you use properties of reflections to prove that $\triangle GHJ$ is equilateral? Explain how you know.

15. How do you know that a triangle is an equilateral triangle?

16. Use the properties of reflections to compare the side lengths.

$GH = $ ⬜ and $HD = $ ⬜

Chapter 9

232

For Exercises 17 and 18, circle the correct answer.

17. Can you determine if $HJ = GH = GJ$ using the properties of reflection? yes / no

18. The properties of reflections can/cannot be used to prove that $\triangle GHJ$ is equilateral.

Lesson Check • Do you UNDERSTAND?

Error Analysis A classmate sketched $R_r(A) = A'$ as shown in the diagram.

a. Explain your classmate's error.

b. Copy point A and line r and show the correct location of A'.

19. Use the properties of reflections to describe how the line of reflection r is related to $\overline{AA'}$.

Line r is the _____ of $\overline{AA'}$.

20. Examine the classmate's drawing. What was the classmate's error? Explain.

_____

_____

21. Draw the correct location of A'.

Math Success

Check off the vocabulary words that you understand.

☐ transformation   ☐ reflection   ☐ line of reflection

Rate how well you can use the properties of reflections.

Lesson 9-2

Vocabulary

● Review

1. What is the name of the tool shown to the right?

2. Draw a line segment to classify each angle measure. Then draw and label the angles on the tool.

90°	*acute* angle
25°	*right* angle
155°	*obtuse* angle

● Vocabulary Builder

rotation (noun) **roh tey shuh n**

Related Words: transformation, preimage, image, center of rotation, angle of rotation

Main Idea: A rotation is a transformation which turns a figure about a fixed point called the center of rotation.

Example: A propeller is fixed to a boat or airplane at a center point. The blades rotate about that center of rotation. To map one blade of this propeller onto the next blade, rotate 90°.

● Use Your Vocabulary

3. Tell if each pair of figures shows a rotation. Write *yes* or *no*.

Rotations preserve distance, angle, and orientation of figures.

Key Concept Rotation About a Point

A **rotation** of $x°$ about a point Q, called the

center of rotation, is a transformation with
these two properties:

- The image of Q is itself (that is, $Q' = Q$).

- For any other point V, $QV' = QV$ and
  $m\angle VQV' = x$.

The positive number of degrees a figure rotates is
the **angle of rotation**.

A rotation about a point is a rigid motion.
You write the $x°$ rotation of $\triangle UVW$ about
point Q as $r_{(x°, Q)}(\triangle UVW) = \triangle U'V'W'$.

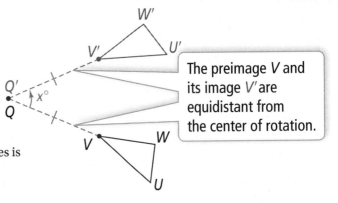

The preimage V and
its image V' are
equidistant from
the center of rotation.

Problem 1 Drawing a Rotation Image

Got It? What is the image of $\triangle LOB$ for a 50° rotation about B?

4. Fill in the blanks to develop your plan.

The image of point B is itself. So, $B' = $ _____ .

The image of $\triangle LOB$ is _____ .

I need to _____ $\triangle LOB$ _____ around point _____ .

I will begin by drawing side _____ .

Then I will draw side _____ .

5. Circle the tools you will need to draw $\triangle L'O'B$.

ruler   compass   protractor   calculator

6. Write T for true and F for false next to each statement.

_____ To draw $\triangle L'O'B$, I will rotate the preimage clockwise.

_____ The sides of the image must be congruent to the sides of the preimage.

_____ I need to use the compass and protractor to draw only 2 sides of the image.

_____ Each angle in $\triangle L'O'B$ is 50° greater than each angle in $\triangle LOB$.

Lesson 9-3

When a figure is rotated 90°, 180°, or 270° about the origin O in a coordinate plane, you can use the following rules.

take note

Key Concept   Rotation in the Coordinate Plane

$r_{(90°, O)}(x, y) = (-y, x)$

$r_{(180°, O)}(x, y) = (-x, -y)$

$r_{(270°, O)}(x, y) = (y, -x)$

$r_{(360°, O)}(x, y) = (x, y)$

Problem 2   Drawing Rotations in a Coordinate Plane

Got It? Graph $r_{(270°, O)}$ (*FGHI*).

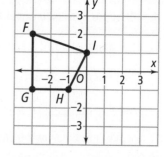

7. Circle the correct ordered pair you use to find $r_{(270°, O)}(x, y)$.

| (x, y) | $(-y, x)$ | $(-x, -y)$ | $(y, -x)$ |

8. Use the rule you circled in Example 7. Fill in the blanks to find the coordinates for each vertex of the image and graph.

$F': r_{(270°, O)}(-3, 2) = (\boxed{}, \boxed{})$ $G': r_{(270°, O)}(\boxed{}, \boxed{}) = (\boxed{}, \boxed{})$

$H': r_{(270°, O)}(\boxed{}, \boxed{}) = (\boxed{}, \boxed{})$ $I': r_{(270°, O)}(\boxed{}, \boxed{}) = (\boxed{}, \boxed{})$

Problem 3   Using Properties of Rotations

Got It? In the diagram, *WXYZ* is a parallelogram, and *T* is the midpoint of the diagonals. Can you use the properties of rotations to prove that *WXYZ* is a rhombus? Explain.

9. Fill in the blanks or circle the word to complete each sentence.

A rhombus is a parallelogram / rectangle with two / four congruent sides.

To prove that *WXYZ* is a rhombus I need to show that $WX = \boxed{} = \boxed{} = \boxed{}$.

Since the lengths of *WX*, *XY*, *YZ*, and *ZW* are known / unknown , you can / cannot use a rotation to prove that *WXYZ* is a rhombus.

Lesson Check • Do you UNDERSTAND?

Reasoning Point $P(x, y)$ is rotated about the origin by 135° and then by 45°. What are the coordinates of the image of point P? Explain.

10. Find the sum of the angles of rotation. Fill in the blank to complete the equation.

$$135° + 45° = \boxed{}$$

11. Match each rotation with the rule you can use to find the coordinates of the image.

$r_{(90°, O)}(x, y)$ $(y, -x)$

$r_{(180°, O)}(x, y)$ (x, y)

$r_{(270°, O)}(x, y)$ $(-y, x)$

$r_{(360°, O)}(x, y)$ $(-x, -y)$

12. Write the rule you need to use to find the coordinates of point P'.

_____

13. Use the graph to show point P and its image, point P'.

14. Explain how you found the coordinates of the image of point P.

_____

_____

Math Success

Check off the vocabulary words that you understand.

☐ rotation   ☐ point of rotation   ☐ angle of rotation

Rate how well you can *use the properties and rules of rotations.*

Vocabulary

● **Review**

Use the transformation below to answer questions 1-3.

1. Fill in the blanks.

   The *image* of $\angle J$ is ____ and the *image* of $\angle K$ is ____.

2. Circle the pair of *corresponding sides*.

   $\overline{JQ}$ and $\overline{J'Q'}$ $\overline{KQ}$ and $\overline{J'Q'}$ $\overline{JK}$ and $\overline{J'Q'}$ $\overline{JQ}$ and JQ'

3. Circle the word that completes the sentence.

   The *transformation* $\triangle JKQ \rightarrow \triangle J'K'Q'$ is a _____.

   translation   reflection   rotation   dilation

● **Vocabulary Builder**

Isometry (noun) $\overline{\text{I}}$ să mə trē

Related Words: transformation, translation, reflection, rotation, glide reflection

Definition: An **isometry** is a transformation that preserves distance, or length.

Example: Translations, reflections, rotations, and glide reflections are **isometries**.

● **Use Your Vocabulary**

4. Underline the correct word to complete each sentence.

   In a transformation, the original figure is the image/preimage .

   The resulting figure is the image/preimage .

5. Circle the type of transformation that maps each (x, y) to $(x - 8, y + 2)$.

   translation   reflection   rotation   glide reflection   dilation

There are only four isometries.

Translation   **Rotation**   **Reflection**   **Glide Reflection**

Theorem 9-1

The composition of two or more isometries is an isometry.

Theorem 9-2   Reflections Across Parallel Lines

A Composition of reflections across two parallel lines is a translation.

You can write this composition as

$R_m \circ R_l(\triangle ABC) = \triangle A''B''C''$

or $R_m(R_l(\triangle ABC)) = \triangle A''B''C''$.

The Composition has the following properties.

- $\overline{AA''}$, $\overline{BB''}$, and $\overline{CC''}$ are all perpendicular to lines l and m.

- $AA'' = BB'' = CC'' = 2PQ$

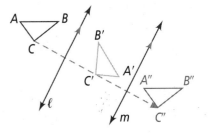

Problem 1 **Composing Reflections Across Parallel Lines**

Got It? Draw parallel lines l and m. Draw J between l and m. What is the image of $(R_m \circ R_l)(J)$? What is the distance of the resulting translation?

6. Reflect J across line l. $PA = AP'$, so $PP' = 2$ [   ].

7. Reflect the image across line m. $P'B = BP''$, so $P'P'' = 2$ [   ].

8. Circle the correct answer.
P moved a total distance $PP'' = P'P'' - PP' = 2BP' - 2AP' = $ [?]

| $0.5AB$ | AB | $1.5AB$ | $2AB$ | $2.5AB$ |

Lesson 9-4

take note

Theorem 9-3 Reflections Across Intersecting Lines

A Composition of reflections across two intersecting lines is a rotation.

You can write this composition as $(R_l \circ R_m)(\triangle ABC) = \triangle A''B''C''$

$R_l(R_m\triangle ABC) = \triangle A''B''C''$.

The composition has the following properties.

- The figure is rotated about the point where the two lines intersect. In this case, point Q.

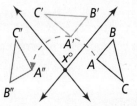

9. Underline the correct word to complete the sentence. $\triangle ABC$ is rotated clockwise/counterclockwise around the point of intersection.

✓ **Problem 3** **Finding a Glide Reflection Image**

Got It? $\triangle TEX$ is shown in the graph to the right. What is the image of $\triangle TEX$ for the glide reflection $(R_{y=-2} \circ T_{<1,0>})(\triangle TEX)$?

Use the information you are given and choose from the following words to fill in the blanks and complete each statement.

reflection   *translate*   *reflect*   *image*

Know	**Need**	**Plan**
Vertices of $\triangle TEX$: $T(\ \square\ ,\ \square\ )$, $E(\ \square\ ,\ \square\ )$, $X(\ \square\ ,\ \square\ )$ Translation rule: $T_{<\square,\square>}$ $(\triangle TEX)$ Reflection line equation: _____	The _____ of $\triangle TEX$ for the glide reflection	First use the translation rule to _____ $\triangle TEX$. Then _____ the translation image of each vertex across the line of _____.

10. Underline the correct word to complete the sentence.

   Use the translation rule $T_{<1,0>}(\triangle TEX)$ to move $\triangle TEX$ right / left / up / down 1 unit.

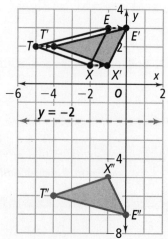

11. Fill in the blanks to make correct statements.

   Reflect the image of $\triangle T'E'X'$ across the line _____ .
   The vertices of $\triangle A''B''C''$ are

   $T''(\ \ ,\ \ )$, $E''(\ \ ,\ \ )$, $X''(\ \ ,\ \ )$.

Lesson Check • Do you UNDERSTAND?

Error Analysis You reflect △ *DEF* first across line *m* and then across line *n*. Your friend says you can get the same result by reflecting △ *DEF* first across line *n* and then across line *m*. Explain your friend's error.

Fill in the blanks in each statement and diagram.

You:

12. Reflect △*DEF* over line ⬚.

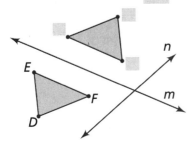

13. Reflect the image of △*DEF* over line ⬚.

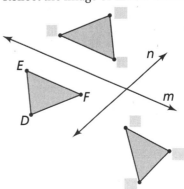

Your friend:

14. Reflect △*DEF* over line ⬚.

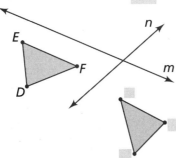

15. Reflect the image of △*DEF* over line ⬚.

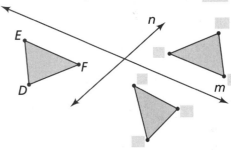

16. Explain your friend's error on the lines below.

_____

_____

Math Success

Check off the vocabulary words that you understand.

☐ glide reflection   ☐ isometry

Rate how well you can *use compositions of isometries*.

Need to review 0 2 4 6 8 10 Now I get it!

Vocabulary

● **Review**

Look at the congruent triangles.

$\triangle ABC \cong \triangle DEF$

1. Draw line segments to match *corresponding sides*.

$\overline{AB}$ $\overline{DE}$

$\overline{BC}$ $\overline{DF}$

$\overline{AC}$ $\overline{EF}$

2. Draw line segments to match *corresponding angles*.

$\angle A$ $\angle E$

$\angle B$ $\angle D$

$\angle C$ $\angle F$

● **Vocabulary Builder**

Congruent (noun) kǎη-grü-ənt

Related Words: corresponding sides, corresponding angles, side length, angle measure

Definition: Two figures are **congruent** if and only if there is a sequence of rigid motions that maps one figure onto the other.

Example: If a triangle is transformed by the composition of a reflection and a translation, the image is **congruent** to the given triangle.

● **Use Your Vocabulary**

3. Circle the transformations that make up a glide reflection.

| translation | reflection | rotation | dilation |

4. When a figure is transformed by an isometry, what is true about the corresponding angles and the corresponding sides of the image and preimage?

_____

_____

Problem 1 **Identifying Equal Measures**

Got It? The composition $(R_t \circ T_{<2,3>})(\triangle ABC) = \triangle XYZ$. List all of the equal angle pairs and all of the equal side lengths.

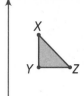

5. Compositions of isometries preserve angle measure, so corresponding angles have equal measures. Fill in the blanks to make true statements.

$m\angle A = m\angle$ ☐ $m\angle B = m\angle$ ☐ $m\angle C = m\angle$ ☐

6. By definition, isometries preserve distance. So, corresponding side lengths have equal measures. Draw line segments to match corresponding side lengths.

AB   YZ

BC   XZ

AC   XY

 Key Concept **Congruent Figures**

Two figures are congruent if and only if there is a sequence of one or more rigid motions that maps one figure onto another.

 Problem 2 **Identifying Congruent Figures**

Got It? Which pairs of figures in the grid are congruent? For each pair, what is a sequence of rigid motions that map one figure to the other?

Underline the correct words to complete each sentence in Exercises 7 and 8.

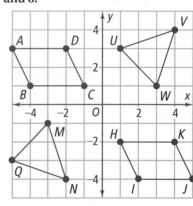

7. To map parallelogram *ABCD* onto parallelogram *HIJK*,
   translate *ABCD* 2 / 5 / 6 units to the right / left and
   3 / 5 / 6 units up / down .

8. To map $\triangle UVW$ onto triangle $\triangle QNM$, reflect $\triangle UVW$
   across y = −1 / 0 / 1 . Then translate $\triangle UVW$ 6 units
   right / left / up / down .

Fill in the blanks to complete Exercises 9 and 10.

9. Because $T_{<\;\;,\;\;>}(ABCD) = HIJK$, the parallelograms are ☐ .

10. Because $(T_{<\;\;,\;\;>} \circ R_{(y=0)}(\triangle UVW) = $ ☐ , the triangles are ☐ .

Lesson 9-5

Got It? What is a congruence transformation that maps △NAV to △BCY?

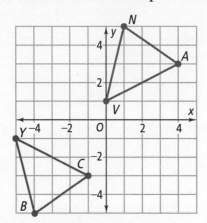

Fill in the blanks and underline to complete the statements.

Know

Preimage	image
N (☐, ☐)	B (☐, ☐)
A (☐, ☐)	C (☐, ☐)
V (☐, ☐)	Y (☐, ☐)

Need
You need to determine the rigid motion, or sequence of rigid motions, that maps _____ onto _____.

Plan
Vertex N corresponds to vertex ☐, vertex A to vertex ☐, and vertex V to vertex ☐. It appears that △NAV has been reflected across the x-axis / y-axis and then translated ☐ units right / left and ☐ units down. Use the vertices to verify the congruence transformation.

Fill in the blanks to complete the statements.

11. Verify that the vertex N corresponds to vertex ☐ .

$R_{x\text{-}axis}(x, y) = (x, -y)$

$R_{x\text{-}axis}(N) = (\boxed{}, \boxed{}) = N'$

$T_{<-5, 0>}(N') = (\boxed{}, \boxed{}) = $ vertex ☐

12. Vertex A corresponds to vertex ☐ .

$R_{\boxed{}}(A) = (\boxed{}, \boxed{}) = A'$

$T_{<\boxed{}, \boxed{}>}(A') = (\boxed{}, \boxed{}) = $ vertex ☐

13. Vertex V corresponds to vertex ☐ .

$R_{\boxed{}}(V) = (\boxed{}, \boxed{}) = V'$

$T_{<\boxed{}, \boxed{}>}(V') = (\boxed{}, \boxed{}) = $ vertex ☐

14. Circle the congruence transformation that maps △NAV onto △BCY.

$T_{<5, 0>} \circ R_{x\text{-}axis}$ $T_{<-5, 0>} \circ R_{x\text{-}axis}$ $T_{<5, 0>} \circ R_{y\text{-}axis}$ $T_{<-5, 0>} \circ R_{y\text{-}axis}$

Problem 4 **Verifying the SAS Postulate**

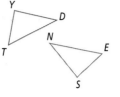

Got It? Verify the SSS Postulate.

Given: $\overline{TD} \cong \overline{EN}$, $\overline{YT} \cong \overline{SE}$, $\overline{YD} \cong \overline{SN}$

Prove: $\triangle YDT \cong \triangle SNE$

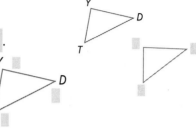

Fill in the blanks to complete each sentence and diagram.

15. Step 1: Rotate $\triangle SNE$ about point ▢ so that $\overline{NE}$ is parallel to ▢.

16. Step 2: Translate $\triangle SNE$ so that points S and ▢ coincide.

Underline the correct choice to complete each sentence.

17. There is / is not a congruence transformation that maps $\triangle SNE$ onto $\triangle YDT$, so

$\triangle YDT \approx$ / $\neq$ / $\cong \triangle SNE$. This verifies the ASA / SSA / SSS / AAS postulate.

Lesson Check • **Do you UNDERSTAND?**

Reasoning Is a composition of a rotation followed by a glide reflection a congruence transformation? Explain.

18. List the four isometries on the line below.

19. Fill in the blank to complete the sentence.

The composition of two or more isometries is an ▢.

20. Is a composition of a rotation followed by a glide reflection a congruence transformation? Explain on the lines below.

Math Success

Check off the vocabulary words that you understand.

☐ congruence transformation   ☐ congruent

Rate how well you can *use congruence transformations*.

245

Lesson 9-5

Vocabulary

● **Review**

1. Identify four *isometries* on the lines below.

   T_____, R_____, R_____, G_____

2. Circle the correct answer to complete the sentence.

   A *mapping* that results in a change in the position, size, or shape of a geometric figure is called a/n   isometry / congruence / transformation .

● **Vocabulary Builder**

Scale factor of a dilation   (noun)   SKĀL FAK **tər dī LĀ tion**

Related Words: dilation, center of a dilation, reduction, enlargement

Definition: The **scale factor of a dilation** is the ratio of a length of the preimage to the corresponding length in the image, with the image length always in the numerator.

Example: If the **scale factor of a dilation** is greater than one, the dilation is an enlargement. If the **scale factor** is less than one, the dilation is a reduction.

● **Use Your Vocabulary**

3. Which of the following shows a dilation?

4. When a figure is transformed by a congruence transformation, what is true about the corresponding angles and the corresponding sides of the image and preimage?

   _____

   _____

take note

Key Concept   Dilation

A **dilation** with **center of dilation** C and scale factor n, $n > 0$, can be written as $D_{(n, C)}$. A dilation is a transformation with the following properties:

- The image of C is itself (that is, $C' = C$).

- For any other point R, R' is on $\overrightarrow{CR}$ and $CR' = n \cdot CR$, or $n = \frac{CR'}{CR}$.

- Dilations preserve angle measure.

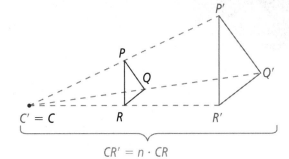

$CR' = n \cdot CR$

5. Circle the equation that is true for the dilation shown to the right.

$$n = \frac{CX}{CX'} \qquad n = \frac{CX'}{CX} \qquad n = \frac{CY}{CY'} \qquad n = \frac{CY'}{CX}$$

Problem 1   Finding a Scale Factor

Got It? Is $D(n, O)(JKLM) = J'K'L'M'$ an enlargement or a reduction? What is the scale factor of the dilation?

Underline the correct choice to complete the sentence.

6. The image $J'K'L'M'$ is larger / smaller than the preimage $JKLM$.

7. The image $J'K'L'M'$ is a(n) enlargement / reduction .

8. Fill in the blanks to identify the coordinates of the preimage $JKLM$.

   $J(\boxed{}, \boxed{})$, $K(\boxed{}, \boxed{})$, $L(\boxed{}, \boxed{})$, $M(\boxed{}, \boxed{})$,

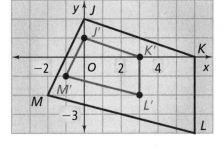

9. Fill in the blanks to identify the coordinates of the image $J'K'L'M'$.

   $J'(\boxed{}, \boxed{})$, $K'(\boxed{}, \boxed{})$, $L'(\boxed{}, \boxed{})$, $M'(\boxed{}, \boxed{})$,

10. Use the distance formula $d = \sqrt{(x_2 - x_1)^2 + (y_2 - y_1)^2}$ to find the lengths of the corresponding sides of the preimage JK and the image $J'K'$ in simplest radical form. Fill in the blanks.

$$JK = \sqrt{(\boxed{} - \boxed{})^2 + (\boxed{} - \boxed{})^2} = \boxed{}\sqrt{\boxed{}}$$

$$J'K' = \sqrt{(\boxed{} - \boxed{})^2 + (\boxed{} - \boxed{})^2} = \sqrt{\boxed{}}$$

11. Fill in the blanks to complete the sentence.

   The scale factor of the dilation is $n = \dfrac{J'K'}{JK} = \dfrac{\boxed{}}{\boxed{}} = \boxed{}$

Lesson 9-6

Problem 2 Finding a Dilation Image

Got It? What are the coordinates of the vertices of $D_{\frac{1}{2}}(\triangle PZG)$?

Fill in the blanks to complete the sentence.

12. The center of the dilation is the [blank] and the scale factor is [blank].

Underline the correct word to complete the sentence.

13. Because the scale factor is less than 1, the dilation is a(n) enlargement / reduction .

14. Use $D_{\frac{1}{2}}(x, y) = \left(\frac{1}{2}x, \frac{1}{2}y\right)$ to find the coordinates of each image vertex and plot $\triangle P'Z'G'$.

$D_{\frac{1}{2}}(P) = \left(\frac{1}{2} \cdot \boxed{}, \frac{1}{2} \cdot \boxed{}\right)$; or $P'\left(\boxed{}, \boxed{}\right)$

$D_{\frac{1}{2}}(Z) = \left(\frac{1}{2} \cdot \boxed{}, \frac{1}{2} \cdot \boxed{}\right)$; or $Z'\left(\boxed{}, \boxed{}\right)$

$D_{\frac{1}{2}}(G) = \left(\frac{1}{2} \cdot \boxed{}, \frac{1}{2} \cdot \boxed{}\right)$; or $G'\left(\boxed{}, \boxed{}\right)$

Problem 3 Using a Scale Factor to Find a Length

Got It? The height of a document on your computer screen is 20.4 cm. When you change the zoom setting on your screen from 100% to 25%, the new image of your document is a dilation of the previous image with scale factor 0.25. What is the height of the new image?

Underline the correct word to complete the sentence.

15. Because the scale factor is 0.25, the dilation is a(n) enlargement/reduction .

Fill in the blanks to complete the statements.

16. A scale factor of 0.25 tells you that the ratio of the image length to the actual length is 0.25.

$$\frac{\boxed{}}{\text{actual length}} = \boxed{}$$

So, image length = scale factor · actual length

$$= \boxed{} \cdot \boxed{}$$

$$= \boxed{} \text{ cm}$$

Lesson Check • Do you UNDERSTAND?

Error Analysis The gray figure is a dilation image of the black figure for a dilation with center *A*. A student made an error when asked to find the scale factor. Explain and correct the error.

Use the diagram to complete Exercises 17 to 22.

17. Circle the image.

$\triangle AB'C'$ $\qquad\qquad$ $\triangle ABC$

18. Circle the preimage.

$\triangle AB'C'$ $\qquad\qquad$ $\triangle ABC$

19. Draw line segments to identify three pairs of corresponding sides of the image and the preimage.

AB	AC'
AC	B'C'
BC	AB'

Fill in the blanks to complete the statements.

20. Find the side lengths.

$AB' = \boxed{}$ $\qquad$ $AC' = \boxed{}$

$AB = \boxed{}$ $\qquad$ $AC = \boxed{}$

21. Find the scale factor for two pairs of corresponding sides.

$n = \dfrac{AB'}{AB} = \dfrac{\boxed{}}{\boxed{}} = \dfrac{\boxed{}}{\boxed{}}$ $\qquad$ $n = \dfrac{AC'}{AC} = \dfrac{\boxed{}}{\boxed{}}$

22. Explain and correct the error on the line below.

_____

_____

_____

_____

Math Success

Check off the vocabulary words that you understand.

☐ dilation $\qquad$ ☐ center of dilation $\qquad$ ☐ scale factor of a dilation

☐ enlargement $\qquad\qquad\qquad$ ☐ reduction

Rate how well you can *use dilations*.

Need to review | 0   2   4   6   8   10 | Now I get it!

Lesson 9-6

9-7 Similarity Transformations

Vocabulary

● Review

1. Underline the correct choice to complete the sentence.

Rigid motions and *dilations* both preserve angle measure / distance .

2. Fill in the blanks with one of the following words to complete the sentence.

rigid motions   *dilations*

[   ] preserve **distance;** [   ] do **not** preserve **distance.**

3. Define similar polygons on the lines below.

_____

_____

● Vocabulary Builder

Similar (noun) SIM ə lər

Related Words: corresponding sides, corresponding angles, scale factor

Definition: Two figures are **similar** if and only if there is a similarity transformation that maps one figure onto the other.

Example: When a figure is transformed by a **similarity transformation** (a composition of rigid motion and dilation), a **similar** figure is formed.

● Use Your Vocabulary

4. The image length of a dilation is 5 cm and the corresponding preimage length is 2 cm. Circle the scale factor of the dilation.

$\frac{1}{5}$ $\frac{2}{5}$ $\frac{5}{2}$ $\frac{5}{1}$

5. The scale factor of a dilation is $\frac{2}{3}$. An image length is 4 ft. Circle the corresponding preimage length.

2 ft   3 ft   4 ft   5 ft   6 ft

Problem 1 Drawing Transformations

Got It? Triangle *LMN* has vertices $L(-4, 2)$, $M(-3, -3)$, and $N(-1, 1)$. Suppose the triangle is translated 4 units right and 2 units up and then dilated by a scale factor of 0.5 with center of dilation at the origin. Sketch the resulting image of the composition of transformations.

Fill in the blanks to complete the statements.

6. Step 1: Draw $T(\triangle LMN)$

$T(x, y) = (x + 4, y + 2)$

$T(L) = L'(\quad, \quad)$ $T(M) = M'(\quad, \quad)$ $T(N) = N'(\quad, \quad)$

Sketch $L'M'N'$.

7. Step 2: Draw the dilation of $L'M'N'$

$D_{0.5}(x, y) = (0.5x, 0.5y)$

$D_{0.5}(L') = L''(\quad, \quad)$

$D_{0.5}(M') = M''(\quad, \quad)$

$D_{0.5}(N') = N''(\quad, \quad)$

Sketch $L''M''N''$.

 Problem 2 Describing Transformations

Got It? What is a composition of rigid motions and a dilation that maps trapezoid *ABCD* to trapezoid *MNHP*?

8. Use the information in the problem to complete the problem-solving model below.

Fill in the blanks to complete the statements.

Know		Need	Plan
Preimage	image	You need to determine which happened.	Choose 2 points and follow their movement from preimage to image.
$A(\quad, \quad)$	$M(\quad, \quad)$	☐ Reflection	
$B(\quad, \quad)$	$N(\quad, \quad)$	☐ Rotation	
$C(\quad, \quad)$	$H(\quad, \quad)$	☐ Translation	
$D(\quad, \quad)$	$P(\quad, \quad)$	☐ Dilation	

9. Follow the Plan. Use preimage points *A* and *D*. Circle the corresponding points in the image.

Point *A* corresponds with: Point *M*   Point *N*   Point *P* .

Point *D* corresponds with: Point *H*   Point *M*   Point *P* .

10. Underline the correct choice to complete each sentence.

Segment *AD* is located on the right / left of figure *ABCD*.

Segment *MP* is located on the right / left of figure *MNHP*.

Copyright © by Pearson Education, Inc. or its affiliates. All Rights Reserved.

Lesson 9-7

11. Circle the one transformation you can use on *ABCD* so that *AD* is parallel to *MP* and the corresponding points are located in the correct quadrant.

dilation   reflection   rotation   translation

12. Underline the correct choice to complete each sentence.

Trapezoid *ABCD* is larger / smaller / the same size as *MNHP*.

To map *ABCD* onto *MNHP*, I need to duplicate / enlarge / reduce *ABCD* by performing a reflection / rotation / translation / dilation .

The scale fator is 0.5 / 2 / 4 .

13. To map *ABCD* to *MNHP*, begin by [ ] *ABCD* across *x* = [ ] . Then perform a [ ] on *A'B'C'D'* using a scale factor of [ ] .

Compositions of rigid motions and dilations form a special class of transformations. These transformations that map preimages to similar images are called **similarity transformations**.

take note

Similar Figures

Two figures are **similar** if and only if there is a similarity transformation that maps one figure onto the other.

Problem 3 **Finding Similarity Transformations**

Got It? Is there a similarity transformation that maps △*JKL* to △*RST* ? If so, identify the similarity transformation and write a similarity statement. If not, explain.

14. Use information from the diagram to complete each statement.

JK = [ ]   *KL* = [ ]   *LJ* = [ ]   *RS* = [ ]   *ST* = [ ]   *TR* = [ ]

15. Underline the correct word to complete each sentence.

Corresponding sides of similar figures are congruent / proportional .

To determine if corresponding sides are proportional, set up a proof / proportion .

16. Circle the proportion you could use to determine if the triangles are similar.

$\frac{JK}{RS} = \frac{KL}{RT}$ $\frac{JK}{RS} = \frac{ST}{RT}$ $\frac{JK}{RS} = \frac{KL}{ST}$

17. Substitute values into the proportion you circled in Exercise 16. Simplify the proportion, then write = or ≠ between the ratios.

          Simplify: $\frac{\boxed{}}{\boxed{}}\boxed{}\frac{\boxed{}}{\boxed{}}$

18. Underline the correct choices to complete each sentence.

Corresponding sides are/are not proportional, so △*JKL* and △*RST* are/are not similar.

There is / is not a similarity transformation that will map △*JKL* to △*RST* .

Open Ended For △ *TUV* shown at the right, give the vertices of a similar triangle after a similarity transformation that uses at least 1 rigid motion.

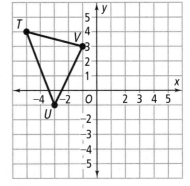

19. Find the vertices of the preimage of △ *TUV*.

$T($,   ) $U($,   ) $V($,   )

20. When a triangle is reflected across a line, what happens to the corresponding angle measures and the length of the corresponding sides of the image triangle?

21. Write the coordinates of the reflection of △ *TUV* across the *y*-axis.

$R_{y\text{-}axis}(x, y) = (-x, y)$

$R_{y\text{-}axis}(T) = T'($,   )

$R_{y\text{-}axis}(U) = U'($,   )

$R_{y\text{-}axis}(V) = V'($,   )

22. When a triangle is dilated by a scale factor, what happens to the corresponding angle measures and the length of the corresponding sides of the image triangle?

23. Draw the dilation of △ *T'U'V'* using a scale factor of 0.5 and the origin as the center of the dilation. $D_{0.5}(x, y) = (0.5x, 0.5y)$

$D_{0.5}(T') = T''($,   ) $D_{0.5}(U') = U''($,   ) $D_{0.5}(V') = V''($,   )

Math Success

Check off the vocabulary words that you understand.

☐ similarity transformation   ☐ similar

Rate how well you can *identify similarity transformations.*

Need to review   0   2   4   6   8   10   Now I get it!

Lesson 9-7

10-1 Areas of Parallelograms and Triangles

Vocabulary

Review

The diagram below shows the different types of *parallelograms*.

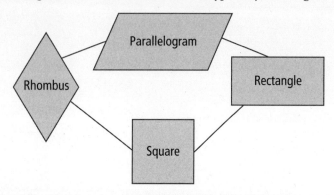

Underline the correct word to complete each sentence.

1. All *parallelograms* are quadrilaterals / rectangles .

2. All *parallelograms* have opposite sides parallel / perpendicular .

3. Some *parallelograms* are trapezoids / rectangles .

Vocabulary Builder

area (noun) EHR ee uh

Definition: **Area** is the number of square units needed to cover a given surface.

Main Idea: You can find the **area** of a parallelogram or a triangle when you know the length of its base and its height.

Use Your Vocabulary

Find the area of each figure.

4.

____ square units

5.

____ square units

6.

____ square units

Theorems 10-1 and 10-2   Area of a Rectangle and a Parallelogram

Theorem 10-1 Area of a Rectangle
The area of a rectangle is the product of its base and height.

$$A = bh$$

Theorem 10-2 Area of a Parallelogram
The area of a parallelogram is the product of a base and the corresponding height.

$$A = bh$$

7. Explain how finding the area of a parallelogram and finding the area of a rectangle are alike.

_____

_____

Problem 1 Finding the Area of a Parallelogram

Got It? What is the area of a parallelogram with base length 12 m and height 9 m?

8. Label the parallelogram at the right.

9. Find the area.

$A = bh$	Write the formula.
$= 12 ()$	Substitute.
$= $	Simplify.

10. The area of the parallelogram is ☐ m^2.

Problem 2 Finding a Missing Dimension

Got It? A parallelogram has sides 15 cm and 18 cm. The height corresponding to a 15-cm base is 9 cm. What is the height corresponding to an 18-cm base?

11. Label the parallelogram at the right.
Let h represent the height corresponding to the 18-cm base.

12. Find the area.

18 cm

13. The area of the parallelogram is ☐ cm^2.

Lesson 10-1

14. Use the area of the parallelogram to find the height corresponding to an 18-cm base.

$A = bh$ Write the formula.

☐ = (☐)h   Substitute.

$\dfrac{135}{\boxed{}} = \dfrac{(\boxed{})h}{\boxed{}}$ Divide each side by the length of the base.

☐ = h   Simplify.

15. The height corresponding to an 18-cm base is ☐ cm.

---

 take note

Theorem 10-3   Area of a Triangle

The area of a triangle is half the product of a base and the corresponding height.

$A = \dfrac{1}{2}bh$

16. Explain how finding the area of a triangle is different from finding the area of a rectangle.

_____

_____

Problem 3   Finding the Area of a Triangle

Got It? What is the area of the triangle?

17. Circle the formula you can use to find the area of the triangle.

$A = bh$ $A = \dfrac{1}{2}bh$

18. Convert the lengths of the base and the hypotenuse to inches.

base   hypotenuse

1 ft = ☐ in.   1 ft 1 in. = ☐ in.

19. Find the area of the triangle.

20. The area of the triangle is ☐ in.^{2}.

Problem 4 Finding the Area of an Irregular Figure

Got It? Reasoning Suppose the base lengths of the square and triangle in the figure are doubled to 12 in., but the height of each polygon remains the same. How is the area of the figure affected?

8 in.
6 in.

21. Complete to find the area of each irregular figure.

Area of Original Irregular Figure

$A = 6(6) + \frac{1}{2}(6)(8)$

$= \boxed{} + 24$

$= \boxed{}$

Area of New Irregular Figure

$A = (2)(6)(6) + \frac{1}{2}(2)(6)(8)$

$= (2)(36) + (2)(\boxed{})$

$= (2)(\boxed{} + \boxed{}) = (2)(\boxed{}) = \boxed{}$

22. How is the area affected?

_____

Lesson Check • **Do you UNDERSTAND?**

$\square ABCD$ is divided into two triangles along diagonal $\overline{AC}$. If you know the area of the parallelogram, how do you find the area of $\triangle ABC$?

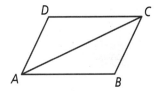

Write T for *true* or F for *false*.

____ **23.** Since $\overline{AC}$ is a diagonal of $\square ABCD$, $\triangle ABC$ is congruent to $\triangle CDA$.

____ **24.** The area of $\triangle ABC$ is greater than the area $\triangle CDA$.

____ **25.** The area of $\triangle ABC$ is half the area of $\square ABCD$.

26. If you know the area of the parallelogram, how do you find the area of $\triangle ABC$?

_____

Math Success

Check off the vocabulary words that you understand.

☐ base of a parallelogram   ☐ height of a parallelogram

☐ base of a triangle   ☐ height of a triangle

Rate how well you can *find the area of parallelograms and triangles*.

Need to review   0   2   4   6   8   10   Now I get it!

Lesson 10-1

Vocabulary

● Review

1. Is a *rhombus* a parallelogram?

Yes / No

2. Are all *rhombuses* squares?

Yes / No

3. Are all squares *rhombuses*?

Yes / No

4. Cross out the figure that is NOT a *rhombus*.

● Vocabulary Builder

kite (noun) **kyt**

Definition: A **kite** is a quadrilateral with two pairs of congruent adjacent sides.

Main Idea: You can find the area of a **kite** when you know the lengths of its diagonals.

Word Origin: The name for this quadrilateral is taken from the name of the flying toy that it looks like.

● Use Your Vocabulary

5. Circle the *kite*.

6. The figure at the right is a *kite*. What is the value of x? Explain.

_____

Theorem 10-4 **Area of a Trapezoid**

The area of a trapezoid is half the product of the height
and the sum of the bases.

$$A = \tfrac{1}{2}h(b_1 + b_2)$$

Underline the correct word to complete each sentence.

7. The bases of a trapezoid are parallel / perpendicular .

8. The height / width of a trapezoid is the perpendicular distance between the bases.

Problem 1 Area of a Trapezoid

Got It? What is the area of a trapezoid with height 7 cm and bases
12 cm and 15 cm?

9. Use the justifications below to find the area of the trapezoid.

$A = \tfrac{1}{2}h(b_1 + b_2)$ Use the formula for area of a trapezoid.

$ = \tfrac{1}{2}(\quad)(\quad + 15)$ Substitute.

$ = \tfrac{1}{2}(\quad)(\quad)$ Add.

$ = \boxed{}$ Simplify.

10. The area of the trapezoid is [   ] cm².

Problem 2 Finding Area Using a Right Triangle

Got It? Suppose h decreases in trapezoid $PQRS$ so that $m\angle P = 45$ while angles
R and Q and the bases stay the same. What is the area of trapezoid $PQRS$?

11. If $m\angle P = 45$, is the triangle still a 30°-60°-90° triangle?   Yes / No

12. Is the triangle a 45°-45°-90° triangle?   Yes / No

13. Are the legs of a 45°-45°-90° triangle congruent?   Yes / No

14. The height of the triangle is [   ] m.

15. The area is found below. Write a justification for each step.

$A = \tfrac{1}{2}h(b_1 + b_2)$

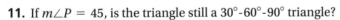

$ = \tfrac{1}{2}(2)(5 + 7)$

$ = \tfrac{1}{2}(2)(12)$

$ = 12$

16. The area of trapezoid $PQRS$ is [   ] m².

259

Theorem 10-5 Area of a Rhombus or a Kite

The area of a rhombus or a kite is half the product of the lengths of its diagonals.

$$A = \frac{1}{2}(d_1 d_2)$$

Rhombus

Kite

17. Describe one way that finding the area of rhombus or a kite is different from finding the area of a trapezoid.

_____

_____

_____

18. Find the lengths of the diagonals of the kite and the rhombus below.

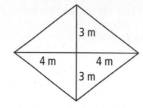

lengths of the diagonals of the kite:

☐ m and ☐ m

lengths of the diagonals of the rhombus:

☐ m and ☐ m

Problem 3 **Finding the Area of a Kite**

Got It? What is the area of a kite with diagonals that are 12 in. and 9 in. long?

19. Error Analysis Below is one student's solution. What error did the student make?

20. Find the area of the kite.

21. The area of the kite is ☐ in.^{2}.

Problem 4 Finding the Area of a Rhombus

Got It? A rhombus has sides 10 cm long. If the longer diagonal is 16 cm, what is the area of the rhombus?

Underline the correct words to complete the sentence.

22. The diagonals of a rhombus bisect each other / side and are parallel / perpendicular .

23. Label the rhombus at the right.

24. The shorter diagonal is [   ] + [   ] , or [   ] .

25. Use the Pythagorean Theorem to find the value of x.

26. Find the area of the rhombus.

27. The area of the rhombus is [   ] cm^2.

 Lesson Check • **Do you UNDERSTAND?**

Reasoning Do you need to know the lengths of the sides to find the area of a kite? Explain.

28. Cross out the length you do NOT need to find the area of each triangle in a kite.

> each leg   hypotenuse

29. Now answer the question.

_____

_____

_____

 Math Success

Check off the vocabulary words that you understand.

☐ kite   ☐ height of a trapezoid

Rate how well you can *find the area of a trapezoid, rhombus, or kite.*

| Need to review | 0   2   4   6   8   10 | Now I get it! |

Lesson 10-2

10-3 Areas of Regular Polygons

Vocabulary

● Review

Write T for *true* or F for *false*.

_____ **1.** In a *regular polygon*, all sides are congruent.

_____ **2.** In a *regular polygon*, all angles are acute.

3. Cross out the figure that is NOT a *regular polygon*.

● Vocabulary Builder

apothem (noun) AP **uh them**

Related Words: center, regular polygon

Definition: The **apothem** is the perpendicular distance from the center of a regular polygon to one of its sides.

● Use Your Vocabulary

4. Underline the correct word to complete the statement.

In a regular polygon, the *apothem* is the perpendicular distance from the center to a(n) angle / side .

5. Label the regular polygon below using *apothem, center,* or *side.*

Problem 1 Finding Angle Measures

Got It? At the right, a portion of a regular octagon has radii and an apothem drawn. What is the measure of each numbered angle?

6. A regular octagon has ☐ sides.

7. Circle the type of triangles formed by the radii of the regular octagon.

equilateral	isosceles	right

8. Use the justifications below to find the measure of each numbered angle.

$m\angle 1 = \dfrac{360}{\boxed{}} = \boxed{}$ Divide 360 by the number of sides.

$m\angle 2 = \boxed{} (m\angle 1)$ The apothem bisects the vertex angle of the triangle formed by the radii.

$\qquad = \frac{1}{2}(\boxed{}) = \boxed{}$

$90 + m\angle 2 + m\angle 3 = \boxed{}$ Triangle Angle-Sum Theorem

$90 + \boxed{} + m\angle 3 = \boxed{}$ Substitute.

$\boxed{} + m\angle 3 = \boxed{}$ Simplify.

$m\angle 3 = \boxed{}$ Subtraction Property of Equality

9. Write the measure of each numbered angle.

$m\angle 1 = \boxed{}$ $m\angle 2 = \boxed{}$ $m\angle 3 = \boxed{}$

---

take note

Postulate 10-1 and Theorem 10-6

Postulate 10-1 If two figures are congruent, then their areas are equal.

The isosceles triangles in the regular hexagon at the right are congruent. Complete each statement.

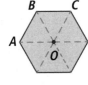

10. If the area of $\triangle AOB$ is 24 in.^{2}, then the area of $\triangle BOC$ is ☐ in.^{2}.

11. If the area of $\triangle BOC$ is 8 cm^2, then the area of $\triangle AOC$ is ☐ cm^2.

Theorem 10-6 Area of a Regular Polygon
The area of a regular polygon is half the product of the apothem and the perimeter.

$A = \frac{1}{2}ap$

Complete.

12. apothem: 10   perimeter: 80   area: $\frac{1}{2}(10) \cdot \boxed{}$

13. apothem: 5   perimeter: $30\sqrt{3}$ area: $\frac{1}{2} \cdot \boxed{} \cdot \boxed{}$

14. apothem: $5\sqrt{3}$ perimeter: 60   area: $\boxed{} \cdot \boxed{} \cdot \boxed{}$

Lesson 10-3

Problem 2 Finding the Area of a Regular Polygon

Got It? What is the area of a regular pentagon with an 8-cm apothem and 11.6-cm sides?

15. Label the regular pentagon with the lengths of the apothem and the sides.

16. Use the justifications below to find the perimeter.

$p = ns$ Use the formula for the perimeter of an *n*-gon.

= □ (11.6)   Substitute for *n* and for *s*.

= □   Simplify.

17. Use the justifications below to find the area.

$A = \frac{1}{2}ap$ Use the formula for the area of a regular polygon.

$= \frac{1}{2} \cdot$ □ · □   Substitute for *a* and for *p*.

= □   Simplify.

18. The regular pentagon has an area of □ cm².

Problem 3 Using Special Triangles to Find Area

Got It? The side of a regular hexagon is 16 ft. What is the area of the hexagon? Round your answer to the nearest square foot.

19. Use the information in the problem to complete the problem-solving model below.

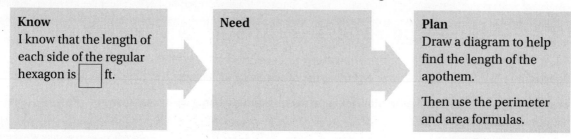

Know
I know that the length of each side of the regular hexagon is □ ft.

Need

Plan
Draw a diagram to help find the length of the apothem.

Then use the perimeter and area formulas.

Use the diagram at the right.

20. Label the diagram.

21. Circle the relationship you can use to find the length of the apothem.

hypotenuse = 2 · shorter leg   longer leg = √3 · shorter leg

22. Complete.

length of shorter leg = □ ft

length of longer leg (apothem) = □ ft

23. Use the formula $p = ns$ to find the perimeter of the hexagon.

24. Now use the perimeter and the formula $A = \frac{1}{2}ap$ to find the area of the hexagon.

25. To the nearest square foot, the area of the hexagon is [   ] ft².

Lesson Check • Do you UNDERSTAND?

What is the relationship between the side length and the apothem in each figure?

square

regular hexagon

equilateral triangle

26. The radius and apothem form what type of triangle in each figure?

square

[   ]°-[   ]°-[   ]° triangle

regular hexagon

[   ]°-[   ]°-[   ]° triangle

equilateral triangle

[   ]°-[   ]°-[   ]° triangle

27. Complete to show the relationship between the side length and the apothem.

square

leg = leg

$a = [\ ]\ s$

regular hexagon

longer leg = $\sqrt{3}$ · shorter leg

$a = \sqrt{3} \cdot [\ ]\ s$

$a = [\ ]\ s$

equilateral triangle

longer leg = $\sqrt{3}$ · shorter leg

$\frac{1}{2}s = \sqrt{3} \cdot [\ ]$

$s = [\ ]\ a$

Math Success

Check off the vocabulary words that you understand.

☐ radius of a regular polygon   ☐ apothem

Rate how well you can *find the area of a regular polygon.*

Lesson 10-3

Vocabulary

● **Review**

1. What does it mean when two figures are *similar*?

_____

2. Are the corresponding angles of *similar* figures always congruent? | Yes / No

3. Are the corresponding sides of *similar* figures always proportional? | Yes / No

4. Circle the pairs of *similar* figures.

● **Vocabulary Builder**

radius (noun) RAY dee us (plural radii)

Related Words: apothem, center

Definition: The **radius** of a regular polygon is the distance from the center to a vertex.

Main Idea: The **radii** of a regular polygon divide the polygon into congruent triangles.

● **Use Your Vocabulary**

5. Cross out the segment that is NOT a *radius* of regular pentagon *ABCDE*.

$\overline{OA}$ $\overline{OD}$ $\overline{OB}$ $\overline{OE}$ $\overline{OC}$ $\overline{OF}$

Underline the correct word(s) to complete each sentence.

6. The *radii* of a regular polygon   are / are not   congruent.

7. The triangles formed by the *radii* and sides of regular pentagon *ABCDE* are / are not   congruent.

take note

Theorem 10-7   Perimeters and Areas of Similar Figures

If the scale factor of two similar figures is $\frac{a}{b}$, then

(1) the ratio of their perimeters is $\frac{a}{b}$ and

(2) the ratio of their areas is $\frac{a^2}{b^2}$.

8. The name for the ratio of the length of one side of a figure to the
length of the corresponding side of a similar figure is the __?__ .

9. If the scale factor of two figures is $\frac{1}{2}$, then the ratio of their perimeters is ▭/▭ .

10. If the scale factor of two figures is $\frac{3}{x}$, then the ratio of their perimeters is ▭/▭ .

11. If the scale factor of two figures is $\frac{3}{5}$, then the ratio of their areas is $\dfrac{▭^2}{▭^2}$.

12. If the scale factor of two figures is $\frac{1}{x}$ then the ratio of their areas is $\dfrac{▭^2}{▭^2}$.

Problem 1 **Finding Ratios in Similar Figures**

Got It? Two similar polygons have corresponding sides in the ratio 5 : 7. What is
the ratio (larger to smaller) of their perimeters? What is the ratio (larger to smaller)
of their areas?

13. Circle the similar polygons that have corresponding sides in the ratio 5 : 7.

5   10   14   8   14   10

Underline the correct word to complete each sentence.

14. In similar figures, the ratio of the areas / perimeters equals the ratio of
corresponding sides.

15. In similar figures, the ratio of the areas / perimeters equals the ratio of the squares
of corresponding sides.

16. Complete.

ratio (larger to smaller) of corresponding sides	ratio (larger to smaller) of perimeters	ratio (larger to smaller) of areas
▭/▭	▭/▭	$\dfrac{▭^2}{▭^2} = \dfrac{▭}{▭}$

Lesson 10-4

Problem 2 Finding Areas Using Similar Figures

Got It? The scale factor of two similar parallelograms is $\frac{3}{4}$. The area of the larger parallelogram is 96 in.^{2}. What is the area of the smaller parallelogram?

Write T for *true* or F for *false*.

_____ **17.** The ratio of the areas is $\frac{3}{4}$.

_____ **18.** The ratio of the areas is $\frac{9}{16}$.

19. Use the justifications below to find the area A of the smaller parallelogram.

$\dfrac{\boxed{}}{16} = \dfrac{A}{96}$ Write a proportion.

$16A = (96)\boxed{}$ Cross Products Property

$16A = \boxed{}$ Multiply.

$\dfrac{16A}{\boxed{}} = \dfrac{\boxed{}}{\boxed{}}$ Divide each side by $\boxed{}$.

$A = \boxed{}$ Simplify.

20. The area of the smaller parallelogram is $\boxed{}$ in.^{2}.

Problem 3 Applying Area Ratios

Got It? The scale factor of the dimensions of two similar pieces of window glass is 3 : 5. The smaller piece costs \$2.50. How much should the larger piece cost?

21. Use the information in the problem to complete the reasoning model below.

Think	Write
The ratio of areas is the square of the scale factor.	Ratio of areas = $3^2 : 5^2$ $= \boxed{} : \boxed{}$

I can use a proportion to find the cost c of the larger piece to the nearest hundredth.	$\dfrac{\boxed{}}{\boxed{}} = \dfrac{2.50}{c}$
	  $\boxed{} \cdot c = 2.50 \cdot \boxed{}$
	  $\boxed{} \cdot c = \boxed{}$
	  $\dfrac{\boxed{} \cdot c}{\boxed{}} = \dfrac{\boxed{}}{\boxed{}}$
	  $c \approx \boxed{}$

22. The larger piece of glass should cost about \$ $\boxed{}$.

Problem 4 Finding Perimeter Ratios

Got It? The areas of two similar rectangles are 1875 ft^2 and 135 ft^2.
What is the ratio of their perimeters?

23. The scale factor is found below. Use one of the reasons listed in the blue
box to justify each step.

$\dfrac{a^2}{b^2} = \dfrac{135}{1875}$ _____

$\dfrac{a^2}{b^2} = \dfrac{9}{125}$ _____

$\dfrac{a}{b} = \dfrac{3}{5\sqrt{5}}$ _____

$\dfrac{a}{b} = \dfrac{3}{5\sqrt{5}} \cdot \dfrac{\sqrt{5}}{\sqrt{5}}$ _____

$\dfrac{a}{b} = \dfrac{3\sqrt{5}}{25}$ _____

> Rationalize the
> denominator.
> Simplify.
> Simplify.
> Take the positive
> square root of
> each side.
> Write a
> proportion.

24. The ratio of the perimeters equals the scale factor ⬚ : ⬚ .

Lesson Check • Do you UNDERSTAND?

Reasoning The area of one rectangle is twice the area of another. What is the ratio of
their perimeters? How do you know?

25. Let x and y be the sides of the smaller rectangle. Complete.

area of smaller rectangle	area of larger rectangle	ratio of larger to smaller areas
xy	⬚ xy	⬚ : ⬚

26. Find the square root of the ratio of larger to smaller areas to find the scale factor.

27. The ratio of perimeters is ⬚ : ⬚ because the scale factor is ⬚ : ⬚ .

Math Success

Check off the vocabulary words that you understand.

☐ similar polygons   ☐ radius   ☐ perimeter   ☐ area

Rate how well you can *find the perimeters and areas of similar polygons.*

Need to review 0 2 4 6 8 10 Now I get it!

Lesson 10-4

Vocabulary

● **Review**

1. Underline the correct word to complete the sentence.

Area is the number of cubic / square units needed to cover a given surface.

2. Circle the formula for the *area* of a triangle.

$A = bh$ $\qquad$ $A = \frac{1}{2}bh$ $\qquad$ $A = \frac{1}{2}h(b_1 + b_2)$ $\qquad$ $A = \frac{1}{2}d_1d_2$

● **Vocabulary Builder**

trigonometry (noun) **trig uh NAHM uh tree**

Other Word Form: trigonometric (adjective)

Related Words: cosine, sine, tangent

Definition: Trigonometry is the study of the relationships among two sides and an angle in a right triangle.

Main Idea: You can use **trigonometry** to find the area of a regular polygon.

● **Use Your Vocabulary**

Complete each sentence with the word *trigonometry* or *trigonometric*.

3. The sine, cosine, and tangent ratios are __?__ ratios.

4. This year I am studying __?__ in math.

Draw a line from each *trigonometric ratio* in Column A to its name in Column B.

Column A	Column B
5. $\dfrac{\text{length of opposite leg}}{\text{length of hypotenuse}}$	cosine
6. $\dfrac{\text{length of adjacent leg}}{\text{length of hypotenuse}}$	sine
7. $\dfrac{\text{length of opposite leg}}{\text{length of adjacent leg}}$	tangent

Problem 1 Finding Area

Got It? What is the area of a regular pentagon with 4-in. sides? Round your answer to the nearest square inch.

8. Underline the correct words to complete the sentence.

To find the area using the formula $A = \frac{1}{2}ap$, you need to know the length of the

apothem / radius and the perimeter / width of the pentagon.

9. In the regular pentagon at the right, label center C, apothem $\overline{CR}$, and radii $\overline{CD}$ and $\overline{CE}$.

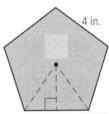

4 in.

10. The perimeter of the pentagon is 5 · ☐ in., or ☐ in.

11. The measure of central angle DCE is $\dfrac{360}{\boxed{}}$, or ☐ .

Complete Exercises 12 and 13.

12. $m\angle DCR = \frac{1}{2}m\angle DCE$
    $ = \frac{1}{2} \cdot \boxed{}$
    $ = \boxed{}$

13. $DR = \frac{1}{2}DE$
    $ = \frac{1}{2} \cdot \boxed{}$
    $ = \boxed{}$

14. Use your results from Exercises 12 and 13 to label the diagram below.

15. Circle the equation you can use to find the apothem a.

$\tan 72° = \dfrac{36}{a}$ $\qquad\qquad$ $\tan 36° = \dfrac{2a}{a}$ $\qquad\qquad$ $\tan 36° = \dfrac{2}{a}$

$\qquad\qquad\quad \tan 36° = \dfrac{a}{2}$ $\qquad\qquad$ $\tan 72° = \dfrac{2}{a}$

16. Use the justifications below to find the apothem and the area.

$\tan 72° = \dfrac{\boxed{}}{a}$ $\qquad\qquad\qquad$ Use the tangent ratio.

$a \cdot \tan 36° = \boxed{}$ $\qquad\qquad\quad$ Multiply each side by a.

$a = \dfrac{\boxed{}}{\tan 36°}$ $\qquad\qquad\qquad$ Divide each side by $\tan 36°$.

$A = \frac{1}{2}ap$ $\qquad\qquad\qquad\qquad\qquad$ Write the formula for the area of a regular polygon.

$ = \frac{1}{2} \cdot \dfrac{\boxed{}}{\tan 36°} \cdot \boxed{}$ $\qquad\qquad$ Substitute for a and p.

$ \approx \boxed{}$ $\qquad\qquad\qquad$ Use a calculator.

17. To the nearest square inch, the area of the regular pentagon is ☐ in.^{2}.

Lesson 10-5

Problem 2 Finding Area

Got It? A tabletop has the shape of a regular decagon with a radius of 9.5 in. What is the area of the tabletop to the nearest square inch?

18. Complete the problem-solving model below.

Know	Need	Plan
		Use trigonometric ratios to find the apothem and the length of a side.

19. Look at the decagon at the right. Explain why the measure of each central angle of a decagon is 36 and $m\angle C$ is 18.

_____

_____

20. Use the cosine ratio to find the apothem a.

$$\cos 18° = \dfrac{a}{\boxed{}}$$

$$\boxed{} \cdot \cos 18° = a$$

21. Use the sine ratio to find x.

$$\sin 18° = \dfrac{x}{\boxed{}}$$

$$\boxed{} \cdot \sin 18° = x$$

22. Use the justifications below to find the perimeter.

$p = \boxed{} \cdot$ length of one side   perimeter = number of sides times length of one side

$= 10 \cdot \boxed{} \cdot x$ The length of each side is $2x$.

$= 10 \cdot \boxed{} \cdot \boxed{}$ Substitute for x.

$= \boxed{} \cdot \sin 18°$ Simplify.

23. Find the area. Use a calculator.

24. To the nearest square inch, the area of the tabletop is $\boxed{}$ in.^{2}.

take note

Theorem 10-8 Area of a Triangle Given SAS

The area of a triangle is half the product of the lengths of two sides and the sine of the included angle.

25. Complete the formula below.

Area of $\triangle ABC = \frac{1}{2}bc(\sin \boxed{})$

Problem 3 Finding Area

Got It? What is the area of the triangle? Round your answer to the nearest square inch.

10 in.
34°
16 in.

26. Complete the reasoning model below.

Think	Write
I know the lengths of two sides and the measure of the included angle.	Side lengths: ☐ in. and 16 in. Angle measure: ☐
I can use the formula for the area of a triangle given SAS.	$A = \frac{1}{2} \cdot$ ☐ $\cdot 16 \cdot \sin$ ☐ ≈ ☐

27. To the nearest square inch, the area of the triangle is ☐ in.²

Lesson Check • Do you UNDERSTAND?

Error Analysis Your classmate needs to find the area of a regular pentagon with 8-cm sides. To find the apothem, he sets up and solves a trigonometric ratio. What error did he make? Explain.

$$\frac{a}{4} = \tan 36°$$
$$a = 4 \cdot \tan 36°$$

28. The lengths of the legs of the triangle in the regular pentagon are ☐ and ☐ cm.

29. The tangent of the 36° angle is $\dfrac{\text{length of opposite leg}}{\text{length of adjacent leg}}$, or $\dfrac{\square}{\square}$.

36°
a
8 cm

30. Explain the error your classmate made.

_____

Math Success

Check off the vocabulary words that you understand.

☐ area   ☐ trigonometry

Rate how well you can use *trigonometry to find area*.

Need to review 0 2 4 6 8 10 Now I get it!

Lesson 10-5

10-6   Circles and Arcs

Vocabulary

● Review

1. Is a *circle* a two-dimensional figure?   Yes / No

2. Is a *circle* a polygon?   Yes / No

3. Is every point on a circle the same distance from the center?   Yes / No

4. Circle the figure that is a *circle*.

● Vocabulary Builder

arc (noun) **ahrk**

Definition: An **arc** is part of a circle.

Related Words: minor arc, major arc, semicircle

Example: Semicircle *AB* is an **arc** of the circle.

Major **arc** *ABC*
Minor **arc** *AC*

● Use Your Vocabulary

Underline the correct word to complete each sentence.

5. A *minor arc* is larger / smaller than a semicircle.

6. A *major arc* is larger / smaller than a semicircle.

7. You use two / three points to name a *major arc*.

8. You use two / three points to name a *minor arc*.

9. Circle the name of $\overset{\frown}{KL}$.

    minor arc   major arc   semicircle   radius

10. Circle the name of $\overset{\frown}{LJK}$.

    minor arc   major arc   semicircle   radius

Got It? What are the minor arcs of ⊙A?

Draw a line from each central angle in Column A to its corresponding minor arc in Column B.

Column A	Column B
11. ∠PAQ	$\overarc{RS}$
12. ∠QAR	$\overarc{SP}$
13. ∠RAS	$\overarc{PQ}$
14. ∠SAP	$\overarc{QR}$
15. ∠SAQ	$\overarc{SQ}$

16. The minor arcs of ⊙A are ▢ , ▢ , ▢ , ▢ , and ▢ .

---

take note

Key Concepts   Arc Measure and Postulate 10-2

Arc Measure

The measure of a minor arc is equal to the measure of its corresponding central angle.

The measure of a major arc is the measure of the related minor arc subtracted from 360.

The measure of a semicircle is 180.

Use ⊙S at the right for Exercises 17 and 18.

17. $m\overarc{RT} = m\angle RST = $ ▢

18. $m\overarc{TQR} = 360 - m\overarc{RT} = 360 - $ ▢ $= $ ▢

Postulate 10-2 Arc Addition Postulate

The measure of the arc formed by two adjacent arcs is the sum of the measures of the two arcs.

$$m\overarc{ABC} = m\overarc{AB} + m\overarc{BC}$$

Use the circle at the right for Exercises 19 and 20.

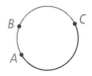

19. If $m\overarc{AB} = 40$ and $m\overarc{BC} = 100$, then $m\overarc{ABC} = $ ▢ .

20. If $m\overarc{AB} = x$ and $m\overarc{BC} = y$, then $m\overarc{ABC} = $ ▢ .

Problem 2 **Finding the Measures of Arcs**

Got It? What are the measures of $\overarc{PR}$, $\overarc{RS}$, $\overarc{PRQ}$, and $\overarc{PQR}$ in ⊙C?

Complete.

21. $m\angle PCR = $ ▢ , so $m\overarc{PR} = $ ▢ .

Lesson 10-6

22. $m\angle RCS = m\angle PCS - m\angle PCR$

$= 180 - \boxed{} = \boxed{}$

23. $m\angle RCS = \boxed{}$, so $m\,\widehat{RS} = \boxed{}$.

24. $m\widehat{PRQ} = m\,\widehat{PR} + m\,\widehat{RS} + m\,\widehat{SQ}$

$= \boxed{} + \boxed{} + \boxed{} = \boxed{}$

25. $m\widehat{PQR} = 360 - m\,\widehat{PR}$

$= 360 - \boxed{} = \boxed{}$

Theorem 10-9   Circumference of a Circle

The circumference of a circle is π times the diameter.

$$C = \pi d \text{ or } C = 2\pi r$$

26. Explain why you can use either $C = \pi d$ or $C = 2\pi r$ to find the circumference of a circle.

_____

_____

_____

Problem 3   Finding a Distance

Got It? A car has a circular turning radius of 16.1 ft. The distance between the two front tires is 4.7 ft. How much farther does a tire on the outside of the turn travel than a tire on the inside?

16.1 ft

4.7 ft

27. The two circles have the same center. To find the radius of the inner circle, do you *add* or *subtract*? _____

Complete.

28. radius of outer circle = $\boxed{}$

radius of inner circle = $\boxed{} - 4.7 = \boxed{}$

29. circumference of outer circle = $2\pi r = 2\pi \cdot \boxed{} = \boxed{} \cdot \pi$

circumference of inner circle = $2\pi r = 2\pi \cdot \boxed{} = \boxed{} \cdot \pi$

30. Find the differences in the two distances traveled. Use a calculator.

$\boxed{} \cdot \pi - \boxed{} \cdot \pi = \boxed{} \cdot \pi$

$\approx \boxed{}$

31. A tire on the outer circle travels about $\boxed{}$ ft farther.

Theorem 10-10 Arc Length

The length of an arc of a circle is the product of the ratio $\frac{\text{measure of the arc}}{360}$ and the circumference of the circle.

32. Complete the formula below.

length of [____] $= \frac{m\,\widehat{AB}}{360} \cdot 2\pi r = \frac{m\,\widehat{AB}}{360} \cdot \pi d$

Write T for *true* or F for *false*.

_____ **33.** The length of an arc is a fraction of the circumference of a circle.

_____ **34.** In $\odot O$, $m\,\widehat{AB} = m\angle AOB$.

Lesson Check • Do you UNDERSTAND?

Error Analysis Your class must find the length of $\widehat{AB}$. A classmate submits the following solution. What is the error?

35. Is $\widehat{AC}$ a semicircle?   Yes / No

36. Does $m\,\widehat{AB} = 180 - 70 = 110$?   Yes / No

37. Is the length of the radius 4?   Yes / No

38. What is the error?

_____

Math Success

Check off the vocabulary words that you understand.

☐ circle   ☐ minor arc   ☐ major arc   ☐ circumference

Rate how well you can *use central angles, arcs, and circumference*.

Vocabulary

● Review

1. Explain how the *area* of a figure is different from the perimeter of the figure.

_____

_____

2. Circle the formula for the *area* of a parallelogram.

$A = bh$	$A = \frac{1}{2}bh$	$A = \frac{1}{2}h(b_1 + b_2)$	$A = \frac{1}{2}d_1d_2$

3. Find the *area* of each figure.

3 m / 5 m

6 cm / 9 cm

6 ft / 10 ft

$A =$ [ ] m^2 $A =$ [ ] cm^2 $A =$ [ ] ft^2

● Vocabulary Builder

sector *RST*

sector (noun) SEK **tur**

Definition: A **sector** of a circle is a region bounded by an arc of the circle and the two radii to the arc's endpoints.

Main Idea: The area of a **sector** is a fractional part of the area of a circle.

● Use Your Vocabulary

4. Name the arc and the radii that are the boundaries of the shaded *sector*.

arc [ ]   radii [ ] and [ ]

5. Circle the name of the shaded *sector*.

sector *ABC*	sector *ACB*	sector *BAC*

6. The shaded *sector* is what fractional part of the area of the circle? Explain.

_____

_____

Theorem 10-11   Area of a Circle

The area of a circle is the product of π and the square of the radius.

$$A = \pi r^2$$

Complete each statement.

7. If the radius is 5 ft, then $A = \pi \cdot$ ☐ $\cdot$ ☐.

8. If the diameter is 1.8 cm, then $A = \pi \cdot$ ☐ $\cdot$ ☐.

Problem 1 **Finding the Area of a Circle**

Got It? What is the area of a circular wrestling region with a 42-ft diameter?

9. The radius of the wrestling region is ☐ ft.

10. Complete the reasoning model below.

42 ft

Think	Write
I can use the formula for the area of a circle.	$A = \pi r^2$
I can subtitute the radius into the formula and then simplify.	$= \pi \cdot$ ☐^{2} $=$ ☐ $\cdot \pi$
I can use a calculator to find the approximate area.	$\approx$ ☐

11. The area of the wrestling region is about ☐ ft^2.

Theorem 10-12   Area of a Sector of a Circle

The area of a sector of a circle is the product of the ratio $\dfrac{\text{measure of the arc}}{360}$ and the area of the circle.

$$\text{Area of sector } AOB = \frac{m\,\widehat{AB}}{360} \cdot \pi r^2$$

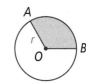

Complete.

measure of the arc	$\dfrac{\text{measure of the arc}}{360}$	area of the sector
12. 60	$\dfrac{60}{360} = \dfrac{1}{\boxed{}}$	$\dfrac{1}{\boxed{}} \cdot \boxed{} \cdot r^2$
13. 120	$\dfrac{\boxed{}}{360} = \dfrac{\boxed{}}{\boxed{}}$	$\dfrac{\boxed{}}{\boxed{}} \cdot \boxed{} \cdot r^2$

Lesson 10-7

Finding the Area of a Sector of a Circle

Got It? A circle has a radius of 4 in. What is the area of a sector bounded by a 45° minor arc? Leave your answer in terms of π.

14. At the right is one student's solution. What error did the student make?

$$\text{area of sector} = \frac{45}{360} \cdot \pi(4)$$
$$= \frac{1}{8} \cdot \pi(4)$$
$$= \frac{1}{2}\pi$$

_____

_____

15. Find the area of the sector correctly.

16. The area of the sector is [ ] in.²

take note

Key Concept **Area of a Segment**

The area of a segment is the difference of the area of the sector and the area of the triangle formed by the radii and the segment joining the endpoints.

 — =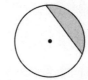

Area of sector — Area of triangle = Area of segment

Problem 3 **Finding the Area of a Segment of a Circle**

Got It? What is the area of the shaded segment shown at the right? Round your answer to the nearest tenth.

17. Use the justifications below to find the area of sector PQR.

$$\text{area of sector } PQR = \frac{m\,\overparen{PR}}{\boxed{}} \cdot \pi r^2 \qquad \text{Use the formula for the area of a sector.}$$

$$= \frac{90}{360} \cdot \pi(\boxed{})^2 \qquad \text{Substitute.}$$

$$= \boxed{} \cdot \pi \qquad \text{Simplify.}$$

18. $\triangle PQR$ is a right triangle, so the base is [ ] m and the height is [ ] m.

19. Find the area of $\triangle PQR$.

20. Complete to find the area of the shaded segment. Use a calculator.

area of shaded segment $=$ area of sector PQR $-$ area of $\triangle PQR$

$$= \boxed{} \cdot \pi - \boxed{}$$

$$\approx \boxed{}$$

 21. To the nearest tenth, the area of the shaded segment is $\boxed{}$ m^2.

Lesson Check • Do you UNDERSTAND?

Reasoning Suppose a sector in $\odot P$ has the same area as a sector in $\odot O$. Can you conclude that $\odot P$ and $\odot O$ have the same area? Explain.

Use the figures at the right for Exercises 22–24.

22. Find the area of sector AOC in $\odot O$.

23. Find the area of sector RPT in $\odot P$.

24. Do the sectors have the same area? Can you conclude that the circles have the same area? Explain.

_____

_____

Math Success

Check off the vocabulary words that you understand.

☐ sector of a circle   ☐ segment of a circle   ☐ area of a circle

Rate how well you can *find areas of circles, sectors, and segments*.

Lesson 10-7

10-8 Geometric Probability

Vocabulary

● Review

Write T for *true* or F for *false*.

_____ **1.** A *point* indicates a location and has no size.

_____ **2.** A line contains a finite number of *points*.

3. Use the diagram at the right. Circle the segment that includes *point S*.

$\overline{PR}$ $\overline{PT}$ $\overline{QR}$

● Vocabulary Builder

probability (noun) **prah buh BIL uh tee**

Related Term: geometric probability

theoretical **probability**

$$P(\text{event}) = \frac{\text{number of favorable outcomes}}{\text{number of possible outcomes}}$$

Definition: The **probability** of an event is the likelihood that the event will occur.

Main Idea: In geometric **probability,** favorable outcomes and possible outcomes are geometric measures such as lengths of segments or areas of regions.

● Use Your Vocabulary

4. Underline the correct words to complete the sentence.

The *probability* of an event is the ratio of the number of favorable / possible

outcomes to the number of favorable / possible outcomes.

5. There are 7 red marbles and 3 green marbles in a bag. One marble is chosen at random. Write the *probability* that a green marble is chosen.

Write as a fraction.	Write as a decimal.	Write as a percent.
		%

Key Concept Probability and Length or Area

Probability and Length

Point S on $\overline{AD}$ is chosen at random. The probability that S is on $\overline{BC}$ is the ratio of the length of $\overline{BC}$ to the length of $\overline{AD}$.

$$P(S \text{ on } \overline{BC}) = \frac{BC}{AD}$$

Complete.

6. $P(S \text{ on } \overline{AC}) = \dfrac{\boxed{}}{AD}$

7. $P(S \text{ on } \overline{AB}) = \dfrac{\boxed{}}{\boxed{}}$

Probability and Area

Point S in region R is chosen at random. The probability that S is in region N is the ratio of the area of region N to the area of region R.

$$P(S \text{ in region } N) = \frac{\text{area of region } N}{\text{area of region } R}$$

8. Find the probability for the given areas.

area of region $R = 11 \text{ cm}^2$ area of region $N = 3 \text{ cm}^2$

$P(S \text{ in } N) = \dfrac{\boxed{}}{\boxed{}}$

✓ Problem 1 Using Segments to Find Probability

Got It? Point H on $\overline{ST}$ is selected at random. What is the probability that H lies on $\overline{SR}$?

9. Find the length of each segment.

length of $\overline{SR} = \left| 2 - \boxed{} \right| = \boxed{}$ length of $\overline{ST} = \left| \boxed{} - \boxed{} \right| = \boxed{}$

10. Find the probability.

$$P(H \text{ on } \overline{SR}) = \frac{\text{length of } \overline{SR}}{\text{length of } \boxed{}} = \frac{\boxed{}}{\boxed{}} = \frac{\boxed{}}{\boxed{}}$$

11. The probability that H is on $\overline{SR}$ is $\boxed{}$, or $\boxed{}$ %.

✓ Problem 2 Using Segments to Find Probability

Got It? Transportation A commuter train runs every 25 min. If a commuter arrives at the station at a random time, what is the probability that the commuter will have to wait no more than 5 min for the train?

12. Circle the time t (in minutes) before the train arrives that the commuter will need to arrive in order to wait *no more than* 5 minutes.

$0 \le t \le 5$	$5 < t \le 10$	$10 < t \le 15$
$15 < t \le 20$	$20 < t \le 25$	

283

Lesson 10-8

13. Circle the diagram that models the situation.

14. Complete.

length of favorable segment = ☐   length of entire segment = ☐

15. Find the probability.

$$P(\text{waiting no more than 5 min}) = \frac{\text{length of favorable segment}}{\text{length of entire segment}}$$

$$= \frac{☐}{☐}, \text{ or } \frac{☐}{☐}$$

16. The probability of waiting no more than 5 min for the train is ☐, or ☐ %.

 Problem 3 **Using Area to Find Probability**

Got It? A triangle is inscribed in a square. Point *T* in the square is selected at random. What is the probability that *T* lies in the shaded region?

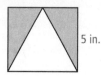

5 in.

17. Complete the model below to write an equation.

Define   Let *s* = the area of the shaded region.

Relate | area of the shaded region | is | area of the square | minus | area of the triangle |

Write   *s* = ☐² − $\frac{1}{2}$ · ☐ · ☐

18. Now solve the equation to find the area of the shaded region.

19. Find the probability.

$$P(\text{point } T \text{ is in shaded region}) = \frac{\text{area of shaded region}}{\text{area of square}}$$

$$= \frac{☐}{☐}, \text{ or } \frac{☐}{2}$$

20. The probability that *T* lies in the shaded region is ☐, or ☐ %.

Problem 4 **Using Area to Find Probability**

Got It? **Archery** An archery target has 5 scoring zones formed by concentric circles. The target's diameter is 122 cm. The radius of the middle zone is 12.2 cm. The width of each of the other zones is also 12.2 cm. If an arrow hits the target at a random point, what is the probability that it hits the middle zone?

21. The radius of the target is $\dfrac{\boxed{}}{2}$, or $\boxed{}$ cm.

22. Find the probability. Write the probability as a decimal.

$$P(\text{arrow hits middle zone}) = \frac{\text{area of middle zone}}{\text{area of entire target}}$$

$$= \frac{\pi(12.2)^2}{\pi(\boxed{})^2} = \frac{\boxed{}}{\boxed{}} = \boxed{}$$

23. Explain why the calculation with π is not an estimate.

_____

24. The probability that the arrow hits the middle zone is $\boxed{}$, or $\boxed{}$ %.

 ## Lesson Check • Do you UNDERSTAND?

Reasoning In the figure at the right, $\dfrac{SQ}{QT} = \dfrac{1}{2}$. What is the probability that a point on $\overline{ST}$ chosen at random will lie on $\overline{QT}$? Explain.

S   Q   T

25. If $SQ = x$, then $QT = \boxed{}$ and $ST = \boxed{}$.

26. What is $P(\text{point on } \overline{QT})$? Explain.

_____

Math Success

Check off the vocabulary words that you understand.

☐ length   ☐ area   ☐ geometric probability

Rate how well you can *use geometric probability*.

Lesson 10-8

11-1 Space Figures and Cross Sections

Vocabulary

● Review

Complete each statement with the correct word from the list.

edge   edges   vertex   vertices

1. A(n) _?_ is a segment that is formed by the intersections of two faces.

2. A(n) _?_ is a point where two or more *edges* intersect.

3. A cube has eight _?_ .

4. A cube has twelve _?_ .

● Vocabulary Builder

polyhedra

polyhedron (noun) **pahl ih HEE drun (plural: polyhedra)**

Related Words: face, edge, vertex

Definition: A *polyhedron* is a space figure, or three-dimensional figure, whose surfaces are polygons.

Origin: The word *polyhedron* combines the Greek prefix *poli-*, meaning "many," and *hedron*, meaning "base."

Examples: prism, pyramid

Non-Examples: circle, cylinder, sphere

Pyramid

Prism

● Use Your Vocabulary

5. Cross out the figure below that is NOT a *polyhedron*.

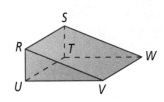

Problem 1 Identifying Vertices, Edges, and Faces

Got It? How many vertices, edges, and faces are in the polyhedron at the right? List them.

6. Identify each description as a *vertex*, an *edge*, or a *face*.

a point where three or more edges intersect
_____

polygon
_____

a segment where two or more faces intersect
_____

7. List the vertices.

8. List the edges. Remember to list the dashed hidden edges.

9. List the faces. Remember to list the hidden faces.

10. The polyhedron has ☐ vertices, ☐ edges, and ☐ faces.

Key Concept   Euler's Formula

The sum of the number of faces (F) and vertices (V) of a polyhedron is two more than the number of its edges (E).

$$F + V = E + 2$$

Problem 2 Using Euler's Formula

Got It? Use Euler's Formula to find the number of faces for a polyhedron with 30 edges and 20 vertices.

11. Use the justifications at the right to find the number of faces.

$F + V = E + 2$ — Use Euler's Formula.

$F + \boxed{} = \boxed{} + 2$ — Substitute with given information.

$F + \boxed{} = \boxed{}$ — Simplify.

$F = \boxed{} - \boxed{}$ — Subtraction Property of Equality

$F = \boxed{}$ — Simplify.

12. A polygon with 30 edges and 20 vertices has ☐ faces.

Lesson 11-1

Problem 3 Verifying Euler's Formula in Two Dimensions

Got It? Use the solid at the right. How can you verify Euler's Formula $F + V = E + 2$ for the solid?

13. Count the number of vertices.

[ ] on the bottom + [ ] on the top = [ ] vertices

14. Count the number of faces.

[ ] bases + [ ] lateral faces = [ ] faces

15. Count the number of edges.

[ ] solid edges + [ ] dashed hidden edges = [ ] edges

16. Now verify Euler's Formula for the values you found.

$F + V = E + 2$ Write Euler's Formula.

[ ] + [ ] = [ ] + 2   Substitute.

[ ] = [ ]   Simplify.

 Problem 4 Describing a Cross Section

Got It? For the solid at the right, what is the cross section formed by a horizontal plane?

Underline the correct word to complete each sentence.

17. A horizontal plane is parallel to the bottom / side of the solid.

18. A view from the side / top of the solid helps you see the shape of the cross section.

19. The cross section is a circle / trapezoid .

Problem 5 Drawing a Cross Section

Got It? Draw the cross section formed by a horizontal plane intersecting the left and right faces of the cube. What shape is the cross section?

20. A *horizontal* plane is parallel to which faces of the cube? Circle your answer.

front and back   left and right   top and bottom

21. Circle the diagram that shows the intersection of the horizontal plane and the left and right faces of the cube.

22. Use the cube to draw and shade the cross section.

23. The cross section is a ___?___

Lesson Check • Do you UNDERSTAND?

Vocabulary Suppose you build a polyhedron from two octagons and eight squares. Without using Euler's Formula, how many edges does the solid have? Explain.

24. Complete the problem-solving model below.

Know	Need	Plan
The octagons and squares are ___?___. An edge is a segment formed by the intersection of two ___?___.	To find the number of ___?___ without using Euler's Formula	Count the number of edges formed by the squares and the top octagon. Count the number of edges formed by the squares and the bottom octagon. Count the number of edges formed by the squares.

25. The intersections of the squares and the top octagon form [ ] edges.

26. The intersections of the squares and the bottom octagon form [ ] edges.

27. The intersection of the eight squares form [ ] edges.

28. The solid has [ ] + [ ] + [ ] = [ ] edges.

Math Success

Check off the vocabulary words that you understand.

☐ polyhedron   ☐ face   ☐ edge   ☐ vertex   ☐ cross section

Rate how well you can *recognize polyhedra and their parts*.

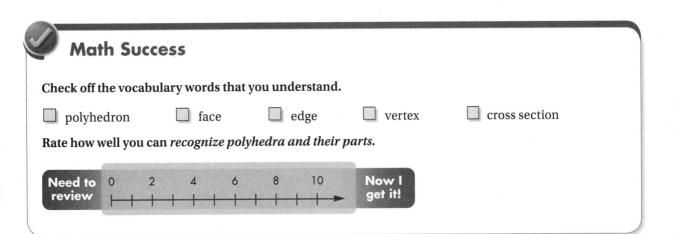

Need to review   0   2   4   6   8   10   Now I get it!

Lesson 11-1

Vocabulary

● Review

Write T for *true* or F for *false*.

1. A *lateral face* is a polygon surface of a solid.

2. *Lateral faces* are surfaces of a polyhedron.

3. A *lateral face* may be a circle.

4. A base is a *lateral face*.

● Vocabulary Builder

oblique (adjective) oh BLEEK

Definition: An **oblique** object is slanting, not straight.

Main Idea: **Oblique** means indirect and not straight to the point.

Other Word Forms: obliquely (adverb)

Math Usage: An **oblique** polyhedron has no vertical edge so an **oblique** prism is not a right prism.

● Use Your Vocabulary

5. Circle the *oblique* prism.

6. Circle the *oblique* cylinder.

7. Complete with *oblique* or *obliquely*.

A right prism is not an __?__ prism.

Your classmate answered the question __?__ .

Problem 1 **Using a Net to Find Surface Area of a Prism**

Got It? What is the surface area of the triangular prism? Use a net.

8. Label the missing dimensions in the net below.

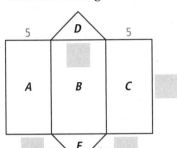

9. The altitude a of each triangle forms a right triangle with legs of lengths a cm and ▢ cm.

10. Use the Pythagorean Theorem to find a.

$$▢^2 + a^2 = 5^2$$

$$a^2 = 25 - ▢$$

$$a^2 = ▢$$

$$a = ▢$$

11. Find the surface area of the prism.

S.A. = L.A. + area of base

= areas of two lateral rectangles + areas of two lateral triangles + area of base

= (Area A + Area C) + (Area D + Area E) + Area B

$$= 5 \cdot ▢ + 5 \cdot ▢ + \frac{1}{2}(▢ \cdot ▢) + \frac{1}{2}(▢ \cdot ▢) + ▢ \cdot ▢$$

$$= ▢ + ▢ + ▢ + ▢$$

$$= ▢$$

12. The surface area of the triangular prism is ▢ cm^2.

Theorem 11-1 **Lateral and Surface Areas of a Prism**

The lateral area of a right prism is the product of the perimeter of the base and the height of the prism.

L.A. = ph

The surface area of a right prism is the sum of the lateral area and the areas of the two bases.

S.A. = L.A. + $2B$

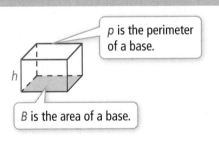

p is the perimeter of a base.

B is the area of a base.

13. Write the formula for S.A. using p and h.

S.A. = ▢ + $2B$

Lesson 11-2

Problem 2 Using Formulas to Find Surface Area of a Prism

Got It? What is the lateral area of the prism at the right?

14. Complete the flow chart below.

L.A. = *ph*

p = perimeter of base

= ☐ · ☐ = ☐

h = height of prism

= ☐

L.A. = ☐ · ☐

= ☐

12 m

6 m

15. The lateral area of the prism is ☐ m².

take note

Theorem 11–2 Lateral and Surface Areas of a Cylinder

16. Use the diagram at the right to complete the formulas below.

The lateral area of a right cylinder is the product of the circumference of the base and the height of the cylinder.

$$L.A. = 2\pi r \cdot h, \text{ or } L.A. = \pi \cdot \boxed{} \cdot h$$

The surface area of a right cylinder is the sum of the lateral area and the areas of the two bases.

$$S.A. = L.A. + 2B$$
$$= \boxed{} + 2\pi r^2$$

B is the area of a base.

Problem 3 Finding Surface Area of a Cylinder

Got It? A cylinder has a height of 9 cm and a radius of 10 cm. What is the surface area of the cylinder in terms of π?

17. Use the information in the problem to complete the reasoning model below.

Think	Write
I can use the formula for the surface area of a cylinder.	$S.A. = L.A. + 2B$
Then I can substitute the formulas for lateral area and area of a circle.	$= \boxed{} + 2 \cdot \boxed{}$
Next I substitute 10 for the radius and 9 for the height.	$= 2\pi \cdot \boxed{} \cdot \boxed{} + 2\pi \cdot \boxed{}^2$
Now I simplify.	$= \boxed{} \cdot \pi + \boxed{} \cdot \pi$ $= \boxed{} \cdot \pi$

18. The surface area of the cylinder is ☐ π cm².

Problem 4 Finding Lateral Area of a Cylinder

Got It? A stencil roller has a height of 1.5 in. and a diameter of 2.5 in. What area does the roller cover in one turn? Round your answer to the nearest tenth.

19. Underline the correct words to complete the sentence. The distance that is covered in one turn is the circumference / diameter of the circular base of the cylinder / prism .

20. Find the area the roller covers in one turn.

21. The roller covers about ___ in.² in one turn.

Lesson Check • Do you UNDERSTAND?

Vocabulary Name the lateral faces and the bases of the prism at the right.

22. Write the name of each of the ___ faces of the prism in the correct region of the Venn diagram.

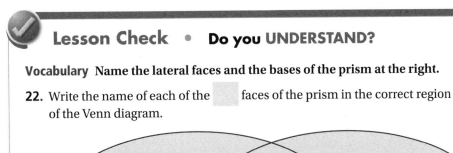

Congruent Faces

≅ and ‖ Faces

Parallel Faces

23. Name the bases of the prism.

24. Name the lateral faces of the prism.

Math Success

Check off the vocabulary words that you understand.

☐ right prism   ☐ oblique prism   ☐ right cylinder   ☐ oblique cylinder

Rate how well you can *find the surface area of a prism and a cylinder.*

Need to review   0   2   4   6   8   10   Now I get it!

Vocabulary

● **Review**

Label each diagram *cone* or *pyramid*.

1.

2.

3.

4.

● **Vocabulary Builder**

slant height (noun) **slant hyt**

slant height, ℓ

Related Words: regular pyramid, lateral face

Definition: The **slant height** ℓ of a regular pyramid is the length of the altitude of a lateral face of the pyramid. The **slant height** ℓ of a cone is the distance from the vertex of a cone to a point on the circumference of the base.

Math Usage: The **slant height** of a regular pyramid divides the lateral face into two congruent right triangles.

● **Use Your Vocabulary**

5. Circle the figure that shows a three-dimensional figure with *slant height* 5 m.

 5 m

 5 m

 5 m

6. Is the *slant height* the same as the *height* of a pyramid or cone?   Yes / No

7. The *slant height* of the cone at the right is ___ in.

2 in.   3 in.

Theorem 11-3   Lateral and Surface Areas of a Pyramid

The lateral area (L.A.) of a regular pyramid is half the product of the perimeter p of the base and the slant height ℓ of the pyramid.

The surface area (S.A.) of a regular pyramid is the sum of the lateral area and the area B of the base.

8. In a square pyramid with base side length s, $p = \boxed{}$.

9. If the base of a regular pyramid has a perimeter of $6q$ and its side length is 6, the pyramid has $\boxed{}$ sides.

Draw a line from each description in Column A to the corresponding formula in Column B.

Column A	Column B
10. lateral area (L.A.) of a pyramid	$\frac{1}{2}p\ell$
11. surface area (S.A.) of a pyramid	$\frac{1}{2}p\ell + B$

Problem 1   Finding the Surface Area of a Pyramid

Got It? A square pyramid has base edges of 5 m and a slant height of 3 m. What is the surface area of the pyramid?

12. Complete the problem-solving model below.

Know	Need	Plan
The base is a square with side length $\boxed{}$ m. Slant height ℓ is $\boxed{}$ m.	Lateral area Surface area	Find the perimeter $\boxed{}$ of the base. Find the area $\boxed{}$ of the base. Use p and ℓ to find $\boxed{}$ Use L.A. and B to find $\boxed{}$

13. Find p.

$p = 4(s)$

$= 4(\boxed{})$

$= \boxed{}$

14. Find B.

$B = s^2$

$= \boxed{}^2$

$= \boxed{}$

15. L.A. $= \frac{1}{2}p\ell$

$= \frac{1}{2}(\boxed{})(\boxed{})$

$= \boxed{}$

16. S.A. $=$ L.A. $+ B$

$= \boxed{} + \boxed{}$

$= \boxed{}$

17. The surface area of the pyramid is $\boxed{}$ m^2.

take note

Copyright © by Pearson Education, Inc. or its affiliates. All Rights Reserved.

295

Lesson 11-3

Problem 2 Finding the Lateral Area of a Pyramid

Got It? What is the lateral area of the hexagonal pyramid at the right? Round to the nearest square foot.

18. Circle the correct equation for the perimeter of the hexagonal base.

$$42 \cdot 36 = 1512 \qquad 6 \cdot 18 = 108 \qquad \frac{1}{2}(36)(18\sqrt{3}) \approx 561 \qquad 6 \cdot 36 = 216$$

19. The slant height ℓ of the pyramid is the hypotenuse of a right triangle. Label the legs of the right triangle at the right.

20. Use the Pythagorean Theorem to find the slant height ℓ of the pyramid.

$$\ell = \sqrt{\boxed{}^2 + \boxed{}^2}$$

$$= \sqrt{\boxed{} + \boxed{}}$$

$$= \sqrt{\boxed{}}$$

21. Use the formula L.A. $= \frac{1}{2}p\ell$ to find the lateral area of the pyramid.

$$\text{L.A.} = \frac{1}{2}(\boxed{})(\boxed{}) \approx \boxed{}$$

22. The lateral area of the hexagonal pyramid is about $\boxed{}$ ft².

take note

Theorem 11-4   Lateral and Surface Areas of a Cone

The lateral area of a right cone is half the product of the circumference of the base and the slant height of the cone.

$$\text{L.A.} = \frac{1}{2} \cdot 2\pi r \cdot \ell, \text{ or L.A.} = \pi r \ell$$

The surface area of a cone is the sum of the lateral area and the area of the base.

23. S.A. $=$ L.A. $+ \boxed{}$

Problem 3 Finding the Surface Area of a Cone

Got It? The radius of the base of a cone is 16 m. Its slant height is 28 m. What is the surface area in terms of π?

24. Use the justifications at the right to find the surface area.

$\text{S.A.} = \text{L.A.} + B$ Use the formula for surface area.

$\quad = \boxed{} + \boxed{}$ Substitute the formulas for L.A. and B.

$\quad = \pi(\boxed{})(\boxed{}) + \pi(\boxed{})^2$ Substitute for r and for ℓ.

$\quad = \pi(\boxed{}) + \pi(\boxed{})$ Simplify.

$\quad = \pi(\boxed{})$ Add.

25. The surface area of the cone in terms of π is $\boxed{}$ m².

Chapter 11

Problem 4 **Finding the Lateral Area of a Cone**

Got It? What is the lateral area of a traffic cone with radius 10 in. and height 28 in.? Round to the nearest whole number.

26. Let ℓ be the slant height of the cone. Label the missing dimensions on the cone at the right.

27. Use the Pythagorean Theorem to find ℓ.

$$\ell = \sqrt{\boxed{}^2 + \boxed{}^2}$$

$$= \sqrt{\boxed{} + \boxed{}}$$

$$= \sqrt{\boxed{}}$$

28. Use the formula for lateral area of a cone.

$$L.A. = \pi(\boxed{})(\boxed{})$$

$$= \pi(\boxed{})(\boxed{})$$

$$\approx \boxed{}$$

29. To the nearest square inch, the lateral area of the traffic cone is $\boxed{}$ in.^{2}.

Lesson Check • **Do you UNDERSTAND?**

Compare and Contrast How are the formulas for the surface area of a prism and the surface area of a pyramid alike? How are they different?

30. Use the descriptions in the list at the right. Write the letter for each description under the correct polyhedron.

Prism	Pyramid

A. Base is a polygon.

B. Faces are rectangles.

C. Faces are triangles.

D. S.A. = L.A. + B

E. S.A. = L.A. + 2B

F. Uses height

G. Uses perimeter

H. Uses slant height

31. How are the formulas alike? How are they different?

_____

_____

_____

_____

Math Success

Check off the vocabulary words that you understand.

☐ pyramid   ☐ slant height   ☐ lateral area   ☐ surface area   ☐ cone

Rate how well you can *find the surface area of pyramids and cones.*

Need to review   0   2   4   6   8   10   Now I get it!

Volumes of Prisms and Cylinders

Vocabulary

● Review

Label each diagram *cylinder* or *prism*.

1.

2.

3.

4.

● Vocabulary Builder

composite (adjective, noun) **kum PAHZ it**

Related Words: compound, combination, component

Definition: **Composite** means put together with distinct parts.

Main Idea: A **composite** is a whole made up of different parts.

● Use Your Vocabulary

Complete each statement with the correct phrase from the list below. Use each phrase only once.

composite function   *composite* map   *composite* number   *composite* sketch

5. A __?__ combines different descriptions of features.

6. A __?__ has factors other than one and the number.

7. A __?__ shows the locations of shopping malls, houses, and roads in one illustration.

8. A __?__ shows how to apply at least one function to another function.

take note

Theorem 11-5 Cavalieri's Principle

If two space figures have the same height and the same cross-sectional area at every level, then they have the same volume.

9. The three prisms below have the same height and the same volume. The first is a square prism. Label the missing dimensions.

10. Circle the solid(s) that may have the same cross-sectional area at every level.

cone   cylinder   prism   pyramid

take note

Theorem 11-6 Volume of a Prism

The volume of a prism is the product of the area of the base and the height of the prism.

$V = Bh$

11. A prism with a base area of 15 m² and a height 4 m has a volume of ▢ m³.

12. A prism with a volume of 81 ft³ and a height of 3 ft has a base area of ▢ ft².

 Problem 1 Finding the Volume of a Rectangular Prism

Got It? What is the volume of the rectangular prism at the right?

13. Circle the measurements of a base of the prism.

3 ft × 4 ft   3 ft × 5 ft   4 ft × 5 ft

14. Underline the correct word to complete the sentence.

The base is a rectangle / square .

15. Find *B*.

$B = $ ▢ · ▢

$= $ ▢ · ▢

$= $ ▢

16. Find *V*.

$V = $ ▢ · ▢

$= $ ▢ · ▢

$= $ ▢

17. Underline the correct word to complete the sentence.

The units for this volume are cubic / square feet .

18. The volume of the prism is ▢ .

Lesson 11-4

Problem 2 Finding the Volume of a Triangular Prism

Got It? What is the volume of the triangular prism at the right?

19. The base is a right triangle with legs of length ☐ m and ☐ m.

20. The height of the prism is ☐ m.

21. Complete the formula for volume of a prism. $V = $ ☐ $\cdot$ ☐

22. Find the area of the base.

$$A = \frac{1}{2} \cdot \boxed{} \cdot \boxed{}$$

$$= \frac{1}{2} \cdot \boxed{}$$

$$= \boxed{}$$

23. Find the volume of the prism.

$$V = \boxed{} \cdot \boxed{}$$

$$= \boxed{}$$

24. The volume of the triangular prism is ☐ m^3.

> **take note**

Theorem 11-7 Volume of a Cylinder

The volume of a cylinder is the product of the area of the base and the height of the cylinder.

$$V = Bh, \text{ or } V = \pi r^2 h$$

25. Shade a base of the cylinder at the right.

26. Describe the shape of the base.

Problem 3 Finding the Volume of a Cylinder

Got It? What is the volume of the cylinder at the right in terms of π?

27. Compete the reasoning model below.

Think	Write
First I need to find the radius.	$r = \dfrac{\boxed{}}{2} = \boxed{}$
I can use the formula $V = \pi r^2 h$ and substitute for r and h.	$V = \pi \cdot \boxed{}^{2} \cdot \boxed{}$
Now I simplify.	$V = \pi \cdot \boxed{}$

28. The volume of the cylinder is ☐ m^3.

Got It? What is the approximate volume of the lunch box shown at the right? Round to the nearest cubic inch.

3 in.
6 in.
6 in.
10 in.

29. The top and bottom of the lunch box are sketched below. Label the dimensions.

30. Find the volume of the top.

$V = \frac{1}{2}\pi r^2 h$

$= \frac{1}{2}\pi(\boxed{}^2)(\boxed{})$

$= \boxed{}$

31. Find the volume of the bottom.

$V = Bh$

$= (\boxed{} \cdot \boxed{})(\boxed{})$

$= \boxed{}$

32. Find the sum of the volumes.

$V = \boxed{}\ \pi + \boxed{}$

$\approx \boxed{}$

33. The approximate volume of the lunch box is $\boxed{}$ in.³.

✓ **Lesson Check** • **Do you UNDERSTAND?**

Reasoning How is the volume of a rectangular prism with base 2 m by 3 m and height 4 m related to the volume of a rectangular prism with base 3 m by 4 m and height 2 m? Explain.

34. Cross out the formula that does NOT give the volume of a rectangular prism.

$V = Bh$	$V = \pi r^2 h$	$V = \ell wh$

35. The Commutative / Identity Property of Multiplication states that the product of factors is the same when listed in a different order.

36. Now answer the question.

_____

✓ **Math Success**

Check off the vocabulary words that you understand.

☐ volume ☐ composite space figure

Rate how well you can *find the volume of prisms and cylinders*.

Need to review   0   2   4   6   8   10   Now I get it!

11-5 Volumes of Pyramids and Cones

Vocabulary

● **Review**

1. Write *L*, *W*, or *H* to label the *length*, *width*, and *height* of the rectangular prism at the right.

2. Explain how the *length, width*, and *height* of a cube are related.

_____

Circle the correct statement in each exercise.

3. The *width* of a cylinder is the radius of a base of the cylinder.

   The *height* of a cylinder is the *length* of an altitude of the cylinder.

4. The *height* of a pyramid is the length of a segment perpendicular to the base.

   The slant *height* of a pyramid is the length of a segment perpendicular to the base.

● **Vocabulary Builder**

| **volume** (noun) VAHL **yoom** |

Related Word: capacity

Main Idea: **Volume** measures quantity of space or amount, such as loudness of sound or a collection of books.

Definition: **Volume** is the amount of space that a three-dimensional figure occupies, measured in cubic units.

Example: The **volume** of a bottle of juice is 2 liters.

● **Use Your Vocabulary**

Write T for *true* or F for *false*.

_____ 5. A synonym for *volume* is capacity.

_____ 6. *Volume* is measured in square units.

_____ 7. You can find the *volume* of a circle.

Chapter 11

302

Copyright © by Pearson Education, Inc. or its affiliates. All Rights Reserved.

Theorem 11-8   Volume of a Pyramid

The volume of a pyramid is one third the product of the area of the base and the height of the pyramid.

8. Complete the formula for the volume of a pyramid.

$$V = \boxed{} \cdot Bh$$

Theorem 11-9   Volume of a Cone

The volume of a cone is one third the product of the area of the base and the height of the cone.

$$V = \frac{1}{3} Bh$$

9. Circle an equivalent formula for the volume of a cone.

$$V = \frac{1}{3}\pi r^2 h \qquad\qquad V = \frac{1}{3} \cdot 2\pi r \cdot h$$

Write the formula for the volume of each figure below.

10.

$$V = \frac{1}{3} \cdot \boxed{} \cdot \boxed{}$$

11.

$$V = \boxed{}$$

Problem 1   Finding Volume of a Pyramid

Got It? A sports arena shaped like a pyramid has a base area of about 300,000 ft² and a height of 321 ft. What is the approximate volume of the arena?

12. Complete the problem-solving model below.

Know	Need	Plan
$B \approx \boxed{}$ $h = \boxed{}$	Volume of the pyramid	Substitute the given values into the formula $\boxed{}$.

13. Solve for V.

14. The approximate volume of the arena is $\boxed{}$ ft³.

Lesson 11-5

Problem 2 Finding the Volume of a Pyramid

Got It? What is the volume of a square pyramid with base edges 24 m and slant height 13 m?

15. Label the pyramid at the right.

16. Find the height of the pyramid.

$$13^2 = h^2 + \boxed{}\,^2$$

$$169 = h^2 + \boxed{}$$

$$h^2 = \boxed{}$$

$$h = \boxed{}$$

17. Find the area of the base.

$$B = \boxed{} \cdot \boxed{}$$

$$= \boxed{}$$

18. Find the volume of the pyramid.

$$V = \boxed{} \cdot Bh$$

$$= \boxed{} \cdot \boxed{} \cdot \boxed{}$$

$$= \boxed{}$$

19. The volume of the pyramid is $\boxed{}$ m^3.

Problem 3 Finding the Volume of a Cone

Got It? A small child's teepee is 6 ft high with a base diameter of 7 ft. What is the volume of the child's teepee to the nearest cubic foot?

20. Label the cone at the right with the dimensions of the teepee.

21. The radius of the teepee is $\boxed{}$ ft.

22. Use the justifications to find the volume of the teepee.

$$V = \boxed{}$$ Use the formula with π for the volume of a cone.

$$V = \boxed{}$$ Substitute for r and h.

$$= \boxed{}$$ Square the radius.

$$= \boxed{}$$ Simplify in terms of π.

$$\approx \boxed{}$$ Use a calculator.

23. The volume of the child's teepee to the nearest cubic foot is $\boxed{}$ ft^3.

Problem 4 Finding the Volume of an Oblique Cone

Got It? What is the volume of the oblique cone at the right in terms of π and rounded to the nearest cubic meter?

12 m

6 m

24. The radius of the base is $\boxed{}$ m and the height is $\boxed{}$ m.

25. Cross out the formula that is NOT a formula for the volume of a cone.

$$V = \tfrac{1}{3}Bh \qquad\qquad V = Bh \qquad\qquad V = \tfrac{1}{3}\pi r^2 h$$

Chapter 11

304

26. Find the volume of the cone.

27. The volume of the cone in terms of π is ▢ m^3.

Rounded to the nearest cubic meter, the volume of the cone is ▢ m^3.

Lesson Check • Do you UNDERSTAND?

Error Analysis A square pyramid has base edges 13 ft and height 10 ft. A cone has diameter 13 ft and height 10 ft. Your friend claims the figures have the same volume because the volume formulas for a pyramid and a cone are the same: $V = \frac{1}{3}Bh$. What is her error?

28. Is $V = \frac{1}{3}Bh$ the volume formula for both a pyramid and a cone? Yes / No

Underline the correct word to complete each sentence.

29. The base of a square pyramid is a circle / polygon .

30. The base of a cone is a circle / polygon .

31. Circle the base used in the formula for the volume of a cone. Underline the base used in the formula for the volume of a square pyramid.

$$B = \pi r^2 \qquad\qquad B = \frac{1}{2}bh \qquad\qquad B = s^2$$

32. Now explain your friend's error.

_____

_____

Math Success

Check off the vocabulary words that you understand.

☐ pyramid   ☐ cone   ☐ oblique   ☐ volume

Rate how well you can *find the volumes of pyramids and cones*.

Need to review   0   2   4   6   8   10   Now I get it!

Lesson 11-5

11-6 Surface Areas and Volumes of Spheres

Vocabulary

● **Review**

Underline the correct word to complete each sentence.

1. The *diameter / radius* of the circle at the right is 5 cm.

2. The circumference of a circle is the product of its *diameter / radius* and π.

3. The *diameter / radius* of a circle is a segment containing the center with endpoints on the circle.

● **Vocabulary Builder**

sphere

sphere (noun) **sfeer**

Related Words: spherical (adjective), hemisphere (noun)

Main Idea: A **sphere** is formed by the revolution of a circle about its diameter.

Definition: A **sphere** is the set of all points in space equidistant from a given point called the *center*.

Example: A basketball is a **sphere**.

Non-Example: A football is not a **sphere**.

● **Use Your Vocabulary**

4. Complete each statement with *sphere* or *spherical*.

   ADJECTIVE   Each _?_ candy looks like a rock.

   NOUN   A baseball is in the shape of a _?_ .

Write T for *true* or F for *false*.

_____ 5. Celestial bodies such as the sun or Earth are often represented as *spheres*.

_____ 6. A *sphere* is a two-dimensional figure.

Theorem 11-10 Surface Area of a Sphere

The surface area of a sphere is four times the product of π and the square of the radius of the sphere.

7. Complete: S.A. = ▢ · ▢ · ▢^{2}

✓ **Problem 1** Finding the Surface Area of a Sphere

Got It? What is the surface area of a sphere with a diameter of 14 in.? Give your answer in terms of π and rounded to the nearest square inch.

8. The radius of the sphere is ▢ in.

9. Find the surface area.

S.A. = $4\pi($▢$)^2$ Use the formula for surface area of a sphere.

    = $4\pi($▢$)^2$ Substitute for r.

    = $\pi($▢$)$ Simplify.

    ≈ ▢   Use a calculator.

10. The surface area in terms of π is ▢ π in.^{2}, or about ▢ in.^{2}.

✓ **Problem 2** Finding Surface Area

Got It? What is the surface area of a melon with circumference 18 in.? Round your answer to the nearest ten square inches.

11. Complete the problem-solving model below.

Know	Need	Plan
The circumference is ▢ in.	The radius r of the sphere The surface area of the sphere	Solve the formula for circumference for ▢. Substitute ▢ into the formula for surface area of a sphere.

12. Find r in terms of π.

$C = 2\pi r$

13. Use your value for r to find the surface area.

S.A. = $4\pi r^2$

14. To the nearest ten square inches, the surface area of the melon is ▢ in.^{2}.

Lesson 11-6

Theorem 11-11   Volume of a Sphere

15. Complete the model below.

Relate | The volume of a sphere | is | four thirds the product of π and the cube of the radius of the sphere. |

Write V =

Draw a line from each measure in Column A to its corresponding formula in Column B.

Column A	Column B
16. surface area of a sphere	$\frac{4}{3}\pi r^3$
17. volume of a sphere	$4\pi r^2$

Problem 3 Finding the Volume of a Sphere

Got It? A sphere has a diameter of 60 in. What is its volume to the nearest cubic inch?

18. Complete the missing information in the diagram.

The volume is $\frac{4}{3}\pi r^3$.

The diameter is 60 in., so the radius is ___ in.

19. Complete to find the volume.

$V = \frac{4}{3}\pi(\quad)^3$

$\quad = \frac{4}{3}\pi(\qquad)$

$\quad = \pi(\qquad)$

$\quad \approx \boxed{\qquad}$

20. The volume is about ___ in.^{3}.

Problem 4 Using Volume to Find Surface Area

Got It? The volume of a sphere is 4200 ft^3. What is its surface area to the nearest tenth?

21. Circle the correct formula for the volume of a sphere.

$V = \frac{4}{3}\pi r^2$ $V = \frac{4}{3}\pi r^3$

22. Complete the reasoning model below.

Think	Write
I need to solve the volume formula for the radius.	$V = \frac{4}{3}\pi r^3$
I can substitute the given volume into the formula.	$\boxed{} = \frac{4}{3}\pi r^3$
Now, I can solve for r^3.	$\boxed{}$
If I take the cube root of both sides, I can solve for r. I need to use a calculator to simplify.	$\sqrt[3]{\boxed{}} = r$ $\boxed{} \approx r$
Then, I can substitute r into the formula for surface area of a sphere.	$\text{S.A.} = 4\pi \cdot \boxed{}^2$
Finally, I can simplify.	$\text{S.A.} \approx \boxed{}$

23. To the nearest tenth of a foot, the surface area is $\boxed{}$ ft^2.

Lesson Check • Do you UNDERSTAND?

Vocabulary What is the ratio of the area of a great circle to the surface area of the sphere?

24. A great circle is a circle whose center is the center of the __?__. $\boxed{}$

25. $A = \boxed{}$

26. S.A. $= \boxed{}$

27. The ratio is $\dfrac{\boxed{}}{\boxed{}}$, or $\dfrac{\boxed{}}{\boxed{}}$.

Math Success

Check off the vocabulary words that you understand.

☐ sphere (radius, diameter, circumference)   ☐ great circle   ☐ hemisphere

Rate how well you can *find surface area and volume of a sphere*.

Need to review 0 2 4 6 8 10 Now I get it!

Lesson 11-6

Vocabulary

● **Review**

Complete each statement with the appropriate word from the list. Use each word only once.

similar   similarities   similarity   similarly

1. There are several __?__ house styles in the neighborhood.

2. The sequel may end __?__ to the original movie.

3. There is not one __?__ between his first and second drawings.

4. You could find several __?__ between the two video games.

● **Vocabulary Builder**

scale factor (noun) **skayl FAK tur**

Main Idea: The **scale factor** for similar polygons is the ratio of the lengths of their corresponding sides.

Definition: The **scale factor** for two similar solids is the ratio of their corresponding linear dimensions.

Example: The **scale factor** of a map may be 1 inch : 5 miles.

● **Use Your Vocabulary**

Write T for *true* or F for *false*.

_____ **5.** You can find the *scale factor* for any two figures.

_____ **6.** You can find the *scale factor* for similar figures.

_____ **7.** You can write a *scale factor* as a ratio $(a : b)$ or as a fraction $\left(\frac{a}{b}\right)$.

_____ **8.** A *scale factor* is always written as the ratio $a : b$.

Problem 1 Identifying Similar Solids

Got It? Are the two cylinders similar? If so, what is the scale factor of the first figure to the second figure?

Underline the correct word to complete each sentence.

9. You can check whether prisms are similar by comparing the ratios of **two / three** dimensions.

10. You can check whether cylinders are similar by comparing the ratios of **two / three** dimensions.

11. Always compare the ratios of **corresponding / similar** dimensions.

12. The ratio of the height of the larger cylinder to the height of the smaller cylinder

    is $\dfrac{}{}$. Simplified, this ratio is $\dfrac{}{}$.

13. The ratio of the radius of the larger cylinder to the radius of the smaller cylinder

    is $\dfrac{}{}$.

14. Underline the correct words to complete the sentence. The ratios you found in Exercises 12 and 13 **are/are not** equal, so the cylinders **are/are not** similar.

15. The scale factor is [   ].

take note

Theorem 11-12   Areas and Volumes of Similar Solids

If the scale factor of two similar solids is $a : b$, then

- the ratio of their corresponding areas is $a^2 : b^2$
- the ratio of their volumes is $a^3 : b^3$

16. Complete the model below.

17. If the scale factor of two similar solids is $1 : 2$, then the ratio of their corresponding

    areas is [   ]^2 : [   ]^2, or [   ] : [   ].

18. If the scale factor of two similar solids is $1 : 2$, then the ratio of their corresponding

    volumes is [   ]^3 : [   ]^3, or [   ] : [   ].

Lesson 11-7

Problem 2 Finding the Scale Factor

Got It? What is the scale factor of two similar prisms with surface areas 144 m² and 324 m²?

19. Complete the reasoning model below.

Think	Write
I can write the ratio of the lesser surface area to the greater surface area.	$\dfrac{a^2}{b^2} = \dfrac{\boxed{}}{\boxed{}}$
I can take the square roots of the surface areas and write the scale factor as $a:b$.	$\sqrt{\dfrac{a^2}{b^2}} = \dfrac{a}{b} = \dfrac{\boxed{}}{\boxed{}}$

20. The scale factor is $\boxed{} : \boxed{}$, which can be simplified to $\boxed{} : \boxed{}$.

Problem 3 Using a Scale Factor

Got It? The volumes of two similar solids are 128 m³ and 250 m³. The surface area of the larger solid is 250 m². What is the surface area of the smaller solid?

21. Let $\dfrac{a}{b}$ represent the scale factor of the similar solids. Circle the simplified ratio of the volume of the smaller solid to the volume of the larger solid.

$$\dfrac{a^3}{b^3} = \dfrac{64}{125} \qquad\qquad \dfrac{a}{b} = \dfrac{64}{125} \qquad\qquad \dfrac{a^3}{b^3} = \dfrac{125}{64}$$

22. Find the scale factor $a:b$.

$$\dfrac{a}{b} = \dfrac{\sqrt[3]{\boxed{}}}{\sqrt[3]{\boxed{}}} = \dfrac{\boxed{}}{\boxed{}}$$

23. Use the scale factor to find the ratio of surface areas.

$$\dfrac{a^2}{b^2} = \dfrac{\boxed{}^2}{\boxed{}^2} = \dfrac{\boxed{}}{\boxed{}}$$

24. Circle the proportion that compares the surface area of the smaller solid to the surface area of the larger solid.

$$\dfrac{a^2}{b^2} = \dfrac{x}{250} \qquad\qquad \dfrac{a}{b} = \dfrac{x}{250} \qquad\qquad \dfrac{a^2}{b^2} = \dfrac{250}{x}$$

25. Now solve for x.

26. The surface area of the smaller solid is $\boxed{}$ m².

Problem 4 **Using a Scale Factor to Find Capacity**

Got It? A marble paperweight shaped like a pyramid weighs 0.15 lb. How much does a similarly shaped marble paperweight weigh if each dimension is three times as large?

27. The scale factor of small paperweight to large paperweight is 1 : ___ .

28. Let $x =$ the weight of the larger paperweight. Use the justifications at the right to find the value of x.

$$\frac{1^3}{\boxed{}^3} = \frac{0.15}{x}$$ The weights are proportional to their volumes.

$$\frac{1}{\boxed{}} = \frac{0.15}{x}$$ Simplify.

$$x = \boxed{}$$ Use the Cross Products Property.

29. The paperweight that is three times as large weighs ___ lb.

 Lesson Check • **Do you UNDERSTAND?**

Error Analysis Two cubes have surface areas 49 cm² and 64 cm². Your classmate tried to find the scale factor of the larger cube to the smaller cube. Explain and correct your classmate's error.

$$\frac{a^2}{b^2} = \frac{49}{64}$$

$$\frac{a}{b} = \frac{7}{8}$$

The scale factor of the larger cube to the smaller cube is 7 : 8.

Underline the correct word(s) to complete each sentence.

30. The larger cube has the greater / lesser surface area.

31. The scale factor of larger cube to smaller cube is greater / less than the scale factor of smaller cube to larger cube.

32. Your classmate found the scale factor of the smaller / larger cube to the smaller / larger cube.

33. Find the correct scale factor.

Begin with the proportion $\frac{a^2}{b^2} = \frac{\boxed{}}{\boxed{}}$. Then, $\frac{a}{b} = \frac{\boxed{}}{\boxed{}}$.

Math Success

Check off the vocabulary words that you understand.

☐ similar solids   ☐ scale factor

Rate how well you can *find and use scale factors of similar solids.*

Lesson 11-7

12-1 Tangent Lines

Vocabulary

● Review

1. Cross out the word that does NOT apply to a *circle*.

| arc | circumference | diameter | equilateral | radius |

2. Circle the word for a segment with one endpoint at the center of a *circle* and the other endpoint on the *circle*.

| arc | circumference | diameter | perimeter | radius |

● Vocabulary Builder

tangent

tangent (noun, adjective) TAN junt

Definition: A **tangent** to a circle is a line, ray, or segment in the plane of the circle that intersects the circle in exactly one point.

Other Word Form: tangency (noun)

Examples: In the diagram, $\overleftrightarrow{AB}$ is **tangent** to the circle at *B*. *B* is the *point of tangency*. $\overrightarrow{BA}$ is a **tangent** ray. $\overline{BA}$ is a **tangent** segment.

Other Usage: In a right triangle, the **tangent** is the ratio of the side opposite an acute angle to the side adjacent to the angle.

● Use Your Vocabulary

3. Complete each statement with *always*, *sometimes*, or *never*.

A diameter is __?__ a *tangent*.

A *tangent* and a circle __?__ have exactly one point in common.

A radius can __?__ be drawn to the point of tangency.

A *tangent* __?__ passes through the center of a circle.

A *tangent* is __?__ a ray.

Theorems 12-1, 12-2, and 12-3

Theorem 12-1 If a line is tangent to a circle, then the line is perpendicular to the radius at the point of tangency.

Theorem 12-2 If a line in the plane of a circle is perpendicular to a radius at its endpoint on the circle, then the line is tangent to the circle.

Theorem 12-3 If two tangent segments to a circle share a common endpoint outside the circle, then the two segments are congruent.

Use the diagram at the right for Exercises 4–6. Complete each statement.

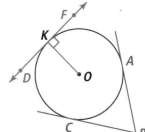

4. Theorem 12-1 If $\overleftrightarrow{DF}$ is tangent to $\odot O$ at K, then ⬜ $\perp$ ⬜ .

5. Theorem 12-2 If $\overleftrightarrow{DF} \perp \overline{OK}$, then ⬜ is tangent to $\odot O$.

6. Theorem 12-3 If $\overline{BA}$ and $\overline{BC}$ are tangent to $\odot O$, then ⬜ $\cong$ ⬜ .

✓ **Problem 1** Finding Angle Measures

Got It? $\overline{ED}$ is tangent to $\odot O$. What is the value of x?

7. Circle the word that best describes $\overline{OD}$.

diameter	radius	tangent

8. What relationship does Theorem 12-1 support? Circle your answer.

$\overline{OD} \perp \overline{ED}$	$\overline{OD} \parallel \overline{ED}$	$\overline{OD} \cong \overline{ED}$

9. Circle the most accurate description of the triangle.

acute	isosceles	obtuse	right

10. Circle the theorem that you will use to solve for x.

Theorem 12-1	Triangle Angle-Sum Theorem

11. Complete the model below.

Relate	sum of angle measures in a triangle	is	38	plus	measure of $\angle D$	plus	measure of $\angle E$
Write	⬜	=	38	+	⬜	+	⬜

12. Solve for x.

13. The value of x is ⬜ .

Lesson 12-1

Got It? What is the distance to the horizon that a person can see on a clear day from an airplane 2 mi above Earth? Earth's radius is about 4000 mi.

14. The diagram at the right shows the airplane at point A and the horizon at point H. Use the information in the problem to label the distances.

15. Use the justifications at the right to find the distance.

☐ $\perp \overline{AH}$	Theorem 12-1
☐$^2 + AH^2 = OA^2$	Pythagorean Theorem
☐$^2 + AH^2 = $ ☐^{2}	Substitute.
☐ $+ AH^2 = $ ☐	Use a calculator.
$AH^2 = $ ☐	Subtract from each side.
$AH = \sqrt{\boxed{}}$	Take the positive square root.
$AH \approx $ ☐	Use a calculator.

16. A person can see about ☐ miles to the horizon from an airplane 2 mi above Earth.

Got It? What is the radius of $\odot O$?

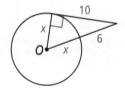

17. Write an algebraic or numerical expression for each side of the triangle.

☐   ☐   ☐

18. Circle the longest side of the triangle. Underline the side that is opposite the right angle.

10	x	$x + 6$

19. Use the Pythagorean Theorem to complete the equation.

☐$^2 + $ ☐$^2 = ($ ☐ $)^2$

20. Solve the equation for x.

21. The radius is ☐ .

Got It? ⊙*O* is inscribed in △*PQR*, which has a perimeter of 88 cm. What is the length of $\overline{QY}$?

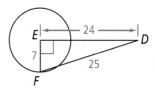

22. By Theorem 12-3, $\overline{PX} \cong$ ▢ , $\overline{RZ} \cong$ ▢ , and $\overline{QX} \cong$ ▢ , so *PX* = ▢ ,

   RZ = ▢ , and *QX* = ▢ .

23. Perimeter *p* = *PQ* + *QR* + *RP*, so *p* = *PX* + ▢ + *QY* + ▢ + *RZ* + ▢
by the Segment Addition Postulate.

24. Use the values in the diagram and your answer to Exercise 23 to solve for *QY*.

 Lesson Check • **Do you UNDERSTAND?**

Error Analysis A classmate insists that $\overline{DF}$ is a tangent to ⊙*E*. Explain how to show that your classmate is wrong.

Underline the correct word or number to complete the sentence.

25. A tangent to a circle is parallel / perpendicular to a radius.

26. If $\overline{DF}$ is tangent to ⊙*E* at point *F*, then $m\angle EFD$ must be 30 / 90 / 180 .

27. A triangle can have at most ▢ right angle(s).

28. Explain why your classmate is wrong.

_____

_____

 Math Success

Check off the vocabulary words that you understand.

☐ circle   ☐ tangent to a circle   ☐ point of tangency

Rate how well you can *use tangents to find missing lengths*.

Lesson 12-1

Vocabulary

● Review

Circle the *converse* of each statement.

1. Statement: If I am happy, then I sing.

If I sing, then I am happy.	If I am not happy, then I do not sing.
If I do not sing, then I am not happy.	

2. Statement: If parallel lines are cut by a transversal, then alternate interior angles are congruent.

If lines cut by a transversal are not parallel, then alternate interior angles are not congruent.	If lines cut by a transversal form alternate interior angles that are not congruent, then the lines are not parallel.	If lines cut by a transversal form alternate interior angles that are congruent, then the lines are parallel.

● Vocabulary Builder

chord (noun) **kawrd**

Definition: A **chord** is a segment whose endpoints are on a circle.

Related Word: arc

chord $\overline{RS}$

● Use Your Vocabulary

3. Complete each statement with *always*, *sometimes*, or *never*.

A *chord* is __?__ a diameter.

A diameter is __?__ a *chord*.

A radius is __?__ a *chord*.

A *chord* __?__ has a related arc.

An arc is __?__ a semicircle.

Theorems 12-4, 12-5, 12-6 and Their Converses

Theorem 12-4 Within a circle or in congruent circles, congruent central angles have congruent arcs.

4. If ∠AOB ≅ [blank] , then $\overset{\frown}{AB}$ ≅ $\overset{\frown}{CD}$.

Converse Within a circle or in congruent circles, congruent arcs have congruent central angles.

5. If $\overset{\frown}{AB}$ ≅ $\overset{\frown}{CD}$, then ∠AOB ≅ [blank] .

Theorem 12-5 Within a circle or in congruent circles, congruent central angles have congruent chords.

6. If ∠AOB ≅ ∠COD, then $\overline{AB}$ ≅ [blank] .

Converse Within a circle or in congruent circles, congruent chords have congruent central angles.

7. If $\overline{AB}$ ≅ $\overline{CD}$, then [blank] ≅ ∠COD.

Theorem 12-6 Within a circle or in congruent circles, congruent chords have congruent arcs.

8. If $\overline{AB}$ ≅ [blank] , then $\overset{\frown}{AB}$ ≅ $\overset{\frown}{CD}$.

Converse Within a circle or in congruent circles, congruent arcs have congruent chords.

9. If $\overset{\frown}{AB}$ ≅ [blank] , then $\overline{AB}$ ≅ $\overline{CD}$.

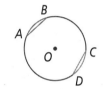

Problem 1 **Using Congruent Chords**

Got It? Use the diagram at the right. Suppose you are given ⊙O ≅ ⊙P and ∠OBC ≅ ∠PDF. How can you show ∠O ≅ ∠P? From this, what else can you conclude?

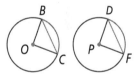

10. Complete the flow chart below to explain your conclusions.

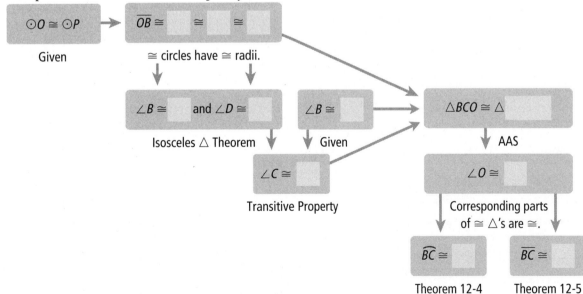

Lesson 12-2

Theorem 12-7 and Its Converse, Theorems 12-8, 12-9, 12-10

Theorem 12-7 Within a circle or in congruent circles, chords equidistant from the center or centers are congruent.

Converse Within a circle or in congruent circles, congruent chords are equidistant from the center (or centers).

11. If $OE = OF$, then $\overline{AB} \cong$ [ ].

12. If $\overline{AB} \cong$ [ ], then $OE =$ [ ].

Theorem 12-8 In a circle, if a diameter is perpendicular to a chord, then it bisects the chord and its arc.

13. If $\overline{AB}$ is a diameter and $\overline{AB} \perp \overline{CD}$, then $\overline{CE} \cong$ [ ] and $\overarc{CA} \cong$ [ ].

Theorem 12-9 In a circle, if a diameter bisects a chord (that is not a diameter), then it is perpendicular to the chord.

14. If $\overline{AB}$ is a diameter and $\overline{CE} \cong \overline{ED}$, then $\overline{AB} \perp$ [ ].

Theorem 12-10 In a circle, the perpendicular bisector of a chord contains the center of the circle.

15. If $\overline{AB}$ is the perpendicular bisector of chord $\overline{CD}$, then [ ] contains the center of $\odot O$.

✓ Problem 2 Finding the Length of a Chord

Got It? What is the value of x? Justify your answer.

16. What is the measure of each chord? Explain.

_____

_____

_____

_____

17. Circle the reason why the chords are congruent.

| Chords that have equal measures are congruent. | Chords that are equidistant from the center of a circle are congruent. |

18. Circle the theorem that you will use to find the value of x.

| Theorem 12-5 | Theorem 12-7 | Converse of Theorem 12-7 |
| Theorem 12-8 | Theorem 12-10 | |

19. Circle the distances from the center of a circle to the chords.

| 16 | 18 | 36 | x |

20. The value of x is [ ].

Problem 3 Using Diameters and Chords

Got It? The diagram shows the tracing of a quarter. What is its radius?

Underline the correct word to complete each sentence. Then do each step.

21. First draw two chords / tangents .

22. Next construct one / two perpendicular bisector(s).

23. Label the intersection *C*. It is the circle's center / chord .

24. Measure the diameter / radius .   **25.** The radius is about ____ mm.

 Problem 4 Finding Measures in a Circle

Got It? Reasoning In finding *y*, how does the auxiliary $\overline{BA}$ make the problem simpler to solve?

26. $\overline{BA}$ is the hypotenuse of a right __?__ , so you can use the __?__ Theorem to solve for *y*.

_____   _____

Lesson Check • **Do you UNDERSTAND?**

Vocabulary Is a radius a chord? Is a diameter a chord? Explain your answers.

27. Circle the name(s) of figure(s) that have two endpoints on a circle. Underline the name(s) of figure(s) that have one endpoint on a circle.

| chord | diameter | radius | ray | segment |

28. Is a radius a chord? Is a diameter a chord? Explain.

_____

_____

Math Success

Check off the vocabulary words that you understand.

☐ circle   ☐ chord   ☐ radius   ☐ diameter

Rate how well you can *use chords to find measures*.

| Need to review | 0 2 4 6 8 10 | Now I get it! |

Lesson 12-2

12-3 Inscribed Angles

Vocabulary

● **Review**

Write *noun* or *verb* to identify how *intercept* is used.

1. Defense tries to *intercept* a touchdown pass.

2. The *y-intercept* of a line is the *y*-value at $x = 0$.

3. Cryptographers *intercept* and decipher code messages.

4. The *x-intercept* of a line is the *x*-value at $y = 0$.

● **Vocabulary Builder**

inscribed (adjective) **in** SKRYBD

Related Word: circumscribed

Definition: *Inscribed* means written, marked, or engraved on. *Circumscribed* means encircled, confined, or limited.

Math Usage: An **inscribed** angle is formed by two chords with a vertex on the circle.

inscribed angle

● **Use Your Vocabulary**

Write *circumscribed* or *inscribed* to describe each angle.

5.

6.

7.

8.

Underline the correct word to complete each sentence.

9. ∠*ABC* with points *A*, *B*, and *C* on a circle is a(n) circumscribed / inscribed angle.

10. An intercepted arc is between the sides of a(n) circumscribed / inscribed angle.

Theorem 12-11   Inscribed Angle Theorem

The measure of an inscribed angle is half the measure of its intercepted arc.

$$m\angle B = \frac{1}{2}\, m\,\widehat{AC}$$

11. Suppose $m\,\widehat{AC} = 90$.

$m\angle B =$ [ ] $\cdot\ m\,\widehat{AC} =$ [ ]

12. Suppose $m\angle B = 60$.

$m\,\widehat{AC} =$ [ ] $\cdot\ m\angle B =$ [ ]

Problem 1 **Using the Inscribed Angle Theorem**

Got It? In $\odot O$, what is $m\angle A$?

13. Complete the reasoning model below.

Think	Write
I know the sides of $\angle A$ are chords and the vertex is on $\odot O$.	$\angle A$ is an inscribed angle.
I can use the Inscribed Angle Theorem.	$m\angle A = \frac{1}{2}$ (measure of the blue arc) $= \frac{1}{2} \cdot$ [ ] $=$ [ ]

Corollaries to Theorem 12-11   Inscribed Angle Theorem

Corollary 1

Two inscribed angles that intercept the same arc are congruent.

Corollary 2

An angle inscribed in a semicircle is a right angle.

Corollary 3

The opposite angles of a quadrilateral inscribed in a circle are supplementary.

Use the diagram at the right. Write T for *true* or F for *false*.

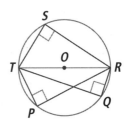

_____ **14.** $\angle P$ and $\angle Q$ intercept the same arc.

_____ **15.** $\angle SRP$ and $\angle Q$ intercept the same arc.

_____ **16.** $\widehat{TSR}$ is a semicircle.

_____ **17.** $\angle PTS$ and $\angle SRQ$ are opposite angles.

_____ **18.** $\angle PTS$ and $\angle SRP$ are supplementary angles.

Problem 2 Using Corollaries to Find Angle Measures

Got It? In the diagram at the right, what is the measure of each numbered angle?

19. Use the justifications at the right to complete each statement.

    $m\angle 4 = \frac{1}{2}(\boxed{} + \boxed{})$ Inscribed Angle Theorem

    $m\angle 4 = \frac{1}{2}(\boxed{})$ Add within parentheses.

    $m\angle 4 = \boxed{}$ Simplify.

20. Circle the corollary you can use to find $m\angle 2$.

    | An angle inscribed in a semicircle is a right angle. | The opposite angles of a quadrilateral inscribed in a circle are supplementary. |

21. Now solve for $m\angle 2$.

22. Underline the correct word to complete the sentence.

    The dashed line is a   diameter / radius .

23. Circle the corollary you can use to find $m\angle 1$ and $m\angle 3$.

    | An angle inscribed in a semicircle is a right angle. | The opposite angles of a quadrilateral inscribed in a circle are supplementary. |

Use your answer to Exercise 23 to find the angle measures.

24. $m\angle 1 = \boxed{}$ 25. $m\angle 3 = \boxed{}$

26. So, $m\angle 1 = \boxed{}$, $m\angle 2 = \boxed{}$, $m\angle 3 = \boxed{}$, and $m\angle 4 = \boxed{}$.

take note

Theorem 12-12

The measure of an angle formed by a tangent and a chord is half the measure of the intercepted arc.

$m\angle C = \frac{1}{2} m\widehat{BDC}$

27. Suppose $m\angle C = 50$.

    $m\widehat{BDC} = \boxed{} \cdot m\angle C = \boxed{}$

28. Suppose $m\widehat{BDC} = 80$.

    $m\angle C = \boxed{} \cdot m\widehat{BDC} = \boxed{}$

29. In the diagram at the right, $\overrightarrow{BC}$ is tangent to $\odot O$ at B.

    $m\widehat{ADB} = \boxed{}$ $m\angle ABC = \boxed{}$

Chapter 12   **324**

Problem 3 Finding Arc Measure

Got It? In the diagram at the right, $\overline{KJ}$ is tangent to $\odot O$. What are the values of x and y?

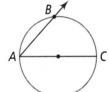

30. Circle the arc intercepted by $\angle JQL$. Underline the arc intercepted by $\angle KJL$.

$\quad\overset{\frown}{JL}\qquad\qquad\overset{\frown}{JQ}\qquad\qquad\overset{\frown}{QL}\qquad\qquad\overset{\frown}{QLJ}$

31. By the Inscribed Angle Theorem, $m\overset{\frown}{JL}$ = ☐ · ☐ = ☐ .

32. By Theorem 12-12, x = ☐ · $m\overset{\frown}{JL}$ = ☐ .

33. The value of x is ☐ .

34. Underline the correct words to complete the sentence.

$\quad\overline{QL}$ is a diameter / radius , so $\angle QJL$ is a(n) acute / right / obtuse angle.

35. Use the justifications at the right to complete each statement.

$\quad m\angle QJL + m\angle JLQ + m\angle LQJ =$ ☐ $\qquad$ Triangle Angle-Sum Theorem

$\qquad\qquad$ ☐ $+ y +$ ☐ $=$ ☐ $\qquad$ Substitute.

$\qquad\qquad\qquad y +$ ☐ $=$ ☐ $\qquad$ Simplify.

$\qquad\qquad\qquad\qquad y =$ ☐ $\qquad$ Subtract from each side.

Lesson Check • Do you UNDERSTAND?

Error Analysis A classmate says that $m\angle A = 90$. What is your classmate's error?

36. Is diameter $\overline{AC}$ a side of $\angle A$? $\qquad\qquad$ Yes / No

37. Is $\angle A$ inscribed in a semicircle? $\qquad\qquad$ Yes / No

38. What is your classmate's error? Explain.

_____

_____

_____

Math Success

Check off the vocabulary words that you understand.

☐ inscribed angle $\qquad\qquad$ ☐ intercepted arc

Rate how well you can *find the measure of inscribed angles*.

Need to review   0   2   4   6   8   10   Now I get it!

Lesson 12-3

12-4 Angle Measures and Segment Lengths

Vocabulary

● Review

1. Underline the correct word(s) to complete the sentence.

The student went off on a *tangent* when he did / did not stick to the subject.

2. A *tangent* to a circle intersects the circle at exactly __?__ point(s).

3. From a point outside a circle, there are __?__ *tangent(s)* to the circle.

● Vocabulary Builder

secant

secant (noun) SEEK unt

Related Word: tangent (noun)

Definition: A **secant** is a line that intersects a circle at two points.

Source: The word **secant** comes from the Latin verb *secare*, which means "to cut."

Examples: In the diagram at the right, $\overleftrightarrow{AB}$ is a **secant**, $\overrightarrow{AB}$ and $\overrightarrow{BA}$ are **secant** rays, and $\overline{AB}$ is a **secant** segment.

● Use Your Vocabulary

Write *secant* or *tangent* to identify each line.

4.

5.

6.

7.

_____ _____ _____ _____

8. Is a chord a *secant*? Explain.

_____

_____

Theorems 12-13, 12-14, and 12-15

Theorem 12-13 The measure of an angle formed by two lines that intersect inside a circle is half the sum of the measures of the intercepted arcs.

$$m\angle 1 = \tfrac{1}{2}(x + y)$$

9. In the diagram at the right, does $m\angle 2 = \tfrac{1}{2}(x + y)$? Explain.

_____

_____

Theorem 12-14 The measure of an angle formed by two lines that intersect outside a circle is half the difference of the measures of the intercepted arcs.

$$m\angle 1 = \tfrac{1}{2}(x - y)$$

10. In the first diagam, the sides of the angle are a secant and a __?__ .

11. In the second diagram, the sides of the angle are a secant and a __?__ .

12. In the third diagram, the sides of the angle are a tangent and a __?__ .

13. Is $m\angle 1 = \tfrac{1}{2}(y - x)$ equivalent to $m\angle 1 = \tfrac{1}{2}(x - y)$?   Yes / No

Theorem 12-15 For a given point and circle, the product of the lengths of the two segments from the point to the circle is constant along any line through the point and the circle.

I.

II.

III.
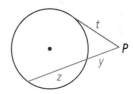

Complete each case of Theorem 12-15.

14. **Case I** $\quad a \cdot b = c \cdot \boxed{}$

15. **Case II** $\quad (w + x)\,w = (\boxed{} + z)\,\boxed{}$

16. **Case III** $\quad (y + z)\,\boxed{} = t^2$

 Problem 1 **Finding Angle Measures**

Got It? What is the value of w?

17. Use Theorem 12-14 to complete the equation.

$$\boxed{} = \tfrac{1}{2}\left(w - \boxed{}\right)$$

Lesson 12-4

18. Now solve the equation.

19. The value of w is ____ .

✓ **Problem 2** **Finding an Arc Measure**

Got It? A departing space probe sends back a picture of Earth as it crosses Earth's equator. The angle formed by the two tangents to the equator is 20°. What arc of the equator is visible to the space probe?

20. Use 20, *F*, *G*, and the words *Earth* and *probe* to complete the diagram below.

E • ____   P ____

21. Complete the flow chart below.

Let $m\widehat{FG} = x$. Then $m\widehat{FEG} = $ ____ $- x$.

The sum of the arc measures is 360°.

$$m\angle FPG = \frac{1}{2}(m\widehat{FEG} - m \boxed{})$$

Theorem 12-14

$20 = \frac{1}{2}(\boxed{} - \boxed{})$ → $20 = \frac{1}{2}(\boxed{})$

Substitute.   Simplify.

$\boxed{} = \boxed{} x$ ← $20 = \boxed{}$

Subtract 180 from each side.   Use the Distributive Property.

$\boxed{} = x$

Divide each side by −1.

22. A $\boxed{}°$ arc of the equator is visible to the space probe.

Problem 3 Finding Segment Lengths

Got It? What is the value of the variable to the nearest tenth?

Underline the correct word to complete each sentence.

23. The segments intersect inside / outside the circle.

24. Write a justification for each statement.

$(14 + 20)14 = (16 + x)16$ _____

$476 = 256 + 16x$ _____

$220 = 16x$ _____

$13.75 = x$ _____

25. To the nearest tenth, the value of x is [   ].

Lesson Check • Do you UNDERSTAND?

In the diagram at the right, is it possible to find the measures of the unmarked arcs? Explain.

26. You can use intercepted arcs to find the value of y.   Yes / No

27. You can use supplementary angles to find the measures of the angles adjacent to $y°$.   Yes / No

28. You can find the sum of the unmarked arcs.   Yes / No

29. Is it possible to find the measure of each unmarked arc? Explain.

_____

_____

Math Success

Check off the vocabulary words that you understand.

☐ chord   ☐ circle   ☐ secant   ☐ tangent

Rate how well you can *find the lengths of segments associated with circles.*

Need to review 0 2 4 6 8 10 Now I get it!

Lesson 12-4

12-5 · Circles in the Coordinate Plane

Vocabulary

● Review

Write T for *true* or F for *false.*

_____ **1.** The *coordinate plane* extends without end and has no thickness.

_____ **2.** Only lines can be graphed in the *coordinate plane.*

_____ **3.** Any polygon can be plotted in the *coordinate plane.*

_____ **4.** (0, 5) and (5, 0) are the same point in the *coordinate plane.*

_____ **5.** The *coordinate plane* is three-dimensional.

_____ **6.** You can find the slope of a line in the *coordinate plane.*

● Vocabulary Builder

standard form (noun) STAN **durd fawrm**

Main Idea: The **standard form** of an equation gives information that can help you graph the equation in the coordinate plane.

Examples: The **standard form** of an equation of a circle is $(x - h)^2 + (y - k)^2 = r^2$. The **standard form** of a linear equation is $Ax + By = C$. The **standard form** of a quadratic equation is $y = ax^2 + bx + c$.

● Use Your Vocabulary

Draw a line from each equation in Column A to its *standard form* in Column B.

Column A	Column B
7. $y = 2x + 3$	$x + y = 0$
8. $y = \frac{3}{4}x - 2$	$2x - y = -3$
9. $y = -x$	$3x - 4y = 8$
10. $0 = 2y - 4x + 3$	$4x - 2y = 3$

Chapter 12

330

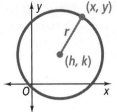

Theorem 12-16 Equation of a Circle

An equation of a circle with center (h, k) and radius r is $(x - h)^2 + (y - k)^2 = r^2$.

Complete each sentence with *center*, *circle*, or *radius*.

11. Each point on a __?__ is the same distance from the center.

12. The equation of a circle with center $(-1, 0)$ and __?__ 6 is $(x + 1)^2 + (y - 0)^2 = 6^2$.

13. Each point on a circle is r units from the __?__ .

14. The Distance Formula is $d = \sqrt{(x_2 - \boxed{})^2 + (y_2 - \boxed{})^2}$

15. How is d in the Distance Formula related to the radius r in the standard equation of a circle?

_____

_____

_____

16. How are the Distance Formula and the standard form of the equation of a circle alike?

_____

_____

_____

Problem 1 Writing the Equation of a Circle

Got It? What is the standard equation of the circle with center (3, 5) and radius 6?

17. The x-coordinate of the center is $\boxed{}$.

18. The y-coordinate of the center is $\boxed{}$.

19. Is the standard equation of a circle $(x - h)^2 + (y - k)^2 = d$ Yes / No

20. Identify the values of h, k, and r.

   $h = \boxed{}$ $k = \boxed{}$ $r = \boxed{}$

21. Write the standard equation of the circle with center (3, 5) and radius 6.

   $(x - \boxed{})^2 + (y - \boxed{})^2 = \boxed{}^2$

22. Simplify the equation in Exercise 21.

   $(x - \boxed{})^2 + (y - \boxed{})^2 = \boxed{}$

Lesson 12-5

Problem 2 Using the Center and a Point on a Circle

Got It? What is the standard equation of the circle with center $(4, 3)$ that passes through the point $(-1, 1)$?

23. Complete the reasoning model below.

Know	Need	Plan
(h, k) is $(\boxed{}, \boxed{})$. $(-1, 1)$ is a point on the circle.	The radius $\boxed{}$ The standard equation of the circle	Use the Distance Formula to find $\boxed{}$. Then substitute for (h, k) and for $\boxed{}$.

24. Use the Distance Formula to find r.

$d = \sqrt{(x_2 - \boxed{})^2 + (y_2 - \boxed{})^2}$ Write the Distance Formula.

$r = \sqrt{(4 - \boxed{})^2 + (3 - \boxed{})^2}$ Substitute.

$r = \sqrt{(\boxed{})^2 + (\boxed{})^2}$ Simplify within parentheses.

$r = \sqrt{(\boxed{}) + (\boxed{})}$ Square each number.

$r = \sqrt{\boxed{}}$ Add.

25. Now write the standard form of the circle with center $(4, 3)$ that passes through the point $(-1, 1)$.

$(x - \boxed{})^2 + (y - \boxed{})^2 = \boxed{}^2$ Use the standard form of an equation of a circle.

$(x - \boxed{})^2 + (y - \boxed{})^2 = \boxed{}^2$ Substitute.

$(x - \boxed{})^2 + (y - \boxed{})^2 = \boxed{}$ Simplify.

Problem 3 Graphing a Circle Given Its Equation

Got It? Suppose the equation $(x - 7)^2 + (y + 2)^2 = 64$ represents the position and transmission range of a cell tower. What does the center of the circle represent? What does the radius represent?

Place a ✓ in the box if the response is correct. Place an ✗ if it is incorrect.

_____ **26.** The transmission range is the same distance all around the cell tower.

_____ **27.** The center of the circle represents the position of the cell tower.

_____ **28.** The center of the circle represents the transmission range.

_____ **29.** The radius of the circle represents the position of the cell tower.

_____ **30.** The radius of the circle represents the transmission range.

Got It? What is the center and radius of the circle with equation $(x - 2)^2 + (y - 3)^2 = 100$? Graph the circle.

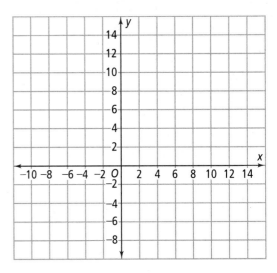

31. The center of the circle is (2,   ).

32. $r^2 = $

33. The radius of the circle is   .

34. Graph the circle on the coordinate plane at the right.

Lesson Check • Do you UNDERSTAND?

Suppose you know the center of a circle and a point on the circle. How do you determine the equation of the circle?

35. Do you know the value of h?   Yes / No

36. Do you know the value of k?   Yes / No

37. Do you know the value of r?   Yes / No

38. How can you find the missing value?

_____

_____

39. Once you know h, k, and r, how do you determine an equation of the circle?

_____

_____

Math Success

Check off the vocabulary words that you understand.

☐ circle   ☐ Distance Formula   ☐ standard form

Rate how well you can *use the standard form of a circle.*

Need to review   0   2   4   6   8   10   Now I get it!

Lesson 12-5

Vocabulary

● Review

Write *plane* or *space* to complete each sentence.

1. The set of all points in three dimensions is __?__ .

2. A __?__ is represented by a flat surface that extends without end and has no thickness.

3. An isometric drawing shows a corner view of a figure in __?__ .

4. Through any three noncollinear points there is exactly one __?__ .

● Vocabulary Builder

locus (noun) ʟᴏʜ **kus**

Other Word Form: The plural of **locus** is **loci** (LOH cy).

Related Words: location, locate

Definition: A locus is a set of points, all of which meet a stated condition.

Main Idea: The locus of points 5 in. from a point on a plane is a *circle* with radius 5 in.

● Use Your Vocabulary

Write T for *true* or F for *false*.

_____ **5.** A square is the *locus* of points equidistant from a given point.

_____ **6.** A sphere is the *locus* of points that are equidistant from a point in space.

_____ **7.** A circle with diameter 3 cm is the *locus* of points 3 cm from a given point.

_____ **8.** The *locus* of points 15 mi from a cell tower is a circle.

Problem 1 Describing a Locus in a Plane

Got It? Reasoning The sketch below shows the locus of the points in a plane 1 cm from $\overline{AB}$. How would the sketch change for the locus of points in a plane 1 cm from $\overleftrightarrow{AB}$?

9. What is the difference between $\overleftrightarrow{AB}$ and $\overline{AB}$? Explain.

_____

_____

_____

10. Would the new sketch have a parallel line segment 1 cm above $\overleftrightarrow{AB}$? Yes / No

11. Would the new sketch have a parallel line segment 1 cm below $\overleftrightarrow{AB}$? Yes / No

12. Would the new sketch have a parallel line 1 cm above $\overleftrightarrow{AB}$? Yes / No

13. Would the new sketch have a parallel line 1 cm below $\overleftrightarrow{AB}$? Yes / No

14. Would the new sketch have semicircles at each end? Yes / No

15. Would the new sketch have anything at each end? Yes / No

16. Sketch the locus of points in a plane 1 cm from $\overleftrightarrow{AB}$.

17. How would the sketch change for the locus of points in a plane 1 cm from $\overleftrightarrow{AB}$?

_____

_____

_____

_____

Lesson 12-6

Problem 2 Drawing a Locus for Two Conditions

Got It? What is a sketch of the locus of points in a plane that satisfy these conditions?

- the points equidistant from two points X and Y

- the points 2 cm from the midpoint of $\overline{XY}$

Use the diagram at the right for Exercises 18–22.

18. Circle the points in a plane that are equidistant from the endpoints of a segment.

| circle | ellipse | perpendicular bisector |

19. Circle the locus of points that are equidistant from X and Y.

| circle with center at the midpoint of $\overline{XY}$ and radius 2 cm | perpendicular bisector of $\overline{XY}$ |

20. Circle the locus of points that are a given distance from a point.

| circle | ellipse | perpendicular bisector |

21. Circle the locus of points 2 cm from the midpoint of $\overline{XY}$.

| circle with center at the midpoint of $\overline{XY}$ and radius 2 cm | perpendicular bisector of $\overline{XY}$ |

22. Points ___ and ___ are the locus of points that satisfy both conditions.

Problem 3 Describing a Locus in Space

Got It? What is the locus of points in a plane that are equidistant from two parallel lines?

Complete each statement with the appropriate word from the list below.

| parallel | perpendicular | plane |

23. Points that are equidistant from two __?__ lines are between the lines.

24. The locus of points in a __?__ that are equidistant from two parallel lines is a line.

25. The distance between parallel lines is the length of a segment __?__ to both lines.

26. What is the locus of points in a plane that are equidistant from two parallel lines?

Got It? What is the locus of points in space that are equidistant from two parallel planes?

27. Cross out the word phrase that does NOT describe the distance between two planes.

length between two points on different planes	length of a segment perpendicular to each plane

28. Circle the word phrase that describes the locus of points in space that are equidistant from two parallel planes.

cylinder	plane halfway between the two parallel planes	plane parallel to the two parallel planes

Lesson Check • Do you UNDERSTAND?

Compare and Contrast How are the descriptions of the locus of points for each situation alike? How are they different?

• in a plane, the points equidistant from points J and K

• in space, the points equidistant from points J and K

29. Place a ✓ in the box if the description is true for the locus of points equidistant from points J and K. Place an ✗ in the box if it is not.

In a Plane	Description	In Space
	$\perp$ bisector of $\overline{JK}$	
	plane containing $\perp$ bisector of $\overline{JK}$	
	plane $\perp$ to plane containing $\overline{JK}$	

30. How are the descriptions of the loci alike?

_____

_____

_____

31. How are the descriptions of the loci different?

_____

_____

_____

Math Success

Check off the vocabulary words that you understand.

☐ locus of points   ☐ plane   ☐ space

Rate how well you can *sketch and describe a locus.*

Lesson 12-6

Vocabulary

● **Review**

Use the following sets to complete Exercises 1–3.

$A = \{1, 2, 3\}$ $B = \{1, 2\}$ $C = \{3, 4, 5\}$

For Execises 1–3, fill in the blanks to complete the statement.

1. What is the *union* of *sets* A and C?

   $A \cup C =$ _____

2. What is the *intersection* of sets A and B?

   $A \cap B =$ _____

3. Which set is a *subset* of set A? _____

For Exercises 4–6, rewrite each fraction as a percentage to one decimal place.

4. $\frac{9}{15}$ _____   5. $\frac{18}{22}$ _____   6. $\frac{118}{150}$ _____

● **Vocabulary Builder**

Probability (noun) **prä-bə-BI-lə-tē**

Related Words: outcome, event, sample space, experimental probability, theoretical probability

Definition: Probability is a measure of the likelihood that an event will occur.

Example: You can write the **probability** of an event as a ratio, decimal, or percent.

● **Use Your Vocabulary**

The words *probability*, *probable*, and *probably* sound alike but have different meanings. In Exercises 7–9, underline the correct choice to complete each sentence.

7. The probability / probable / probably of rain today is 60%.

8. It will probability / probable / probably rain today.

9. It is probability / probable / probably that it will rain today.

Key Concept   Probability

Definition

If the outcomes in a sample space are equally likely to occur, the **theoretical probability** of an event P(event) is a numerical value from 0 to 1 that measures the likelihood of an event.

$$P(\text{event}) = \frac{\text{number of favorable outcomes}}{\text{number of possible outcomes}}$$

An event with a probability close to 0 is unlikely to occur.

An event with a probability close to 1 is likely to occur.

10. A coin is tossed. On the number line what do you think will be the probability of heads?

| 0 | 0.25 | 0.5 | 0.75 | 1 |

You can find the probability of an event by using the results of an experiment.

Key Concept   Experimental Probability

The **experimental probability** of an event measures the likelihood that the event occurs based on the actual results of an experiment.

$$P(\text{event}) = \frac{\text{number of times the event occurs}}{\text{number of times the experiment is done}}$$

11. A coin is tossed 100 times. It comes up heads 60 times. Circle the experimental probability it comes up heads.

| 0 | 0.4 | 0.5 | 0.6 | 1 |

Problem 1   Calculating Experimental Probability

Got It? A park has 538 trees. You choose 40 at random and determine that 25 are maple trees. What is the experimental probability that a tree chosen at random is a maple tree? About how many trees in the park are likely to be maple trees? Give your answer to one decimal place.

12. In the question, circle the event. Then underline the number of times the experiment is done.

13. Use the information to complete the equation $P(\text{event}) = \dfrac{}{} = = $

Lesson 13-1

14. The experimental probability that a tree chosen at random is a maple tree is [_____].

15. Select the correct equation to find how many trees in the park are likely to be maple trees, and use it to calculate the probable number of maple trees in the park.

[_____] a. number of maple trees in the park = P(maples) · total number of trees

[_____] b. number of maple trees in the park = P(maples) + total number of trees

[_____] c. number of maple trees in the park = total number of trees ÷ P(maples)

16. The number of maple trees in the park is probably about [_____].

Theoretical probability describes the likelihood of an event based on mathematical reasoning.

 Problem 2 **Calculating Theoretical Probability**

Got It? What is the probability of getting each sum when rolling two standard number cubes?

a. 9   **b.** 2

	1	2	3	4	5	6
1	1,1	2,1	3,1	4,1	5,1	6,1
2	1,2	2,2	3,2	4,2	5,2	6,2
3	1,3	2,3	3,3	4,3	5,3	6,3
4	1,4	2,4	3,4	4,4	5,4	6,4
5	1,5	2,5	3,5	4,5	5,5	6,5
6	1,6	2,6	3,6	4,6	5,6	6,6

17. Underline the correct choice to complete each statement.

I am looking for a sum / difference / product / quotient .

The first step in finding the answer is:

add the numbers in each box together.

multiply the numbers in each box together.

subtract the smaller number from the larger number in each box.

Fill in the blanks to complete Exercises 18–21.

18. To set up a probability ratio, I need the number of [_____] outcomes and the total number of [_____] outcomes. The possible outcomes are all the pairs.

19. In the number box, circle all pairs that have a sum of 9. There are [____] pairs of numbers that have a sum of 9.

20. P(rolling a sum of 9) $= \dfrac{\text{number of favorable outcomes (sum of 9)}}{\text{total number of possible outcomes (any sum)}} = \dfrac{[\ \ ]}{36} = \dfrac{1}{[\ \ ]}$

21. P(rolling a sum of 2) $= \dfrac{\text{number of favorable outcomes (sum of [\ ])}}{\text{total number of possible outcomes (any sum)}} = \dfrac{[\ \ ]}{[\ \ ]}$

The **complement** of an event consists of all the possible outcomes not part of the event.

Key Concept **Probability of a Complement**

The sum of probabilities of an event and the probability of its complement is 1.

$$P(\text{event}) + P(\text{not event}) = 1 \qquad P(\text{not event}) = 1 - P(\text{event})$$

Problem 3 Using Probabilities of Events and Their Complements

Got It? A jar contains 10 red marbles, 8 green marbles, 5 blue marbles, and 6 white marbles. What is the probability that a randomly chosen marble is *not red*?

22. Underline the word that will complete the statement. The number of *not red* marbles in the jar is the probability / complement of the number of *red* marbles in the jar.

23. Circle the rule(s) you could use to find the probability that the marble will *not* be red.

$P(\text{not red}) = 1 - P(\text{red})$ $P(\text{red}) + P(\text{not red}) = 1$ $P(\text{not red}) - P(\text{red}) = 1$

24. Use a rule you circled in Exercise 23 and solve for the number of not red marbles.

Lesson Check • Do you UNDERSTAND?

Find the Error Your friend says that the probability of a six-sided number cube rolling a number less than 7 is 100. Explain your friend's error and the correct probability.

25. List all the possible outcomes that are less than 7 when rolling a six-sided number cube.

26. What is the probability of rolling a number cube and getting a number less than 7?

$P(\text{rolling a number less than 7}) = \dfrac{}{} = \boxed{} = \boxed{}$

27. Explain your friend's error and the correct probability on the lines below.

Math Success

Check off the vocabulary words that you understand.

☐ experimental probability   ☐ theoretical probability   ☐ complement of an event

Rate how well you can *find probabilities*.

Lesson 13-1

Vocabulary

● Review

1. Write the ratio 3:4 as a fraction, a decimal and a percent.

_____   _____   _____

2. What is the difference between *experimental probability* and *theoretical probability*?

_____

_____

3. Draw line segments to match the term and its definition

outcome   an outcome or group of outcomes

event   the total number of outcomes

sample space   one possible result of a situation or experiment

● Vocabulary Builder

Relative frequency (noun) RE-lə-tiv FRĒ-kwən(t)-sē

Related Words: ratio, frequency table, probability, probability distribution

Definition: The **relative frequency** is the ratio of the number of times an event occurs to the total number of events in the sample space.

Example: The **relative frequency** is an approximation of the overall probability of the result.

● Use Your Vocabulary

Complete each statement with a word from the list. Use each word only once.

    frequency   frequent   frequently

4. His _?_ interruptions disrupted the lecture.   _____

5. How _?_ does he interrupt the lecture?   _____

6. The _?_ of his interruptions increased over time.   _____

Key Concept   Relative Frequency

The **relative frequency** is the ratio of the number of times an event occurs to the total number of events in the sample space.

7. In a survey of 100 people, 30 say their favorite color is red. Circle the relative frequency that a person selects red as their favorite color.

| 0 | 0.3 | 0.5 | 0.7 | 1 |

 Problem 1   Finding Relative Frequencies

Got It? The results of a survey of students' music preferences are organized in this frequency table. What is the relative frequency of each type of music?
a. classical   b. hip hop   c. country

Type of Music Preferred	Frequency
Rock	10
Hip Hop	7
Country	8
Classical	5
Alternative	6
Other	4

8. How do you determine the total frequency for types of music preferred? What is the total frequency?

_____

9. For this survey, what does the total frequency represent?

_____

For Exercises 10–12, fill in the blanks to complete the statements.

10. relative frequency (classical) $= \dfrac{\text{frequency of classical music preference}}{\text{total frequency}} = \dfrac{\quad}{\quad} = \dfrac{\quad}{\quad}$

11. relative frequency (hip hop) $= \dfrac{\text{frequency of hip hop music preference}}{\text{total frequency}} = \dfrac{\quad}{\quad}$

12. relative frequency (country) $= \dfrac{\text{frequency of country music preference}}{\text{total frequency}} = \dfrac{\quad}{\quad} = \dfrac{\quad}{\quad}$

For a larger sample space, you can use relative frequency to approximate the probabilities of events that are not equally likely to occur.

 Problem 2   Calculating Probability by Using Relative Frequencies

Got It? A student conducts a probability experiment by spinning the spinner shown. Using the results in the frequency table, what is the probability of the spinner pointing at 4 on the next spin?

Spinner Result	1	2	3	4
Frequency	29	32	21	18

Lesson 13-2

13. The frequency of the spinner pointing at 4 is [ ].

The total frequency for all possible results is [ ] + [ ] + [ ] + [ ] = [ ].

14. Circle the ratio you could use to find the relative frequency of the spinner pointing to 4.

$$\frac{\text{frequency of spinner pointing at 4}}{\text{frequency of spinner not pointing at 4}}$$

$$\frac{\text{frequency of spinner pointing at 4}}{\text{total frequency}}$$

$$\frac{\text{total frequency}}{\text{frequency of spinner pointing at 4}}$$

15. Use the ratio you circled in Exercise 14 to determine the relative frequency of the spinner pointing at 4.

Problem 3 Finding a Probability Distribution

Got It? On a math test there were 10 scores between 90 and 100, 12 scores between 80 and 89, 15 between 70 and 79, 8 between 60 and 69, and 2 scores below 60. What is the probability distribution for the test scores?

16. Use the following words/expressions to complete the Know, Need, Plan model.

probability   distribution   score ranges   table   number of scores for each range

Know	Need	Plan
You are given: _____ _____ _____	You need to find the _____ of each outcome, or test score range.	I will find the _____ for each range. Then I will construct a _____ to show the probability _____.

17. What is the total number of test scores recorded? [ ]

18. Follow your plan. Fill in the blanks to find the probability of each outcome.

$P(90 - 100) = \dfrac{}{47}$ $P(80 - 89) = \dfrac{}{}$ $P() = \dfrac{}{}$

$P() = \dfrac{}{}$ $P() = \dfrac{}{}$

19. A frequency table should include the following test score ranges:

[   ] , [   ] , [   ] , [   ] , and [   ]

20. What is the probability distribution for the test scores? Complete the table.

Probability Distribution of Test Scores

Percentage Score Range					
Frequency	☐	☐	☐	☐	☐
Probability	___	___	___	___	___

Lesson Check • Do you UNDERSTAND?

Error Analysis A friend says that her sweepstakes ticket will either win or not win, so the theoretical probability of it winning must be 50%. Explain your friend's error.

Use the situation below to answer Exercises 21–24.

> Out of 10,000 people who bought sweepstakes tickets, you bought one.
> One sweepstakes ticket will be selected at random to win the sweepstakes.

21. Draw line segments to match the frequencies with their values.

frequency of the number of tickets you bought   10,000

total frequency of the outcomes   1

22. Fill in the blanks for the formula for relative frequency.

$$\text{relative frequency} = \frac{}{}$$

23. What is the probability that you will win the sweepstakes?

24. Explain your friend's error on the lines below.

_____

_____

Math Success

Check off the vocabulary words that you understand.

☐ frequency table   ☐ relative frequency   ☐ probability distribution

Rate how well you can *use relative frequency*.

Need to review   0   2   4   6   8   10   Now I get it!

Lesson 13-2

Vocabulary

● Review

Fill in the blanks to complete each sentence.

1. You find _____ when you perform an experiment and divide the number of times an event occurs by the total number of times the experiment is done.

2. You find _____ when you use mathematical reasoning to find the quotient of the number of favorable outcomes divided by the number of total possible outcomes.

3. What does a *probability distribution* show? Answer the question on the line below.

   _____

● Vocabulary Builder

Permutation (noun) pər-myü-TĀ-shən

Related Words: combination, factorial

Definition: A **permutation** is an arrangement of items in which the order of the objects is important.

Example: The number of permutations for the way 4 different people can stand in line at the movie theater is 24.

● Use Your Vocabulary

The words *arrange, arrangement,* and *arranging* sound alike but have different meanings. In Exercises 4–6, underline the correct choice to complete each sentence.

4. The audience enjoyed the unique arrange / arrangement / arranging for the concert.

5. She was arrange / arrangement / arranging the flowers when the client arrived.

6. He worked quickly to arrange / arrangement / arranging their travel plans.

You can use the Fundamental Counting Principal to calculate the number of possible ways to choose objects from different sets.

Key Concept Fundamental Counting Principle

If event M occurs in m ways and event N occurs in n ways, then event M followed by event N can occur in $m \cdot n$ ways.

7. If you have 3 pairs of pants and 5 shirts, then event M is 3 pairs of pants and event N is _____, so $m =$ [ ] and $n =$ [ ]. Then there are $m \cdot n$ ways to combine 3 pairs of pants and 5 shirts. Circle the number of different outfits that are available.

| 3 | 5 | 8 | 15 | 35 |

Problem 1 Using the Fundamental Counting Principle

Got It? Suppose that a computer generates passwords that begin with a letter followed by 2 digits, like R38. The same digit can be used more than once. How many different passwords can the computer generate?

8. How many letters are in the alphabet? [ ]   How many digits are there? [ ]

9. Circle the expression you could use to find the number of different passwords.

| $26 \cdot 26 \cdot 10 \cdot 10$ | $26 \cdot 10 \cdot 10$ | $26 \cdot 26 \cdot 10 \cdot 10 \cdot 10$ |

10. Use the expression you circled in Exercise 9 to find how many different passwords the computer can generate.

Problem 2 Finding the Number of Permutations

Got It? In how many different ways can you arrange 12 books on a shelf?

11. Circle the correct word to complete this sentence: Order does / does not matter in this arrangement.

12. After you choose the first book to arrange in the first spot, how many books are left to arrange in the remaining spots? [ ] After the second book is chosen? [ ]

13. If you use the Fundamental Counting Principle will you add, subtract, multiply or divide these numbers? [ ]

14. How many different ways you can arrange 12 books on a shelf?

[ ] · [ ] · [ ] · [ ] · [ ] · [ ] · [ ] · [ ] · [ ] · [ ] · [ ] · [ ] = [ ]

Lesson 13-3

You can use factorial notation to write a formula for the permutation of n objects arranged r at a time.

Key Concept Permutation

The number of permutations of n items of a set arranged r items at a time is

$$_nP_r = \frac{n!}{(n-r)!} \text{ for } 0 \le r \le n.$$

15. $_5P_3 = \frac{\boxed{}!}{(\boxed{})!} = \frac{5 \cdot \boxed{} \cdot \boxed{} \cdot \boxed{} \cdot \boxed{}}{\boxed{} \cdot \boxed{}} = \boxed{}$

Problem 3 Finding a Permutation

Got It? Twelve swimmers compete in a race. In how many possible ways can the swimmers finish first, second, and third?

Fill in the blanks for Exercises 16–18.

16. There are $\boxed{}$ swimmers, arranged $\boxed{}$ at a time; so, $n = \boxed{}$ and $r = \boxed{}$.

17. Substitute your values for n and r into the formula and solve.

$$_{\boxed{}}P_{\boxed{}} = \frac{\boxed{}!}{\left(\boxed{} - \boxed{}\right)!} = \frac{\boxed{}}{\boxed{}} = \boxed{}$$

18. The swimmers can finish first, second, and third in $\boxed{}$ possible ways.

A combination is a selection of items in which order is *not* important.

Key Concept Combination

The number of combinations of n items chosen r at a time is

$$_nC_r = \frac{n!}{r!(n-r)!} \text{ for } 0 \le r \le n.$$

19. $_5C_3 = \frac{\boxed{}!}{3!(\boxed{})!} = \frac{\boxed{} \cdot \boxed{} \cdot \boxed{} \cdot \boxed{} \cdot \boxed{}}{3 \cdot 2 \cdot 1 \cdot (\boxed{} \cdot \boxed{})} = \boxed{}$

Problem 4 Using the Combination Formula

Got It? A service club has 8 freshmen. Five of the freshmen are to be on the clean-up crew for the town's annual picnic. How many different ways are there to choose the 5 member clean-up crew?

20. $_{\boxed{}}C_{\boxed{}} = \frac{\boxed{}!}{(8-5)!} = \frac{\boxed{}\boxed{}\boxed{}\boxed{}\boxed{}}{\boxed{}\boxed{}} = \frac{\boxed{}}{\boxed{}} = \boxed{}$

21. There are $\boxed{}$ different 5-member clean-up crews that can be formed.

Problem 5 Identifying Combinations and Permutations

Got It? A yogurt shop allows you to choose any 3 of the 10 possible mix-ins for a Just Right Smoothie. How many different Just Right Smoothies are possible?

22. Underline the correct choice to complete each sentence.

For a combination, order does / does not matter.

For a permutation, order does / does not matter.

In this scenario, order does / does not matter, so it is a combination / permutation .

23. Circle the formula you will use to find the number of ways to arrange the mix-ins.

$$_nC_r = \frac{n!}{r!(n-r)!} \qquad _nP_r = \frac{n!}{(n-r)!}$$

24. Use the formula you circled in Exercise 23 to find the number of different smoothies.

Lesson Check • Do you UNDERSTAND?

Compare and Contrast How are combinations and permutations similar? How are they different?

Is the situation a permutation or a combination? Circle the correct choice.

25. arrange 5 books on a shelf

    permutation   combination

26. select a committee of 3 people out of 15 people

    permutation   combination

27. read 4 books from a list of 20 books

    permutation   combination

28. How are combinations and permutations similar? How are they different?
    Write your answer on the lines.

    _____

    _____

Math Success

Check off the vocabulary words that you understand.

☐ Fundamental Counting Principle   ☐ *n* factorial   ☐ permutation   ☐ combination

Rate how well you can *use permutations* and *combinations*.

Lesson 13-3

13-4 Compound Probability

Vocabulary

● Review

Fill in the blanks to complete each sentence.

1. For the spinner on the right, what is the probability of the spinner landing on each number?

   P(1) = ☐   P(2) = ☐   P(3) = ☐

Fill in the blank to complete each sentence.

2. An ☐ is an outcome or a group of outcomes

3. The probability of an *impossible* event is ☐ .

   The probability of a *certain* event is ☐ .

● Vocabulary Builder

> **Independent events** (noun) in-də-PEN-dənt i-VENTS
>
> **Related Words:** compound event, dependent events, mutually exclusive events
>
> **Definition:** If the occurrence of an event does not affect how another event occurs, the events are called **independent events**.
>
> **Example:** Being odd and being even are independent events.

● Use Your Vocabulary

Complete each statement with a word from the list. Use each word only once.

independence   independent   independently

4. The contest rules required that each participant complete the tasks _?_ .

5. During the American Revolution, the Thirteen Colonies fought for their _?_ from Great Britain.

6. The pharmaceutical company hired an _?_ research group to verify its latest results.

If the occurrence of an event does not affect how another event occurs, the events are **independent events**.

Key Concept Probability of *A* and *B*

If *A* and *B* are independent events, then $P(A \text{ and } B) = P(A) \cdot P(B)$.

Circle the independent event. Underline the dependent event.

7. A bag contains 10 white marbles, 8 black marbles, 6 red marbles, 4 green marbles, and 4 yellow marbles.

A marble is drawn from a bag, then another marble is drawn from the bag.	A marble is drawn from a bag and replaced, then another marble is drawn from the bag.

Problem 1 Identifying Independent and Dependent Events

Got It? You roll a number cube. Then you flip a coin. Are the events independent or dependent? Explain.

8. Underline the choice that correctly completes each sentence: The result of rolling a number cube does / does not affect the coin flip result. The events are independent / dependent .

Problem 2 Finding the Probability of Independent Events

Got It? You roll a standard number cube and spin the spinner at the right. What is the probability that you roll a number less than 3 and the spinner lands on a vowel?

For Exercises 9–10, fill in the blanks to complete the statements.

9. Let *A* = rolling a number less than 3 on a standard number cube. Find *P(A)*.

$$P(A) = \frac{\boxed{}}{6} = \frac{\boxed{}}{\boxed{}}$$

10. There is $\boxed{}$ vowel on the spinner. Let *B* = spinner lands on a vowel. Find *P(B)*.

$$P(B) = \frac{\boxed{}}{\boxed{}}$$

11. Underline each choice that correctly completes the sentence: *P(A)* and *P(B)* are dependent/independent , so to find *P(A and B)*, add / multiply *P(A)* and *P(B)*.

12. $P(A \text{ and } B) = P(A) \cdot P(B) = \frac{\boxed{}}{\boxed{}} \cdot \frac{\boxed{}}{\boxed{}} = \frac{\boxed{}}{\boxed{}} \approx \boxed{}$

Events that cannot happen at the same time are **mutually exclusive events**.

Key Concept Probability of Mutually Exclusive Events

If *A* and *B* are mutually exclusive events, then $P(A \text{ and } B) = 0$, and $P(A) \text{ or } P(B) = P(A) + P(B)$.

Lesson 13-4

Problem 3 Finding the Probability of Mutually Exclusive Events

Got It? Student athletes at a local high school may participate in only one sport each season. In the spring season, 15% of the athletes play baseball and 23% are on the track team. What is the probability of an athlete either playing baseball or being on the track team?

13. Underline the choice that correctly completes each statement.

In this scenario, playing baseball or running track are the events / probabilities .
Because athletes participate in only one sport each season, the events are
independent / mutually exclusive .

14. Circle the correct formula to find the probability of an athlete either playing baseball or being on the track team.

$P(A \text{ or } B) = P(A) + P(B)$ $P(A \text{ or } B) = P(A) \cdot P(B)$ $P(A \text{ or } B) = P(A) - P(B)$

15. Use the formula you circled in Exercise 14 to solve for the probability.

Events that have outcomes in common are called **overlapping events.**

Key Concept Probability of Overlapping Events

If A and B are overlapping events, then $P(A \text{ or } B) = P(A) + P(B) - P(A \text{ and } B)$.

16. 75% of students at a school participate in sports. 40% are on the honor roll. 30% participate in sports and are on the honor roll. Find the probability that a randomly selected student either participates in sports or is on the honor roll.

$P(\text{participate in sports or on honor roll}) = P(\text{participate in sports}) + P(\text{on honor roll}) -$

$P(\text{participate in sports and on honor roll}) = \boxed{} + \boxed{} - \boxed{} = \boxed{}$.

Problem 4 Finding Probabilities of Overlapping Events

Got It? What is the probability of rolling either an odd number or a number less than 4 when rolling a standard number cube?

Fill in the blanks to complete the statements.

Know
The odd numbers on a number cube are ☐, ☐, and ☐.
The numbers less than 4 are ☐, ☐, and ☐.
The numbers that are odd **and** less than 4 are ☐ and ☐.

Need
You need the probability of rolling an ☐, the probability of rolling a ☐ and the probability of rolling an odd number that is also less than 4.

Plan
Find the probabilities and use the formula for probabilities of ☐.

17. $P(\text{odd}) = \dfrac{}{} = \dfrac{}{}$ $P(\text{less than 4}) = \dfrac{}{} = \dfrac{}{}$

$P(\text{odd number and less than 4}) = \dfrac{}{} = \dfrac{}{}$

18. $P(\text{odd or less than 4}) = P() + P() - P($ and

$)$

$= \dfrac{}{} + \dfrac{}{} - \dfrac{}{} = \dfrac{}{}$

Lesson Check • Do you UNDERSTAND?

Error Analysis Your brother says that the probability that it is cloudy tomorrow and the probability that it rains are independent events. Explain your brother's error.

19. Circle the probability that it rains if the probability that it is cloudy is 0.

| 0 | 0.25 | 0.5 | 0.75 | 1 | undetermined |

20. Circle the probability that it rains if the probability that it is cloudy is 100%.

| 0 | 0.25 | 0.5 | 0.75 | 1 | undetermined |

21. Underline the correct choice to complete the sentence.

The probability that it is cloudy does/does not affect the probability that it rains.

22. Explain your brother's error on the lines below.

_____

_____

Math Success

Check off the vocabulary words that you understand.

- ☐ compound event
- ☐ compound probability
- ☐ independent events
- ☐ dependent events
- ☐ mutually exclusive events

Rate how well you can *find compound probabilities*.

Lesson 13-4

Vocabulary

● Review

Fill in the blanks to complete each sentence.

1. A _____ shows how often an item appears in a category.

2. A probability distribution table shows the _____ of each possible _____ and can be shown in a frequency table or graph.

3. Give an example of *mutually exclusive events* and how to find their *probabilities*.

_____

_____

4. Circle the formula for **theoretical probability** *P*(event).

$$P(\text{event}) = \frac{\text{number of times the event occurs}}{\text{number of times the experiment is done}} \qquad P(\text{event}) = \frac{\text{number of favorable outcomes}}{\text{number of possible outcomes}}$$

● Vocabulary Builder

Two-way frequency table (noun) FRĒ-kwən(t)-sē

Related Words: conditional probability, probability distribution

Definition: A **two-way frequency table**, or contingency table, displays the frequencies of data in two different categories.

Example: A **two-way frequency table**, or contingency table, can be used to find probabilities.

● Use Your Vocabulary

Complete each statement with a word from the list. Use each word only once.

   continent   contingency   contingent

5. Before they battled the blaze, the firefighters prepared for every _?_.

6. Which _?_ has the greatest population density?

7. Our rock climbing plans are _?_ on the weather.

Problem 1 Using a Contingency Table to Find Probability

Got It? The two-way frequency table shows the number of male and female students by grade level on the prom committee. What is the probability that a member of the prom committee is a male who is a junior?

Year	Male	Female	Totals
Juniors	3	4	7
Seniors	3	2	5
Totals	6	6	12

8. From the problem and the list of **Totals** on the table, mark which of the following you need to find the answer to the question.

_____ total males on the committee   _____ total seniors on the committee

_____ total students on the committee   _____ total juniors on the committee

_____ junior females on the committee

9. From the problem and the table, which other group will you need to know to answer the question?

_____ juniors   _____ seniors   _____ males   _____ females

_____ junior males   _____ junior females   _____ senior males   _____ senior females

10. Circle which ratio to use to find the probability that a member of the prom committee is a male who is a junior.

$$\frac{3}{7} \qquad \frac{3}{4} \qquad \frac{3}{9} \qquad \frac{3}{12}$$

11. Fill in the blank to complete the sentence.

The probability that a member of the prom committee is a male who is a junior is [   ]%.

 Problem 2 Finding Probability

Got It? Respondents of a recent poll were asked whether they were for, against, or had no opinion about a state bill that would increase the minimum wage. What is the probability that a randomly selected person is 30–45 years old given that the person is in favor of the minimum wage bill?

Age Group	For	Against	No Opinion	Totals
18–29	310	50	20	380
30–45	200	30	10	240
45–60	120	20	30	170
Over 60	150	20	40	210
Totals	780	120	100	1000

Lesson 13-5

The formula for probability is $P(\text{event}) = \dfrac{\text{number of favorable outcomes}}{\text{number of possible outcomes}}$.

12. Put a check next to the subset of people the question is asking about.

☐ those against the bill   ☐ those for the bill

☐ those with no opinion   ☐ all of the people polled

13. How many possible outcomes are there for people polled for the group you selected? ☐

14. Out of the possible outcomes, which age group is considered a favorable outcome? ☐

15. Circle the number of favorable outcomes there are in the age group you selected in Exercise 14.

10   30   200   240

16. Use the formula to find the probability that a randomly selected person is 30–45 years old, given that the person is in favor of the minimum wage bill.

$P(\text{event}) = \dfrac{\quad}{\quad} \approx$ ☐

Problem 3 Using Relative Frequencies

Got It? A company has 150 sales representatives. Two months after a sales seminar, the company vice-president made the table based on sales results. What is the probability that a randomly selected sales representative, who did not attend the seminar, did not see an increase in sales?

	Attended Seminar	Did not Attend Seminar	Totals
Increased Sales	0.48	0.02	0.5
No Increase in Sales	0.32	0.18	0.5
Totals	0.8	0.2	1

17. Which subset of sales representatives is the question asking about?

☐ attended seminar   ☐ had increased sales

☐ did not attend seminar   ☐ did not have increased sales

18. What is the possible outcome for the group you selected? ☐

19. Out of the outcomes in number 18, which group is considered a favorable outcome? ☐   What is the frequency? ☐

20. Use the probability formula to find the probability that a randomly selected sales representative did not attend the seminar and did not see an increase in sales. Fill in the blanks to solve.

$P(\text{event}) = \dfrac{P\ \boxed{}}{P\ \boxed{}} = \boxed{} = \boxed{}\ \%$

Lesson Check • Do you UNDERSTAND?

Error Analysis The table below shows the results of a poll. A student was asked the question, "If a Republican from this polled group is randomly selected, what is the probability that they do not support the issue?" The student calculated the relative frequency as $\frac{33}{33 + 36} \approx 0.478$. What error did the student make?

	Supports the Issue	Does Not Support the Issue	Totals
Democrat	24	36	60
Repulican	27	33	60
Totals	51	69	120

Use the two-way frequency table to find the probability.

21. Circle the number of people in the possible outcome group.

    69   51   60   120

22. Circle the number of people in the favorable outcome group.

    24   36   27   33

23. Fill in the blanks to find the probability of being a Republican who does not support the issue.

$P(\text{Republican who does not support the issue}) = \dfrac{\rule{1cm}{0.4pt}}{\rule{1cm}{0.4pt}} = \dfrac{\rule{1cm}{0.4pt}}{\rule{1cm}{0.4pt}} = \rule{1cm}{0.4pt}\ \%$

24. Explain what mistake the student made in his computation.

_____

_____

_____

Math Success

Check off the vocabulary words that you understand.

☐ two-way frequency table   ☐ conditional probability

Rate how well you can *use probability models*.

Need to review   0   2   4   6   8   10   Now I get it!

Lesson 13-5

13-6 Conditional Probability

Vocabulary

● Review

1. Fill in the blank to complete each sentence.

A _____ is the total number of *outcomes*.

The final entry in the totals row and column of a probability distribution is always ____ .

2. Draw a line segment to match the type of event to its definition.

independent events   the occurrence of one event does not affect how the other event occurs

dependent events   the occurrence of one event does affect how the other event occurs

● Vocabulary Builder

Conditional (adjective) kən-DISH-nəl

Related Words: conditional probability, two-way frequency table, probability distribution

Definition: Depending on another circumstance or situation.

Example: A **conditional** raise in salary is dependent upon whether the employees meet their yearly goals.

● Use Your Vocabulary

Complete each statement with a word from the list. Use each word only once.

condition   conditional   conditioning   conditions

3. The buyer's offer was __?__, depending on the results of the independent inspection.

_____

4. Due to the pristine __?__ of the vehicle, the owner was offered more money than the listed value.

_____

_____

5. The __?__ were perfect so we began the hike early.

_____

In the following sentences the result depends on some condition. Underline the condition.

6. If it rains tomorrow, there will be no picnic.   **7.** The patient gets better, when she listens to her doctor.

Key Concept   Conditional Probability Formula

For any two events A and B occurring, **given that event A has occurred**, is

$P(B|A) = \dfrac{P(A \text{ and } B)}{P(A)}$, where $P(A) \neq 0$.

A student rolls an even number on a standard number cube. What is the probability the student rolled a 2? Fill in the blanks to complete Exercises 8-10.

8. What are the possible outcomes, given you know the number rolled is even?

This makes the total number of possible outcomes   .

9. How many of those outcomes are favorable, if the student wants a result of 2?

10. $P(B|A) = P(2 \mid \text{even})$ is read, "What is the probability of rolling a 2, given the roll is even?"

Find $P(2 \mid \text{even}) = \dfrac{P(EVEN \text{ and } 2)}{P(EVEN)} = \dfrac{\quad}{\quad} = \dfrac{\quad}{\quad}$

11. Put a T next to the statements which are true about the part of the statement that is the given.

_____   The given limits the possible outcomes.   _____   The given reduces the sample space.

_____   The given is the A in $P(B|A)$.   _____   The given becomes the denominator of the fraction.

✓ Problem 1   Using Conditional Probabilities

Got It? In a study designed to test the effectiveness of a new drug, half of the volunteers received the drug. The other half of the volunteers received a placebo, a tablet or pill containing no medication. The probability of a volunteer receiving the placebo and having his or her health improve was 20%. What is the conditional probability of a volunteer who received the placebo, having his health improve?

12. Mark the possible outcomes in this problem.

_____   all the volunteers

_____   volunteers who received the drug

_____   volunteers who received the placebo

13. Mark the favorable outcome in this problem.

_____   health does not improve   _____   health improves

14. Rewrite the Conditional Probability Statement $P(B|A)$ using your answers to Exercises 12–13.

Fill in the blanks to complete Exercises 15–16.

15. Half the volunteers received the placebo, so $P(\text{placebo}) = $ [ ] .

16. $P(\text{receive the placebo and volunteer's health improves}) = $ [ ]

17. Replace the statements in Exercise 14 with the numeric values and solve for $P\left(\dfrac{B}{A}\right)$.

18. Write out a statement answering the question.

_____

_____

 Problem 2 **Comparing Conditional Probabilities**

Got It? In a survey of pet owners, 45% own a dog, 27% own a cat, and 12% own both a dog and a cat. The survey also showed that 5% of the pet owners own a dog, a cat, and at least one other type of pet.
a. What is the conditional probability that a pet owner owns a cat and some other type of pet given that they own a dog?
b. What is the conditional probability that a pet owner owns a dog and some other type of pet given that they own a cat?

Fill in the blanks to complete the statements and compare the conditional probabilities.

19. $P(\text{owns dog and cat and other} \,|\, $ [ ] $) = \dfrac{p()}{p()} = \dfrac{\%}{\%} \approx$ [ ] %

20. $P(\text{owns dog and cat and other} \,|\, $ [ ] $) = \dfrac{p()}{p()} = \dfrac{\%}{\%} \approx$ [ ] %

Because $P(A \,|\, B) = \dfrac{P(A \text{ and } B)}{P(B)}$, then $P(A \text{ and } B) = P(B) \cdot P(A \,|\, B)$.

 Problem 3 **Using a Tree Diagram**

Got It? A soccer team wins 65% of its games on muddy fields and 30% of its games on dry fields. The probability of the field being muddy for its next game is 70%. What is the probability that the team will win its next game?

21. Fill in the probabilities to complete the tree diagram.

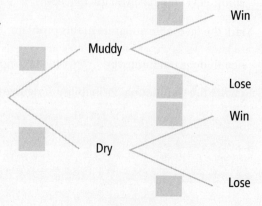

Fill in the blanks to complete each statement.

22. Use $P(A \text{ and } B) = P(B) \cdot P(A \mid B)$.

$P(\text{muddy and } \boxed{}) = P(\text{muddy}) \cdot P(\boxed{} \mid \text{muddy}) = \boxed{} \cdot \boxed{} = \boxed{}$

$P(\text{dry and } \boxed{}) = P(\text{dry}) \cdot P(\boxed{} \mid \text{dry}) = \boxed{} \cdot \boxed{} = \boxed{}$

The combined probability that the team will win their next game is:

$P(\boxed{} \text{ and } \boxed{}) + P(\boxed{} \text{ and } \boxed{}) = \boxed{} + \boxed{} = \boxed{}$

23. The probability that the team will win their next game is $\boxed{}$ %.

Lesson Check • Do you UNDERSTAND?

Error Analysis Your friend says that the conditional probability of one event is 0% if it is independent of another given event. Explain your friend's error.

Consider the events rolling a 6 on a number cube and flipping a coin that shows heads.

24. Are the events independent? Explain your answer.

_____

_____

Fill in the blanks to find the probabilities.

25. What is the probability of rolling a 6 on a number cube? $P(6) = \dfrac{\boxed{}}{\boxed{}}$

26. What is the probability of flipping a coin that shows heads? $P(\text{H}) = \dfrac{\boxed{}}{\boxed{}}$

27. What is the probability of rolling a 6 on a number cube given that the coin shows heads?

$P(6 \mid \text{H}) = \dfrac{\boxed{}}{\boxed{}}$

28. What is the probability of the coin showing heads given that a 6 is rolled on the number cube?

$P(\text{H} \mid 6) = \dfrac{\boxed{}}{\boxed{}}$

29. Explain your friend's error on the lines below.

_____

_____

Math Success

Check off the vocabulary words that you understand.

☐ conditional probability

Rate how well you can *use conditional probability*.

Lesson 13-6

13-7 Modeling Randomness

Vocabulary

● Review

1. Circle the formula for conditional probability.

$$\frac{P(A \text{ and } B)}{P(B)} \qquad P(A) \cdot P(B) \qquad P(A) + P(B) \qquad P(A) + P(B) - P(A \text{ and } B)$$

2. Circle the formula for probability of independent events.

$$\frac{P(A \text{ and } B)}{P(B)} \qquad P(A) \cdot P(B) \qquad P(A) + P(B) \qquad P(A) + P(B) - P(A \text{ and } B)$$

3. Fill in the blank to complete the sentence.

Events that cannot happen at the same time are called _____ events.

● Vocabulary Builder

Expected value (noun) ik-SPEKT-id VAL-(□)yü

Related Words: theoretical probability, experimental probability, outcome, experiment

Definition: The sum of each outcome's value multiplied by its probability.

Example: If the prize in a raffle is $100.00 and your probability of winning is 0.02, then your **expected value** is $2.

● Use Your Vocabulary

For Exercises 4 – 6 use the words below to fill in the blanks and complete each sentence. Use each word only once.

    expected   *expectation*   *expect*

4. The rock climbing trip exceeded her _____.

5. He did not _____ the weather to hold.

6. She _____ the bus to wait for her at the stop.

7. Underline the correct choice to complete the sentence.

If you buy a raffle ticket, the actual "value" is always/ sometimes / never the same as the expected value.

You can use randomly generated numbers to help you make fair decisions.

 Problem 1 **Making Random Selections**

Got It? A teacher wishes to choose three students from a class of 25 students to raise the school's flag. What numbers on the alphabetical list should be chosen based on this line from the random number table?

> 65358 70469 87149 89509 72176 18103 55169 79954 72002 20582

8. Fill in the blanks to group the line into two-digit numbers. Cross out any two-digit numbers less than 1 and greater than 25.

9. Write the first three two-digit numbers that are not crossed out.

_____ , _____ , _____

10. The teacher should choose numbers _____ , _____ , and _____ on the alphabetical list.

 Problem 2 **Modeling a Real-World Situation**

Got It? Suppose that to win a game, you must roll a standard number cube until all of the sides show at least one time. In this simulation how many times will you have to roll the number cube before each side shows at least one time? Use the randomly generated number list below.

> 5 2 5 6 6 2 6 3 1 2 3 2 3 5 1 2 2 3 6 5 3 3 1 2 4 5 3

Fill in the blanks to complete each statement.

11. Let the digits from _____ to _____ represent the sides of the number cube.

12. After six rolls, which sides have not shown yet?

_____

13. Circle how many times you have to roll before each side shows at least one time.

| 9 | 15 | 23 | 24 | 25 | 26 | 27 |

The **expected value** is the sum of each outcome's value multiplied by its probability. If you know what *should* happen mathematically, you make better decisions in problem situations.

 Key Concept **Calculating Expected Value**

If A is an event that includes outcomes $A_1, A_2, A_3, \ldots$ and Value (A_n) is a quantitative value associated with each outcome, the expected value of A is given by

$$\text{Value}(A) = P(A_1) \cdot \text{Value}(A_1) + P(A_2) \cdot \text{Value}(A_2) + \ldots$$

Lesson 13-7

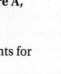

Problem 3 Calculating an Expected Value

Got It? How many points can you expect to get for the dart board shown if you receive these points: 30 points for area A, 15 points for area B, and −10 points for area C? The areas for each region are A, 36 in.^{2}; B, 108 in.^{2}; and C, 432 in.^{2}. The total area is 576 in.^{2}.

14. Substitute the ratio of each area to the total area and the points for each section and solve.

Value (points)

= P(area A)(area A points) + P(area B)(area B points) + P(area C)(area C points)

$$= \frac{}{576} \cdot \boxed{} + \frac{}{} \cdot \boxed{} + \frac{}{} \cdot \boxed{}$$

$$= \boxed{} + \boxed{} + \boxed{} = \boxed{}$$

15. Since points are calculated with whole numbers, the expected points are approximately $\boxed{}$.

Problem 4 Making Decisions Based on Expected Values

Got It? On the opening drive, a football coach must decide whether to kick a field goal or go for a touchdown. A field goal will give his team 3 points. His team will get 7 points if the touchdown is successful. If the probability for a field goal is 80% and the probability for a touchdown is 30%, which play should the coach choose?

16. Fill in the blanks to complete the table.

17. Underline the correct word to complete the sentence.

To find the expected value for each play,

add / subtract / multiply / divide the number of points

and the probability.

18. Fill in the blanks to find the expected value of both plays.

Field Goal: 3 · $\boxed{}$ = $\boxed{}$ points

Touchdown: 7 · $\boxed{}$ = $\boxed{}$ points

Possible Outcomes		
Field Goal or Touchdown		
Possible Outcomes	Points	Probability
Field Goal	$\boxed{}$	$\boxed{}$%
Touchdown	$\boxed{}$	$\boxed{}$%

Fill in the blanks for Exercise 19. Then, complete Exercise 19 and 20 by underlining the correct choice(s) to complete each sentence.

19. Because $\boxed{}$ > $\boxed{}$, a touchdown / field goal has the greater expected value.

20. The coach should choose a field goal / touchdown .

Lesson Check • Do you UNDERSTAND?

Writing Describe how you can use a random number generator to model the results of tossing a coin a hundred times.

Use the following random number table to find probabilities.
81638 36566 42709 33717 59943 12027 46547

Fill in the blanks or underline to complete each sentence.

21. The possible outcomes of flipping a coin are [____] and [____].

22. The possible outcomes are / are not equally likely.

23. Describe on the lines below how you can divide the numbers into two equally likely sets.

24. In the random number table above there are [___] even and [___] odd numbers.

25. If getting an even number in the random number table is heads and getting an odd number is tails, use all the random numbers in the table above to find the probabilities below.

$$P(\text{H}) = \frac{\quad}{\quad} \qquad\qquad P(\text{T}) = \frac{\quad}{\quad}$$

26. Describe how you can use a random number generator to model the results of tossing a coin on the lines below.

27. How could you modify your plan to model the results of tossing a coin a hundred times?

Math Success

Check off the vocabulary words that you understand.

☐ expected value   ☐ random event

Rate how well you can *use expected value*.

Need to review   0   2   4   6   8   10   Now I get it!

Lesson 13-7